RETRIEVING KNOWLEDGE

A Socratic Response to Skepticism

Kelly Fitzsimmons Burton

Public Philosophy Press
Phoenix, USA

First Edition published in 2018 by Public Philosophy Press, LLC.

©2018 Kelly Fitzsimmons Burton
All rights reserved

Library of Congress Cataloging-in-Publication Data pending

Burton, Kelly Fitzsimmons 1972 -
Retrieving Knowledge: A Socratic Response to Skepticism

Includes bibliographical references
Includes index
ISBN: 978-0-692-18486-8 (paper)

1. Title. 2. Philosophy - Epistemology 3. Plato
4. Philosophy - History 5. Nietzsche 6. Public Philosophy
7. Public Discourse

Cover design by Beth Ellen Nagel

Printed in the United States of America
This book is printed on acid-free paper

www.publicphilosophypress.com

Table of Contents

Acknowledgments 5

Introduction: Reason and Public Discourse 7
    I. Socrates, Gettier, and Plantinga on Knowledge . . 21
    II. Some Concerns About Rationalism 36
    III. Nietzsche and the Post-Nietzschean Philosophy . 41

Chapter 1: The Search for a *Logos* and Plato's *Theaetetus* . 47
    I. The First Search for a *Logos* 48
    II. Ancient Empiricism and Skepticism 54
    III. Ancient Metaphysics and the Problems
        of Materialism 62
    IV. Ancient Sophism and Relativism 68
    V. The *Logos* 75

Chapter 2: Socrates, *Logos*, and the Definition
        of Knowledge 78
  I. The Contemporary Problem of Skepticism. . . . 79
  II. Socrates vs. Empiricism and its
     Skeptical Implications 86
  III. Plato and the TOA Definition of Knowledge . 107
  IV. Gettier and the JTB Definition of Knowledge . 133

Chapter 3: *Logos* and Anti-*Logos*: Epistemology
        after Nietzsche. 146
  I. *Logos* and Reason 149
  II. Nietzsche and Anti-*Logos* 170
  III. Nietzsche's Break 186

Chapter 4: Post-*Logos* Philosophy 201
  I. A Genealogy of Post-Nietzschean Skepticism. . 205
  II. "Philosophy" is Not Philosophy:
     The Rectification of the Discipline 268

Chapter 5: Reason and Public Discourse:
        What Can We Learn from Socrates? . . . 273
  I. A Return to the Search for a *Logos* 277
  II. Socratic Principles for Public Philosophy . . . 282

Epilogue: Ancient Philosophy's Search
        for the *Logos* and John's Gospel 292

Bibliography 313

Index 327

Acknowledgments

My love of the *Logos* goes back to the first Philosophy class I attended at Paradise Valley Community College with my mentor, Surrendra Gangadean. I am grateful for his groundbreaking work in philosophy, direction and guidance, and encouragement over the years. I met Owen Anderson shortly after that first Philosophy class at PVCC and we have shared a common pursuit of the good since then. This book developed out of my doctoral dissertation which I completed at Faulkner University in the Spring of 2017. I am most grateful to my committee members Jason Jewell, Mark Linville, Robert Woods, and Owen Anderson for their example in scholarship, guidance in inquiry, and faithfulness in pursuit of what is True, Good, and Beautiful. Although not directly involved in the production of this work, I would be remiss if I did not acknowledge the influence of my graduate professors during the many years I spent at Arizona

State University in both the Philosophy and Religious Studies programs. ASU is where I first felt the challenge of skepticism and experienced the depth of institutional pragmatism. It is because I love the Academy and my students that I took up the challenge of skepticism. I hope that this work is a first step in responding to the challenge.

I dedicate this book to my students, past, present, and future for whom I desire the True, the Good, and the Beautiful. I would like to acknowledge the constant love of my Mother, who always said I could do what I set my mind to, even when I set my mind towards being a philosopher. And finally, I would like to thank David, my husband, for being a true partner in seeking the Good. He is a patient and wise man who has all of my heart.

A significant portion of Chapter 2 and a section of Chapter 5 was published in the *Faulkner Law Review,* Vol. 7, Spring 2016, Issue 2, as "Reason and Public Discourse: What Can We Learn from Socrates? With an Application to Law." The Epilogue was presented as a paper for the Spring 2018 Evangelical Philosophical Society West Coast conference.

Introduction

Reason and Public Discourse

The central topic of this book is reason and public discourse. It is an invitation to a conversation regarding how to navigate difficult topics. Currently, the West is experiencing the results of unreason and the lack of a shared public discourse. Western Civilization seems to be in a crisis of legitimacy in the face of a plurality of competing belief systems within a new level of global interaction. There is a push by some for global unity, but on what basis? The process of secularization has resulted in the celebration of pluralism, diversity, and multiculturalism on the one hand, and the privatization and minimization of national, cultural, and religious particularity on the other. Politically correct (PC) language is used as a means to navigate our diversities and has become the fallback language of the public sphere. However, politically correct language does not provide any content. Instead, PC is a negative guide to what ought not to be said because what is said may be deemed insensitive. PC is the language of tolerance in the face of difference. Social justice has become the fallback ethics of a public that lacks a shared set of values. So since there is no shared source of authority — cultural, religious, traditional, or otherwise — there is no common ground for public discourse. What we currently see in the public sphere are expressions of emotional outrage or the imposition of a will to power, often by protests that verge on civil unrest by the populace, or legal fiat by the elite. Words are emptied of meaning, and we experience the phenomenon of "fake news" and "alternative facts."[1] Instead of engaging in the rational exchange of ideas to explain what one means, ad hominem attacks are often used to defend oneself or to oppose those with whom one disagrees.

Thomas Szasz has named the phenomenon of emptying words of meaning "semanticide." He says: "To concepts like suicide, homicide, and genocide, we should add 'semanticide' — the murder of language. The deliberate (or quasi-deliberate) misuse of language through hidden metaphor and professional mystification breaks the basic contract between people, namely the tacit agreement on the proper use of words."[2] The murder of language has a history and is rooted in an earlier murder of reason (logicide). This book will chart the root of semanticide in the West. Semanticide is not a new phenomenon, nor is it only a Western phenomenon. Chinese Confucian philosophy recog-

---

1   See Scherer, Michael. "Is Truth Dead?" Time Magazine, March 22, 2017. http://time.com/4710614/donald-trump-fbi-surveillance-house-intelligence-committee/ Accessed 3/31/2017.
2   Szasz, Thomas. *The Second Sin*. (New York: Anchor Press, 1973), 22-23.

nizes the danger of semanticide and proffers its cure in "the rectification of names." Confucian philosopher Hsun Tsu (310-238 BCE) says the following about the rectification of names:

> ...When sage-kings instituted names, the names were fixed actualities distinguished. The sage-kings' principles were carried out, and their wills understood. Then the people were carefully led and united. Therefore, the practice of splitting terms and arbitrarily creating names to confuse correct names, thus causing much doubt in people's minds and bringing about much litigation, was called great wickedness. It was a crime, like private manufacturing of credentials and measurements, and therefore the people dared not rely on strange terms created to confuse correct names. Hence the people were honest. Being honest, they were easily employed. Being easily employed, they achieved results. Since the people dared not rely on strange terms created to confuse correct names, they single-mindedly followed the law and carefully obeyed orders. In this way, the traces of their accomplishments spread. The spreading of traces and the achievement of results are the highest point of good government. This is the result of careful abiding by the conventional meaning of names.
>
> Now the sage-kings are dead, and the guarding of names has become lax, strange terms have arisen, and names and actualities have been confused. As the standard of right and wrong is not clear, even the guardians

of law and the teachers of natural principles are in a state of confusion.³

Semanticide is the murder of language through the misuse of names, either intentionally, or through becoming "lax" in guarding the meaning of names. It involves the confusion of words, and what those words represent. Semanticide fails to identify and distinguish the "fixed actualities" that names represent. It leads to disunity, confusion, and doubt (skepticism); lawsuits (will to power); wickedness, fraud, and dishonesty (distrust); unemployment, disobedience to law, and bad government. Semanticide has a cure. The cure is the rectification of names: identifying actualities and calling them by the correct name. The cure must go deep. It must go to the heart of the most fundamental discipline in the academy. The cure must begin with the discipline of philosophy. The sages charged with "the guarding of names" in the West — the philosophers — are often the very people who have promoted and propagated semanticide in our day. Some in the academy are currently proclaiming the death of philosophy. Philosophy, which once stood as the foundation of Western Civilization, is dead. What then becomes of Western Civilization? What becomes of our shared culture, traditions, and language? What becomes of the West in the face of globalization, multiculturalism, and secularization? What will be the source of unity for humankind in this context? What will determine whether we have named things aright? Will a political person or body determine the proper names of things?

To reiterate: This is a book about reason and public discourse. We will ask the question "what is reason?" Moreover, we

---

3   Chan, Wing-Tsit (translator). *A Source Book in Chinese Philosophy*. (Princeton: Princeton University Press, 1969), 124.

will engage the question "how may reason be a shared source of authority for all human beings?" Minimally, reason is the laws of thought.[4] Furthermore, we will ask "how can we use reason as common ground in a global, multicultural, secular context?" The means of exploring reason and public discourse is through the discipline of philosophy, and more specifically by examining a previous period of philosophical crisis similar to our own. The problem and diagnosis of semanticide go to the question of reason in itself, reason's application to being, and its expression in the proper use of words to express being. Reason and being have been the two fundamental concepts in the history of philosophy, and the denial of reason and being are at the root of semanticide today.

The main argument of this work is that we are currently living through a crisis of public discourse. This crisis is rooted in skepticism, the view that knowledge is not possible. Specifically, skepticism is the view that we cannot have shared knowledge about metaphysics (what is real) or ethics (what is Good). The crisis of public discourse is primarily a philosophical problem that requires a philosophical solution. The first era of philosophy began with a search for a *logos* (a rational explanation) and *ontos* (the nature of being). The first era of philosophy almost ended with the skepticism of the Sophists because the first philosophers could not connect *logos* with *ontos* given their materialist and empiricist assumptions.[5] Socrates addresses the assumptions of the first philosophers and the Sophists in Plato's dialogue, *Theaetetus*, and argues for a means for connecting *lo-*

---

[4] The laws of thought include the law of identity; *a* is *a*; the law of non-contradiction, not both *a* and non-*a* in the same respect and at the same time; and the law of excluded middle, either *a* or non-*a*.

[5] This thesis is developed in Chapter 1.

gos and *ontos*.⁶ Socrates' conception of reason (rationalism) and being (realism) is one of the dominant positions in the history of philosophy until the Modern period when moderate empiricism⁷ slowly comes to replace Socrates' rationalism. At the end of the Modern period, Friedrich Nietzsche critiques moderate empiricism and proposes a radical empiricism turned skepticism that rejects the Socratic isomorphism between reason and being.⁸ Some philosophers, following Nietzsche, accept this radical empiricism and skepticism and press Nietzsche's assumptions to their logical conclusion, which results in the current crisis of public discourse.⁹ Philosophy, as we now know it, can either end in pragmatism, or philosophers can return to a search for the way in which reason and being are connected, as first philosophy sought to do. Socrates provides a method and example of how philosophy may return to its original search, and how this pursuit may take place as rational public discourse.¹⁰

We are currently living through a time of great epistemological skepticism. This skepticism, particularly as represented within the academy, is at a point of crisis in public discourse. The root of contemporary skepticism may be found in the lack of shared common ground. The contemporary crisis of public discourse is a crisis of reason stemming from the end of the Modern period in philosophy, what will be termed "post-Nietzschean" philosophy. Friedrich Nietzsche provides the philosophical underpinnings of the materialist-empiricist-skeptical

---

6   This thesis is developed in Chapter 2.
7   "Moderate empiricism" is a term used by Laurence BonJour and will be discussed further later in the Introduction.
8   This thesis is developed in Chapter 3.
9   This is the thesis of Chapter 4.
10 This is the thesis of Chapter 5.

worldview that dominates the academy and the institutions of culture today, resulting in institutional skepticism and pragmatism. Specifically, Nietzsche embraces a Heraclitan flux doctrine in which all is becoming, and there is no permanent being. Connected with his embrace of the flux doctrine, Nietzsche denies that there is an isomorphism between reason and being, which isomorphism is as old as philosophy itself. The consequence of this denial is that knowledge of reality is not possible. Nietzsche claims to philosophize with a hammer and sets out to expose the lie that he thinks philosophers tell us. The lie of the philosophers, according to Nietzsche, is that knowledge of what is True is possible. Nietzsche claims that his insights will usher in a "new" kind of philosopher of the future.

These new philosophers of the future are called the post-Nietzschean philosophers in this work. The post-Nietzschean philosophers are all those philosophers who accept Nietzsche's assumption that there is no isomorphism between reason and being. Post-Nietzschean philosophy is represented by the analytic, continental, and pragmatic strains of American philosophy. Not all those philosophers after Nietzsche accept the assumption that there is no isomorphism between reason and being. Those philosophers who still affirm the isomorphism between reason and being we will call pre-Nietzschean. Many contemporary philosophers are pre-Nietzschean. These philosophers are in the minority, and they do not hold positions of influence within the academy in large number. Instead, the post-Nietzschean philosophers — those who reject the isomorphism between reason and being — dominate in the American academy.[11] The dominance of post-Nietzschean skeptical and

---

11 One could argue that the post-Nietzschean philosophers dominate in the Western academy, but this work will deal primarily with the American academy.

pragmatic philosophy in the academy has influenced the institutions of culture, resulting in an institutional skepticism. This institutional skepticism is similar to what Charles Taylor has called the immanent frame. Taylor says that:

> ...The power of materialism today comes not from the scientific "facts", but has rather to be explained in terms of the power of a certain package uniting materialism with a moral outlook, the package we could call "atheist humanism", or exclusive humanism. What gives the package its power? I have been trying to answer this above in terms of certain values which are implicit in the immanent frame, such as disengaged reason, which pushed to the limit, generate the science-driven "death of God" story.[12]

What Taylor calls "disengaged reason" is similar to the divorce of reason from being. It is instrumental reason or practical rationality, that does not address questions of being. Because reason does not address questions of being in the immanent frame, the "death of God" is the assumed metaphysics. The death of God is the outcome of Nietzsche's separation of reason from being. The immanent frame is life in the world without reference to God or recourse to a transcendent reality. It is the assumed position of the dominant philosophy of our day. And since philosophy is foundational in the academy, this position is the assumed framework of all the disciplines of the academy. Furthermore, since the academy is the institution of culture that certifies the professions of our society, the academy, with its immanent frame, influences all of the other institutions of culture.

---

12 Taylor, Charles. *A Secular Age*. Cambridge: (The Belknap Press of Harvard University Press, 2007), 568.

The prevailing opinion — both in the academy and in popular culture — is that we cannot really know anything for sure. The view that we cannot have knowledge — certainty — about anything is the essence of skepticism. As Taylor has noted, contemporary skepticism is closely related to the empiricism and materialism assumed in much of the Modern era of Western philosophy. Empiricism is the epistemological claim that all of our knowledge is through sensory experience. Few doubt this claim today. Materialism is the metaphysical position that all that exists is material (i.e., there is no non-physical reality such as God or the human soul). If all that exists is matter, then it is natural to assume that all that may be known is the material world. The coupling of empiricism and materialism does not yield knowledge but results in skepticism. If all that exists is matter — and we add that matter is constantly in motion and is changing — then I am material, and I am changing, as are the phenomena that I observe. We will see this position unfold with the post-Nietzschean philosophers. They will argue that there is no constant and fixed being that is a knower and no fixed being that may be known. If being is not fixed but is in a constant state of flux, then our faculties of perception are subject to change and are unreliable for producing knowledge of the changing reality around us. Humans are merely physical and are part of nature and cannot rise above the natural world to some "God's eye view" of objectivity. Human faculties are part of the natural world and are also in the state of flux. There is no permanent knower and no permanent known. Thus, empiricism and materialism lead to skepticism. We really cannot know anything for sure. It is impossible to live consistently with skepticism, and we need to get on with the business of life. Besides, we cannot avoid living in community with others; thus we need to find a means for communal living and communication in the public sphere of life. What determines the rules for public life when nothing is fixed — when there are no objective standards — and all is relative to the perceiver? Institutional skepticism leads to pragmatism. Since there is no objective "Truth," truth is what works for any given circumstance.

Contemporary skepticism uncritically assumes empiricism and materialism.[13] So entrenched is this philosophical dogma that some have pronounced the death of philosophy.[14] There is a crisis in contemporary public life that is rooted in the failure of contemporary philosophy to address the longstanding assumptions of empiricism and skepticism. The skepticism resulting from Modern empiricism and materialism is not new. In fact, the complex of empiricism-materialism-skepticism was a reality for the first era of philosophy going back to Thales, Heraclitus, Parmenides, and Protagoras. The era of first philosophy almost came to an end with a failure of philosophy and crisis of public life similar to that of our age, but it did not end because a philosopher dared to question the assumptions of empiricism,

---

13 Laurence BonJour attributes contemporary empiricism and materialism to something like a philosophical fad. He says that the rejection of rationalism by contemporary analytic philosophers is "relatively superficial in character, that it is due more to arbitrary winds of philosophical fashion and a certain philosophical failure of nerve than to serious argument." See BonJour, Laurence. *In Defense of Pure Reason: A Rationalist Account of A Priori Justification.* (Cambridge: Cambridge University Press, 1998), 100.

14 See Baynes, Kenneth, James Bohman, and Thomas McCarthy. *After Philosophy: End or Transformation?* Cambridge: (The MIT Press, 1987); Rorty, Richard. *Philosophy and the Mirror of Nature.* (Princeton: Princeton University Press, 1979); Rajchman, John. and Cornel West (eds). *Post-Analytic Philosophy.* (New York: Columbia University Press, 1985).

materialism, and resulting skepticism and relativism. That daring philosopher was Socrates, closely followed by Plato and Aristotle in method and purpose. These three philosophers questioned old assumptions and proposed new solutions to counter the intellectual crisis of their day, beginning with the proper naming of things.

This book will engage in a close reading of Plato's dialogue *Theaetetus*, the Platonic dialogue that most explicitly addresses issues of epistemology, to analyze how Socrates approaches the problems of empiricism, materialism, skepticism, and resulting sophism. The argument will be made that contemporary skepticism and the ensuing crisis of public discourse has roots similar to those at the end of the first era of philosophy. Likewise, a means to address the contemporary crisis of public discourse may be found in the way which Socrates addresses the problem of skepticism in his day. Socrates set out to find a *logos*, or an account, by which to ground true opinion and obtain knowledge. For Socrates, knowledge is true opinion with an account — *logos* — or reason. Reason is what counts as evidence for belief through a process of reasoning. This *logos* is a publicly accessible grounding for knowledge claims and is what is needed as a source of common ground for public discourse today. A close reading of the *Theaetetus* implies that the *logos* is reason, that it allows for the exchange of reasons for true opinion, and that reason is a source of common ground for dialogue. Reason begins with the laws of thought, as explained by Aristotle in Book IV of his *Metaphysics*. Aristotle argues that the laws of thought are also the laws of being. There is an isomorphism between thinking and being. One of the significant sources of epistemological skepticism, both in the period of first philosophy and in our day, is the separation of the isomorphism between thinking and being. If our thinking does not apply to being, then our thoughts are not shared and are merely subjective. If our thinking is subjective, then there is no shared public source of authority, and knowledge about the nature of reality is impossible, ethics is based upon emotional preference, and politics is based upon power. Additionally, there is no shared meaning for the words that we use, thus allowing for the phenomenon of semanticide. Without reason as a shared source of authority, there can be no common ground and no common life based upon the common good.

The argument will be made, with Aristotle, that reason is ontological — the laws of thought are also the laws of being — and that reason is a shared source of authority. Reason is the basis for public discourse. What is public is shared. Reason is "publicly accessible" as a shared source of authority to which all involved in public discourse have equal access. All human beings, as rational beings, have recourse to the laws of thought. If anything, human beings are excellent in the application of reason to discover contradictions within the statements or beliefs of our opponents. We have difficulty finding the contradictions within our own beliefs or set of beliefs. Public discourse is the common conversation by which we may discover the contradictions within our own beliefs, and those of others, and rule them out as impossible because they are contradictory. The public sphere should be a place where all views may be expressed, whether religious or non-religious, those promoting belief or those promoting unbelief. All views expressed are also subject to the scrutiny of reason, the laws of thought. If a view is found to violate the laws of thought or is found to be meaningless because it is not connected with reality, then those views ought not to be given attention, but instead, they ought to be silenced through argument or counterargument exposing nonsense. Socrates provides a model for how this kind of exchange of reasons in the public sphere may proceed and how an interlocutor may be silenced.[15]

The claim will be made that reason, minimally in the form of the laws of thought (assumed by Plato in the *Theaetetus* and made explicit by Aristotle in *Metaphysics IV*) is the shared source of authority. Reason is used to identify and to distinguish what *is*. When correctly identified, we can name what a thing *is*. Furthermore, reason is used to provide an account (a *logos*, or reason) for true opinion. Public discourse is a shared give and take of reasons, which assumes a shared system of meaning and language. This shared give and take of reasons is thwarted by the presence of skepticism — particularly by the separation of reason from being. Both ancient and contemporary skepticism, rooted in empiricism and materialism, say that we cannot know the nature of ultimate reality. If reason is ontological, then reason applies to being. We can know the nature of reality using reason, the laws of thought, identifying what *is*. Furthermore, if reason, the laws of thought, is a shared source of authority for all human beings because all human beings have access to these laws, then reason is the source of common ground for public discourse. Given this common ground for the public sphere, we can engage with one another to accurately identify and distinguish what *is*. We can engage in the rectification of names. We would have a shared method for a public philosophy

---

15   Silencing an interlocutor via argument is opposed to the artificial silencing of limiting free rational discourse by the exercise of power.

that engages in discussion with regards to metaphysics and ethics.[16] We could begin to remove the obstacles to knowing that have accumulated during the Modern and Postmodern periods of philosophy and begin to rebuild the foundations of philosophy. We can begin to diagnose our contemporary philosophical crisis by examining a previous period of similar philosophical skepticism.

The roots of the skepticism of Socrates' day go back to the efforts of the pre-Socratic, or First Philosophers, and their failed attempt to find the basis for a *logos*. The first chapter of the book will explore the development of the concept and definition of *logos* (reason) and its connection with *dialogos* (dialogue). This exploration will include the background assumptions of the First Philosophers, including Heraclitus, Parmenides, and the Atomists, whom Socrates addresses in *Theaetetus*, and their search for a *logos*. It will be shown that the first era of philosophy ended in a crisis of skepticism given certain empirical assumptions entangled with materialist assumptions, which are not a sufficient basis for a *logos*. The skepticism at the end of the era of first philosophy results in the rise of Sophism, ethical relativism, and pragmatism. Aristotle's assessment of the skepticism of Gorgias, as well as the fragments of Protagoras, will be used to show the depth of the skepticism at the end of the era of first philosophy.

---

16 We would have a method for engaging in ethics on the basis of reason, what *is*, and what a human being *is*. We could engage in a the pursuit of what is good for human beings, not merely based upon the proliferation, and often contradictory, secular ethical theories such as deontology or consequentialism, but we could return to discussing teleological ethics based upon human nature as Aristotle proposes in his *Nicomachean Ethics*.

I. Socrates, Gettier, and Plantinga on Knowledge

The second chapter will address the content of Plato's dialogue, *Theaetetus*, in which Socrates attempts to define knowledge as true opinion with a *logos*. The chapter will explore the meaning of *logos* as it is used in the dialogue, the relation of *logos* to reason, and the significance of having a *logos* for knowing in Plato's epistemology. We will see that Socrates, in the process of searching for a definition of knowledge with Theaetetus, meets the challenges of empiricism, materialism, skepticism, and sophism raised by the era of first philosophy. He has provided a significant model for how one may achieve knowledge, even though some scholars disagree as to whether the dialogue itself explicitly provides an adequate definition of knowledge.[17] Socrates assumes an isomorphism between thinking and being — that our thoughts are about reality, and that knowledge is rational rather than merely empirical — as well as assuming that reason, the laws of thought, is an authority to which all human beings have access. These assumptions are vital for understanding Socrates, Plato, and Aristotle's "realist" metaphysics, which are dominant in Western philosophy until recently when these assumptions have come under attack at the end of the Modern period and into the Postmodern period. Post-Nietzschean rejection of the Socratic definition of knowledge is one of the most significant challenges of contemporary philosophy.

---

17 For a review of the literature regarding the discussion as to whether Plato provides a positive definition of knowledge. See Desjardins, Rosemary. *The Rational Enterprise: Logos in Plato's Theaetetus*. (Albany: State University of New York Press, 1990).

Philosophers have generally defined two ways of knowing: knowledge by acquaintance and propositional knowledge.[18] Knowledge by acquaintance is "direct, unmediated, and non-inferential access to what is known whereas knowledge by description is a type of knowledge that is indirect, mediated, and inferential."[19] Propositional knowledge is a form of "knowledge by description." There are two ways to have knowledge by acquaintance: "1) S is directly acquainted with p."[20] In this form of knowledge, one has immediate awareness. For example, one is immediately aware that one is in pain. "2) S knows by direct acquaintance that p."[21] In this form of knowledge, one must have a belief with propositional content about p which is properly based on one's direct acquaintance with p. Knowledge by acquaintance theories tend to be empiricist and foundationalist. Bertrand Russell was the first to articulate the distinction between knowledge by acquaintance and knowledge by description:

> Russell used the distinction between knowledge by acquaintance and description to articulate a foundationalist epistemology where knowledge by acquaintance is the most basic kind of knowledge and knowledge by description is inferential (Russell 1910 and 1912, ch. 5). "All our knowledge," wrote Russell, "rests upon acquaintance for its foundation" (Russell 1912, p. 48). Knowledge by acquaintance, therefore, is a direct kind

---

18 DePoe, John M. "Knowledge by Acquaintance and Knowledge by Description." Internet Encyclopedia of Philosophy. Accessed 4/14/2014. http://www.iep.utm.edu/knowacq/
19 Ibid.
20 Ibid.
21 Ibid.

of knowledge; it is a kind of knowledge that does not depend on inference or mediation.[22][23]

The question that arises in the context of this work is, which kind of knowledge does Socrates refer to in the *Theaetetus*? Interpreters of the dialogue have differed over whether Socrates is defining knowledge as acquaintance or as propositional. The dominant view and the view expressed in this work is that Socrates is defining propositional knowledge.[24]

Philosophers have made the distinction between knowledge as certainty, or infallibility, and knowledge as fallibility. Certainty is indubitability. One may have psychological certainty, where one cannot doubt based upon a strong feeling of being sure. And, one may have philosophical certainty, where one

---

22   Ibid.
23   Russell advances a moderate empiricism that is articulated as knowledge by acquaintance in the way described here. His moderate empiricism and related knowledge by acquaintance will later be critiqued by Wilfred Sellars, who is a radical empiricist. The move from moderate to radical empiricism by some analytic philosophers is discussed in Chapter 4. DePoe makes this observation about Sellars' critique of Russell: "...the Sellarsian dilemma appears to leave no viable alternative for the defender of direct acquaintance: (i) if experiences are non-propositional, then they cannot stand in justificatory relations to propositional beliefs; (ii) if experiences are propositional, then there must be some further basis for one to be justified in holding the propositional content of the experiences. The first option alleges that deriving justification from non-propositional content is mysterious and inexplicable. The second option alleges that granting propositional content to experiences does not stop the regress of reasons. Either way, the foundational and unique role that is supposed to be filled by knowledge by acquaintance is undermined," DePoe, John M. "Knowledge by Acquaintance and Knowledge by Description." Accessed 4/14/2014. http://www.iep.utm.edu/knowacq/
24   That knowledge is propositional will be discussed in Chapter 2.

cannot doubt based upon logical necessity. Where "certainty" is discussed in this work, it refers to philosophical certainty unless noted otherwise. Knowledge as fallibility includes the possibility of error. Fallibilists may allow for grades of knowledge based upon different kinds of evidence for justification. But ultimately, it seems one must fall within the categories of infallibilism or fallibilism. Stephen Hetherington states the following:

> So there is a key choice, between infallibility and fallibility, in what standard we are to require of knowing. To demand infallibility is to court the danger of scepticism. Again ... settling for fallibility may seem overly accommodating of the possibility of mistake. This is a substantial choice to make in thinking philosophically about knowledge. Most epistemologists profess not to be infallibilists. They aim to understand knowing as needing only to satisfy a fallibilist standard. Think of everyday situations in which people attribute knowledge: 'I know that you are a good person. And I know that you are sitting down.' The knowledge being attributed is not being thought to involve infallibility. Nonetheless, we do claim or attribute knowledge casually yet literally, all day, every day. In practice, we are fallibilists in that respect. (Still, in practice we also often could have infallibilist moments: 'You're not sure? Then you don't know.' The situation is complex. Maybe we are not always consistent about this.).[25]

---

25   Hetherington, Stephen. "Knowledge." Internet Encyclopedia of Philosophy. Accessed 4/14/2017. http://www.iep.utm.edu/knowledg/

The position taken in this book is that Socrates is an infallibilist when it comes to propositional knowledge regarding philosophical issues not accessible to the senses. He is a fallibilist concerning true opinion, which is supported by sensation, the content of which is the world of appearance.

Philosopher Edmund Gettier, in his landmark essay "Is Justified True Belief Knowledge?"[26] simultaneously defines knowledge as "justified true belief," and then calls that definition into question. Chapter 2 will draw attention to a distinction between the way that Socrates defines knowledge and the way contemporary analytic philosophers define knowledge. Socrates defines knowledge as true opinion with an account. This will be called the TOA definition of knowledge and will be distinguished from the contemporary justified true belief (JTB) definition of knowledge. The difference between the two definitions of knowledge rest in the difference between "giving an account" and providing "justification." "Giving an account," for Socrates, is through reason and argument and is decidedly not by means of sensory evidence. "Justification," for Gettier and contemporary philosophers, is by means of sense experience, or experience of the ordinary world. Socrates thinks that knowledge is indubitable, and that knowledge is only obtained through reason, thus ruling out evidence using the senses as providing an account for true belief. Socrates does allow for the senses to provide evidence for true opinion. He thinks that true opinion is sufficient to motivate right action. He argues that knowledge is better than true opinion because knowledge is "tied down" by reason and will not quickly be forgotten, whereas true opinion

---

[26] Gettier, Edmund J. "Is Justified True Belief Knowledge?" *Analysis*. Vol. 23 No. 6 (Jun. 1963), 121-123.

may quickly be forgotten. In addition, knowledge is unchanging, and opinion, or even true opinion, is changeable.

Since Socrates rejects that knowledge is through evidence provided by the senses, some may be concerned that what we can be sure of is very limited.[27] If knowledge by reason limits us, we can consider several alternative options: 1) We can be comfortable knowing a few fundamental things using reason, such as what *is*, what a human is, and what the True, the Good, and the Beautiful are. 2) We can reject Socrates' definition that knowledge is through reason and explore other logical options such as true belief is tied down employing common sense, intuition, science, testimony, or scripture. It seems that to explore these other logical options, we would have to employ reason and the method of Socrates to test these alternative methods

---

[27] Plato acknowledges that our knowledge of the world may be limited in a passage from the *Timaeus* in which the character Timaeus says: "So accounts of what is stable and fixed and transparent to understanding are themselves stable and unshifting. We must do our very best to make these accounts as irrefutable and invincible as any account may be. On the other hand, accounts we give of that which has been formed to be like that reality since they are accounts of what is a likeness, are themselves likely, and stand in proportion to the previous accounts, i.e., what being is to becoming, truth is to convincingness. Don't be surprised then, Socrates, if it turns out repeatedly that we won't be able to produce accounts on a great many subjects — on gods or the coming to be of the universe — that are completely and perfectly consistent and accurate. Instead, if we can come up with accounts no less likely than any, we ought to be content, keeping in mind that both I, the speaker, and you, the judges, are only human" Plato, John M. Cooper, and D. S. Hutchinson. *Complete Works*. (Indianapolis, IN: Hackett Pub., 1997), *Timaeus* 29b6-d, 1235-1236. In this passage, there are "irrefutable and invincible" accounts, and there are "likely accounts." What is irrefutable and invincible is knowledge and is grasped by reason, what is likely is probable and is grasped by the senses. What we know may turn out to be limited.

to see if they do provide knowledge. 3) Alternatively, we could modify the definition of knowledge a bit to satisfy both Socrates and those wanting evidence through the senses. We could say that knowledge is justified true belief. To believe is to affirm a proposition. True is what corresponds with reality. Then we can say that there are two ways to justify a true belief. The first way to justify a true belief is what we will call "weak justification," or *prima facie* justification. Weak justification is sensory data that yields a high probability of truth. When I park my car in the parking lot and walk to my classroom and later form the belief "my car is in the parking lot," it is highly probable that my car is in the parking lot, based on the evidence that I possess, namely seeing the car in the lot earlier in the day and remembering leaving the car in the lot. I "know" in the weakly justified way that "my car is in the parking lot." Weak justification is sufficient for most of our everyday beliefs about the world. We should probably be fallibilists concerning beliefs that have weak justification because there is the possibility that we are mistaken. Perhaps when I form the belief, later in the day while in my classroom, "my car is in the parking lot," the car has been stolen, or I have forgotten that I took the bus to work today and I am misremembering leaving the car in the parking lot. I could be wrong. We could say that we should believe just as much as the degree of evidence will allow for.

Weak justification would apply to most Gettier problems,[28] where the justification in question is based on sensory data or

---

28   There are many examples of "Gettier problems." One of the more creative is the "sheep in the field" example: "*The sheep in the field* (Chisholm 1966/1977/1989). Imagine that you are standing outside a field. You see, within it, what looks exactly like a sheep. What belief instantly occurs to you? Among the many that could have done so, it happens to

based upon the testimony of another. Also, weak justification applies to Alvin Plantinga's definition of knowledge as "warranted true belief." Where a belief is warranted it is formed by cognitive faculties functioning properly in an appropriate environment, according to a good design plan.[29] The problem with weak justification in the Gettier definition of knowledge as "justified true belief" is that sometimes weak justification is not sufficient for knowledge, as the Gettier problems are meant to show. Plantinga's contribution to the contemporary discussion about the definition of knowledge seems to be that he recognizes three faults in the definition of knowledge as "justified true belief." He says that "the main story of twentieth-century epistemology is the story of three connected notions: justification, internalism, and deontology."[30] Justification is evidence for one's belief, where evidence almost always is empirical. Internalism is the view that the evidence one has for belief is internally accessible. One has justification by "looking" within. Lastly, deontology is connected to the "right" to believe based on our justification, or the "duty" that we have to provide evidence for belief. Plantinga sees the contemporary "justified true belief" defini-

---

be the belief that there is a sheep in the field. And in fact you are right, because there is a sheep behind the hill in the middle of the field. You cannot see that sheep, though, and you have no direct evidence of its existence. Moreover, what you are seeing is a dog, disguised as a sheep. Hence, you have a well justified true belief that there is a sheep in the field. But is that belief knowledge?" Hetherington. Stephen. "Gettier Problems." Internet Encyclopedia of Philosophy. http://www.iep.utm.edu/gettier/#H4. Accessed 3/31/2017.

29 See: Plantinga, Alvin. *Warrant and Proper Function*. (New York: Oxford University Press, 1993); Plantinga, Alvin. *Warrant: The Current Debate*. (New York: Oxford University Press, 1993); Plantinga, Alvin. *Warranted Christian Belief*. New York: (Oxford University Press, 2000).

30 Plantinga, *Warrant: The Current Debate*, 5.

tion of knowledge as carrying a moral obligation. He thinks that the seemingly interminable debate regarding justification, starting with Gettier, is a problem with these three "connected notions."

Plantinga's response to the post-Gettier "justification" debate is to redefine knowledge as "warranted true belief." Warrant is an externalist view, rather than an internalist view, of securing true belief. An externalist view does not merely draw evidence from "looking" within. Externalist accounts of true belief look at the external conditions of the person forming the belief. Plantinga's externalist account will argue that a belief must be formed by cognitive faculties that function properly. He will argue that an environment must be conducive to forming belief. Brains work best in the environment fit for brains. I may not form true beliefs on Alpha Centauri because it is not a good environment for my cognitive faculties. Plantinga argues that when one's cognitive faculties are functioning properly, in an appropriate environment, one that is according to a good design plan, then one will naturally form the following properly basic beliefs: I had eggs for breakfast; there are other minds in the room; the material world exists; and God exists.[31] Plantinga thinks that properly basic beliefs are warranted until we encounter a defeater. Defeaters are counter-evidence that may either rebut or undercut one's warrant.[32] He says:

> This defeater structure is to be found across the length and breadth of our cognitive structure, and nearly any belief is possibly subject to defeat. I say nearly any belief; perhaps a few beliefs — such beliefs about my own

---
31 See Plantinga, *Warrant and Proper Function*, 46-47.
32 Ibid., 41.

mental life as that I am in pain or that I am being appeared to in some way, or that I exist, together with those that are wholly self-evident and accepted with maximal degree of belief, for example — are not thus subject to defeat.[33]

There are a few important things to notice about what Plantinga says here. First, it is not knowledge that is undercut by defeaters; it is belief that is undercut. If one encounters a defeater, one loses their warrant for belief. Second, nearly all of our beliefs may encounter defeaters. Third, warrant and belief come in degrees. We can learn more about the degrees of belief from Plantinga's summary statement about warrant:

> A belief has warrant for me only if (1) it has been produced in me by cognitive faculties that are working properly (functioning as they ought to, subject to no cognitive dysfunction) in a cognitive environment that is appropriate for my kinds of cognitive faculties, (2) the segment of the design plan governing the production of that belief is aimed at the production of true beliefs, and (3) there is a high statistical probability that a belief produced under those conditions will be true. Under those conditions, furthermore, the degree of warrant is an increasing function of degree of belief.[34]

Given these two quotes from Plantinga, we can infer that warrant comes in degrees and that one can lose one's warrant for belief based upon either rebutting or undercutting defeaters. How does one obtain maximal warrant so as to have maximal

---

33 Ibid.
34 Ibid., 46-47.

belief? How does one defeat a defeater that rebuts or undercuts one's belief? It would seem that to reach maximal belief, which presumably would be for the most critical kinds of beliefs, such as maintaining one's belief in God in the face of a defeater, one would need maximal warrant. Also, to maintain warrant for maximal belief, such as belief in God when presented with a defeater, one would need indefeasibility to defeat all possible defeaters. Thus, we need not only "weak justification" by means of empirical data, but we also need to establish "strong justification," or *ultima facie* justification.

Just before addressing "strong justification," a word should be said about Plantinga's externalism, and possibly externalism in general. Externalism arises as a response to the "Gettier problems" that are supposedly driven by internalism. The argument at the end of Chapter 2 of this book is that the "justified true belief" definition of knowledge is a formulation of knowledge that is provided within the post-Nietzschean context of empiricism and naturalism. Plantinga's externalism is a "naturalized epistemology."[35] Ted Poston says in his essay on "Internalism and Externalism in Epistemology" that:

> It's important to stress the context in which these externalist accounts arose. As we have seen the recognition that the traditional justified true belief (JTB) account of knowledge failed led epistemologists to re-

---

35 Although Plantinga's naturalized epistemology is one that assumes a "supernaturalism in anthropology," one wonders if all versions of externalism are naturalized. It seems that externalist theories are empiricist and naturalist. By naturalist is meant they do not rest upon any non-physical mental substance to have warrant. Proper function is of physical, mental processes.

think the connection between true belief and knowledge. It is widely recognized that the traditional JTB account was largely explicated within a rationalist understanding of justification. Justification, on this tradition, invoked concepts such as *implication, consistency, coherence*, and more broadly, *reasons of which the subject was aware*. The introduction of the Gettier problem led epistemologists to question whether this traditional assumption was correct. Externalist analyses attempted to explain how natural relations like causation and reliability could provide the key to understanding noninferential knowledge.[36]

Though couched in "rationalist" and internalist language, the context of the internalist-externalist question is a post-Nietzschean problem that has already assumed empiricism and (versions of) naturalism. It would be anachronistic to apply this problem to Socrates and his definition of knowledge as true opinion with an account. It also seems that Gettier or Plantinga do not necessarily address the "rationalist understanding of justification" that appears to be the source of the problems mentioned in this quote.

A means of overcoming the problems associated with Gettier's "justified true belief" definition of knowledge as not sufficient and overcoming problems with Plantinga's definition of knowledge as "warranted true belief," where warrant can be rebutted or undercut by defeaters, is to have a second kind of justification in addition to the "weak justification" of ordinary

---

36   Poston, Ted. "Internalism and Externalism in Epistemology." *Internet Encyclopedia of Philosophy*. Accessed 3/31/2017. http://www.iep.utm.edu/int-ext/#SH3c

everyday beliefs. What is needed in addition to the highly probable empirical "weak justification" is "strong justification." Strong justification is rational justification based upon reason and argument such that the opposite position is shown to be logically impossible. Consider the example of a person believing in God on the basis of weak empirical justification, call this Person A. Say Person A believes on the basis of an evidential argument for God, perhaps something like the argument from miracles. Person A then encounters a counter-argument to that belief, such as David Hume's argument against miracles. This person would no longer be rationally justified in believing in God.

Consider a second example, where Person B has a properly basic belief in God. This person sees the beauty of the Grand Canyon and finds themselves believing that God is the source of this beauty. According to Plantinga, this person is warranted in believing in God because this belief is formed by their cognitive faculties, functioning properly, in an appropriate environment, one that was created by God to be just as it is. Now consider Person B meeting Person C, a committed atheist, who is also visiting the Grand Canyon. Person C, the atheist, has just formed the belief that this giant hole in the ground is the product of time and change over millions of years, and does not find themselves believing in God at all. On the contrary, they are more confirmed in their non-belief in God through this experience. On the face of it, Person C seems to be warranted in their non-belief in God. In addition, Person C is a defeater to Person B's warranted belief in God. Person B now seems to require a defeater-defeater to maintain their warrant. Plantinga may say that Person C has formed a false belief when they commit themselves to atheism. Moreover, this false belief is due to cognitive malfunction, which is what Plantinga calls "sin."[37] It is difficult to see how God could fault Person C for his "sin" if he cannot help the fact that his cognitive faculties are not functioning properly.[38] It is also difficult to see how Person C is not warranted in their unbelief, and how they are not a defeater to Person B.

In the example where Person A believes in God based upon "weak" Gettier justification, and in the example where Person B believes in God based upon Plantinga's proper basicality, both persons' belief in God may be deemed "irrational" in the presence of a counter argument or a defeater. For rational belief in God, it would seem that one needs strong justification. Strong justification is consistent with Socrates' true opinion with an account, where an account is what "ties down" true belief such that it is certain. It may be that most beliefs can be supported with "weak justification," but for some fundamental, almost always philosophical beliefs such as the existence of God, human nature, and the Good, "strong justification" is necessary. Maximally essential beliefs require maximal justification.

Perhaps the concern remains, that strong justification does not provide knowledge of much. It seems that knowledge is not piecemeal but is rather systematic. For example, if one could be certain that God exists,[39] then one could argue on the basis of

---

37 See Plantinga, *Warranted Christian Belief.*

38 Owen Anderson deals with some of the problems with Plantinga's view of sin in his work: Anderson, Owen. *The Clarity of God's Existence: The Ethics of Belief After the Enlightenment.* (Oregon: Wipf & Stock, 2008).

39 The certainty of God's existence is a worry for many, and is outside the purview of this work, but has been dealt with by Surrendra Gangadean and Owen Anderson. See: Gangadean, Surrendra. *Philosophical Foundation: A Critical Analysis of Basic Beliefs.* (Lanham: University Press of America, 2008). Anderson, Owen. *The Clarity of God's Existence: The Ethics of Belief After the Enlightenment.* (Oregon: Wipf & Stock, 2008).

knowing that God exists that other truths, such as God created beings with natures, and created human beings with human nature, can be known. One could argue that God created human beings with minds that are fitted to understanding the world.[40] Furthermore, one could argue that human nature has certain universal features that are the basis for objective moral standards. Knowledge is systematic and relies upon the certainty of our "first principles." If our first principles are mistaken, our system of belief will be mistaken. Public discourse should be about our most basic disagreements such as differences in first principles. When we converse with one another about these differences, we do not often appeal to empirical data as evidence for our first principles. Instead, we ask one another for reasons. If one were to disagree with Socrates regarding his definition of knowledge, one would present Socrates with a counter-argument. One would not present him with a scientific finding, or other empirical data. The fundamental tool for doing philosophy is reason, not the senses. In public discourse, we are exchanging reasons with one another. Reason, the laws of thought, is the most fundamental standard to which we hold one another. Both rationalists and empiricists are consistent in their assumption of and use of the laws of thought, especially the law of non-contradiction when engaging in philosophy. The laws of thought are neither a rationalist nor an empiricist assumption but are assumed by all who engage in rational discourse.

---

40   This does, in fact, seem to be what the Apostle John claims in the Prologue to his Gospel when providing a Christian interpretation of the *logos*. See the Epilogue for more.

II. Some Concerns About Rationalism

Socrates' definition of knowledge as true opinion with an account, where an account is a reason/*logos*, is a rationalist account. Rationalism is a worry for some. Three main concerns with rationalism will be addressed before introducing the remaining chapters of the book. These concerns are: 1) There is no non-circular *a priori*[41] argument for *a priori*, necessary justification. Or, put another way, there is no noncircular way to justify a rationalist epistemology. 2) Rationalism has no way to justify inductive arguments. 3) Rationalism usually comes packaged with metaphysical assumptions, such as Platonism.[42]

Objection 1) states that there is no non-circular way of justifying *a priori*, necessary, justification. One response is that any justification, *a priori* or *a posteriori*, already assumes *a priori* the laws of thought. The laws of thought are inescapable in the process of any justification. As will be argued in Chapter 3, to

---

41 *A priori* belief is belief not based upon empirical data, but rather upon understanding, or rational insight, or the mind grasping a concept. *A posteriori* belief is belief on the basis of empirical data.

42 There may be other concerns with rationalism, but these seem to be the primary concerns. Laurence BonJour has presented a full-bodied defense of post-Nietzschean rationalism in his work: BonJour, Laurence. *In Defense of Pure Reason: A Rationalist Account of* A Priori *Justification*. (Cambridge: Cambridge University Press, 1998). In this work, he argues against moderate empiricism, which are empirical views that allow for some version of *a priori* analytical beliefs, and he argues against radical empiricism which denies any and all *a priori* beliefs. BonJour's arguments are compelling. The moderate empiricists that BonJour identifies, such as the logical positivists, are the same as what this work has called the pre-Nietzschean and the early analytic empiricists. The radical empiricists that BonJour identifies, such as W.V.O Quine, are what are termed post-Nietzschean philosophers in this work. BonJour argues for a "moderate rationalism" on the basis of a failed empiricism.

say anything significant is to assume the laws of thought. One could argue in the following way for a non-circular *a priori*, necessary, justification: It is self-evident that we think. It is self-evident that there are laws of thought. When we think, we employ the laws of thought. One cannot meaningfully deny the laws of thought because they are the self-evident first-principles of all thought and all discourse (the verbal expression of thought),[43] and are what make meaningful thought and discourse possible. The laws are presupposed in any and all meaningful thinking and discourse. It is also self-evident that we have sensations. Sensations are not self-certifying but are processed (minimally) by using the laws of thought in the act of identifying and distinguishing what is perceived. The laws of thought are before experience and are *a priori* necessary for interpreting all of the experiences that we have. Thus, the laws of thought are *a priori* necessary for any meaningful experience. All *a priori* and all *a posteriori* forms of justification assume the self-evident laws of thought. The laws are not part of a circular method of justification; instead, they are the necessary pre-condition for any form of justification.

Objection 2) states that there is no *a priori*, rationalist, way to justify inductive beliefs. While it was suggested earlier that if one could establish one's first principles via *a priori* reasoning that one could argue from those first principles to other aspects of reality, Laurence BonJour provides another way of securing *a priori* inductive beliefs without reference to God. In his

---

43   This argument is fleshed out more fully in Chapter 3 in an analysis of Aristotle's *Metaphysics* IV.

chapter "The Justification of Induction," he argues "that only[44] an *a priori* justification of induction has any chance of success and, second, that the prospects for such an a priori justification, contrary to widespread belief (or prejudice), are quite good."[45] BonJour first attempts to dispel "general prejudices" of *a priori* knowledge. He relies on the assumption that he claims to have proven in his first chapter that "a rationally justified transition from the premises to the conclusion of *any* argument, whether it be classified as deductive or as inductive or as falling under some further rubric, can ultimately only be made on an *a priori* basis; and the result arrived at is merely the application of this general result to the specific case of induction."[46] BonJour has two central theses for his *a priori* argument for induction. The first thesis states: "(I-1) In a situation in which a standard inductive premise obtains, it is highly likely that there is some

---

44   He thinks "only" an *a priori* justification for induction will work because Hume's problem of induction has not successfully been met with empiricist counter-arguments. BonJour summarizes the results of Hume's problem of induction in the following way: "As Hume, along with many others, points out, the conclusion that inductive reasoning is unjustifiable appears to decisively undermine the rational credentials of both the scientific and the commonsense views of the world. Not only does it render epistemically unjustified all inductively supported beliefs in a world of enduring objects and, via memory, in one's own past history seem to rely ultimately on such regularities, the unjustifiability of induction arguably leads to perhaps the most radical form of skepticism imaginable: a solipsism in which my epistemically justified beliefs are restricted entirely to my own present experience. Such an extreme version of skepticism is obviously enormously implausible from an intuitive standpoint, thus providing an equally strong intuitive reason for thinking that a satisfactory justification for inductive reasoning must be available and making it seem intellectually scandalous if none can be found." Bonjour, 191.

45   Ibid., 188.

46   Ibid., 203.

explanation (other than mere coincidence or chance) for the convergence and constancy of the observed proportion (and the more likely, the larger the number of cases in question."[47] He thinks that this thesis is "sufficiently obvious" and does not require much discussion. He addresses the question of coincidences and chance, ruling them out. He then says that this thesis would seem to hold in all possible worlds. He acknowledges that the thesis implies that there are then some objective lawful facts about the world (that is, there is an isomorphism between reason and being). BonJour's second thesis:

> (I-2) So long as the possibility that observation itself affects the proportion of *As* that are *Bs* is excluded, that is, the most likely to be true, for the truth of a standard inductive premise is the straight inductive explanation, namely that the observed proportion m/n accurately reflects (within a reasonable degree of approximation) a corresponding objective regularity in the world (and this likelihood increases as the number of observations and the variety of the collateral circumstances of observation increases).[48]

He seems to argue, on the basis of I-1 and I-2, that barring the observer does not affect what is being observed, the most likely explanation for the regularity we observe through science or common sense is "the straight inductive explanation" and furthermore, "it is likely *a priori*, relative to this same assumption, that if a standard inductive premise is true, the cor-

---

47   Ibid., 208.
48   Ibid., 212.

responding standard inductive conclusion is true also."[49] It is interesting to note that BonJour not only thinks that he has shown *a priori* support for induction, he also thinks that his argument works against "what might be called *skeptical noninductive explanations*: explanations that postulate some sort of entity or mechanism, such as a Cartesian demon, which does not fall within the common-sens-cum-scientific world view and which allegedly produces or shapes the observational evidence so that it does not accurately reflect the proportion of As that are Bs, if any, that actually exist in the world."[50] He thinks these skeptical noninductive explanations are not counter-arguments to the "straight inductive explanation" that he offers. One need not accept BonJour's theses; they are offered here only to show that it is possible to argue for *a priori* justification of induction. Such an argument is not a lost cause and not an impossible cause. It is a cause that anyone who does philosophy seriously ought to address. It is the kind of argument that this work would welcome into the conversation of public philosophical discourse.

The third objection to rationalism is 3) Rationalism usually comes packaged with metaphysical assumptions, such as Platonism. This objection seems to be the primary objection of Nietzsche and the post-Nietzschean philosophers. Because of their materialist commitments they cannot accept a non-physical supranatural aspect to reality. There are two responses to this objection. BonJour provides the first response. He observes that although rationalism may be the epistemological assumption of Platonism, it is not necessary for a rationalist to assume the metaphysics of Platonism.[51] One can be a rationalist with-

---

49 Ibid., 212.
50 Ibid., 216.
51 Ibid., 158.

out embracing the Platonist view of reality. He observes that rationalism "requires Platonism only if Platonism is the only possible metaphysical account that can accommodate"[52] the existence of the beings of thought. However, Platonism is not the only metaphysical account that supports the existence of the beings of thought so that one may be a rationalist and not a Platonist. The second response to objection 3) is that the materialist assumption is inescapably a metaphysical assumption. Just because Nietzsche and the post-Nietzschean philosophers eschew metaphysics does not mean they do not do metaphysics; instead, they assume their metaphysics and do not prove them. Rational public discourse would engage in the critical examination of all metaphysical assumptions, testing them for rational consistency and coherence. Touching upon the three concerns with rationalism, we will proceed to a discussion of Chapter 3, Nietzsche's rejection of the isomorphism between reason and being on empiricist and materialist grounds.

III. Nietzsche and the Post-Nietzschean Philosophy

The third chapter of the book will examine Nietzsche's revaluation of Plato, and his suggestion that the pre-Socratic philosophers were more accurate in their assessment of reality — especially Heraclitus' "flux doctrine" — and were more honest in their skepticism. Nietzsche, in connection with his reading of the pre-Socratics and his rejection of the Platonic *logos*, develops an anti-*logos*, anti-reason, philosophy. We will explore Aristotle's *Metaphysics* IV and his argument that reason, the laws of thought, apply to being as well as to thought; that there is

---

52   Ibid., 158.

an isomorphism between reason and being. He argues that to break the isomorphism between reason and being is to give up significant speech. It will be made abundantly clear from the literature that Nietzsche explicitly denies an isomorphism between reason and being. This explicit denial has implications for Nietzsche's madness and the silence of not producing any creative work for the last ten years of his life. The denial of the isomorphism between thinking and being, lauded by Nietzsche, results in his "death of God" philosophy. Martin Heidegger develops the post-Nietzschean philosophy and the program for the revaluation of values, preparing the way for the "new philosophers of the future."

Chapter 4 traces how Nietzsche influences the analytic, pragmatic, and continental strains of American philosophy. Nietzsche's critique of Plato and the development of an anti-*logos* philosophy is traced to the analytic philosophers through the "linguistic turn" in philosophy. The "linguistic turn" is typified by Bertrand Russell, Gottlob Frege, the Vienna Circle. The pragmatic and neo-pragmatic strain of post-Nietzschean philosophy is explored through William James, John Dewey, and Richard Rorty. The continental strain of post-Nietzschean philosophy is typified by Jacques Derrida and his critique of "logocentrism" and the doctrine of "presence," and by Michel Foucault in the emphasis on "knowledge as power dynamics." The primary epistemological issue for post-Nietzschean philosophy is whether reason applies to being, or whether reason merely applies to thinking and our "language games," resulting in skepticism, instrumental reason, practical rationality, and general pragmatism concerning truth.

The fourth chapter argues that Nietzsche's denial of the isomorphism between thinking and being heavily influences institutional skepticism through the academy. Also, those who teach skepticism in the academy are analogous to the Sophists of Socrates day. The contemporary crisis in public discourse, particularly within the academy, has roots in the skepticism and sophism of post-Nietzschean philosophy inspired by the Nietzschean rejection of Plato and the *logos*. It is the source of contemporary semanticide. Finally, a consideration of contemporary projections of the future of philosophy are explored. Philosophers such as Ludwig Wittgenstein and Richard Rorty, given the fruitless nature of the linguistic turn in philosophy, have suggested that philosophy now serves as a form of therapy, that philosophy is not meant to deliver knowledge. This position is often referred to as "Quietism" in the literature and is a gentler version of the silence of the madness of Nietzsche's rejection of reason. The effect is the same: philosophy's rejection of the *logos*/reason leads to silence. The logical options for the future of philosophy are: 1) Continue the rejection of reason as ontological and continue with the materialist-empiricist assumption that leads to current skepticism, semanticide, and which leads to silence, possibly through the death of philosophy and the West. 2) Alternatively, consider the abandonment of the materialist-empiricist assumption and a return to reason in search for a *logos*, which enables and encourages public discourse with regards to metaphysics.

The last chapter of the book draws upon how Socrates addresses the empiricism, materialism, skepticism, and resulting sophism of his day to address similar problems in our day. Both continental and analytic objections to knowledge share common assumptions in the rejection of reason as ontological and as authoritative. For philosophy to proceed and to thrive, philosophy must return to the search for a *logos* in reason. A *logos* is necessary for public discourse, or *dialogos*. A number of "Socratic principles" are drawn from the *Theaetetus* that are useful for guiding a healthy public discourse with regards to difficult and seemingly irresolvable topics that affect contemporary public life. The argument is made that a public philosophy with a robust discussion of metaphysics is not only justified by reason as ontological but is necessary for the survival of philosophy and the West.

The unique contributions of this work is found in defense of the definition of knowledge, from the *Theaetetus*, as true opinion with a *logos*, where the *logos* is reason; the redressing of Nietzsche's objection to the *logos* as understood by Socrates, Plato and Aristotle; and finally in the proposal of a model for public discourse based upon what are called "Socratic Principles" gleaned from the *Theaetetus*. This model is an example of retrieval philosophy. In defending the definition of knowledge as true opinion with an account/*logos*, contemporary objections to the definition of knowledge are addressed with the goal of overcoming some forms of skepticism related to empiricism. In addressing Nietzsche's objections, a post-Nietzschean reading of Plato is offered, which addresses the central objection raised by Nietzsche: that reason does not apply to being, and that reason in human communication is merely a construct. By overcoming Nietzsche's objection, the positive argument is made, with Plato and Aristotle, that reason applies to both being and thought, and that reason is an objective universal standard for knowing, accessible to all persons. Since reason is accessible to all, it serves as a universal standard for public discourse and is the source of the rectification of names. Reason can bring us to knowledge — true opinion with a *logos* — and in public discourse knowledge (vs. emotion or will) should be our goal. The *Theaetetus* provides "Socratic Principles" that further elucidate the method, content, and virtues for pursuing knowledge in a diverse and contentious public sphere.

The methodological approach of the project is a critical analysis of epistemological assumptions through examination of aspects of the history of philosophy. It is an act of retrieval. Tools from analytic philosophy and continental philosophy will be drawn upon, but ultimately a classical approach to the study of philosophy will be assumed and defended. The classical approach is exemplified by Socrates and begins with understanding the meaning of the terms being used and then proceeds to test truth claims. It assumes a connection between the true (epistemology), the beautiful (being/metaphysics), and the good (ethics). Lastly, the approach assumes that ideas have consequences for both individuals and society. When individuals cannot agree on what words mean, and how or whether we can have knowledge, there is a resulting lack of unity among individuals and this in turn results in a lack of unity for society. This lack of unity results in social breakdown and the absence of a shared common good.

The overall argument of this book is significant because it not only focuses on how Socrates addresses the intellectual challenges of his day, and attempts the first definition of knowledge, but it also helps us to understand what we ought to be looking for as a *logos*. Socrates provides us with a method and with principles for identifying and addressing the intellectual challenges of our day. Emphasis will be placed upon an often-overlooked matter with regards to the centrality of the philosophical question as to whether there is an isomorphism between thinking and being with an attempt to reorient our attention to the centrality of reason as authoritative within philosophy and for public discourse. And finally, the conclusion of the book argues that there are universal principles that Socrates discovered that continue to be relevant, despite the criticisms raised by Nietzsche and the post-Nietzschean philosophers. Furthermore, the *logos* may be a source of common ground for public discourse, the means for the rectification of names, and the basis for a public philosophy, in a time of skepticism and resulting erosion of public life.

The Epilogue follows the philosophical search for the *Logos* from the first philosophers to the Prologue to the Apostle John's Gospel. The argument is made that the Apostle, in his Prologue, directly addresses the philosophical search for the *Logos* and provides a source, or termination of the search, in the God of Christian theism. The Epilogue provides a blueprint for how Christians might use the *Logos* doctrine to engage in public philosophical discourse.

Chapter 1

The Search for a *Logos* and Plato's *Theaetetus*

Let this, then, suffice to show that the most indisputable of all beliefs is that contradictory statements are not at the same time true ... But on the other hand there cannot be an intermediate between contradictories, but of one subject we must either affirm or deny any one predicate. This is clear, in the first place, if we define what the true and the false are. To say of what is that it is not, or of what is not that it is, is false....[1]

---

1   Jonathan Barnes. *The Complete Works of Aristotle: The Revised Oxford Translation* (Princeton: Princeton University, 1984) *Metaphysics* IV.6.1011b 13-15 & 23-24, 1597.

I. The First Search for a *Logos*

THE HISTORY OF philosophy is characterized by the search for what is rational, an often-resulting failure to find what is rational, an ensuing skepticism, and then a renewed search for the rational from a new (hopefully deepened) perspective. First philosophy is about *logos* and *ontos* — reason and being. First philosophy almost ends with the Skepticism of the Sophists because of the first philosophers' failed attempt to connect *logos* and ontos. The first philosophers[2] were primarily concerned with a rational explanation of metaphysical questions — questions about the nature of being, the infinite, the one, and the many. Historian W.K.C. Guthrie says that "the Presocratics may fairly be said to have been preoccupied with the nature of reality and its relation to sensible phenomena."[3] These philosophers were led to various answers, each of which posed new and troubling questions.[4] The multiplicity, and seeming irreconcilability, of answers to these metaphysical questions, resulted in skepticism after a few hundred years of philosophical inquiry[5] as exemplified in an observation by Aristotle:

---

2   Whether we should call these philosophers "Pre-Socrates" or "first philosophers" is addressed by Eva Brann. "Pre-Socratics or First Philosophers." *The Imaginative Conservative.* http://www.theimaginativeconservative.org/2016/01/pre-Socratics-or-first-philosophers.html. "First philosophers" will be used in this work.
3   W.K.C. Guthrie, *The Sophists* (London: Cambridge University Press, 1971), 4.
4   Aristotle's *Metaphysics* Books I-IV deals with much of the history of the problems these first philosophers had encountered.
5   The time between Thales (585 BC), the first philosopher, and Plato (427-347 BC) is about 240 years.

Gorgias declares that nothing exists, and if anything exists it is unknowable, and if it exists and is knowable, yet it cannot be known to others. To prove that nothing exists he collects the statements of others, who in speaking about what is seem to assert contrary opinions (some trying to prove that what is is one and not many, others that it is many and not one; and some that existents are ungenerated, others that they have come to be), and he argues against both sides.[6]

Gorgias' statement expresses a deep metaphysical skepticism (which Aristotle proceeds to address after this quote), as well as a deep frustration with the state of philosophical inquiry. Gorgias is a Sophist and has a way of participating in public life despite his skepticism. The word "sophist" is derived from the Greek word *sophistes* and is associated with the poets and those reputed to be teachers of wisdom. The Sophists, such as Gorgias and Protagoras, claimed to teach a "special skill" related to what is "practical, whether in the fields of conduct and politics or the technical arts."[7] They do not teach propositional knowledge, but rather practical skills or "know-how." We shall return to Gorgias and the skepticism of some of the other Sophists later in the chapter.

Socrates, the teacher of Plato and main character of most of Plato's dialogues, engages with philosophy at the height of this skeptical period and the waning of first philosophy. Socrates engages with the ideas of the first philosophers, viewing them as providing challenges to be overcome in the pursuit of a

---

6   Aristotle. *Melissus, Xenophanes, and Gorgias*, 979, 11-15.
7   Guthrie, 30.

logos.[8] A *logos* is a rational account, and is what the first philosophers were also pursuing, but failed to achieve. In the *Theaetetus*, Socrates addresses a more fundamental question than that of the first philosophers in his pursuit of a definition of knowledge. In this dialogue, Socrates attempts to find an account for an "account" by defining knowledge itself. It is not apparent from the literature that the first philosophers had directly addressed this question. Defining knowledge had become necessary by the time of Socrates. The skepticism of the Sophists asserts that knowledge is not possible. Yet, what *is* knowledge itself? A definition is necessary to see whether the Sophists, such as Gorgias, are correct.

In the *Theaetetus*, Socrates addresses the question, 'what is knowledge?' with an entailed question, 'how do we know?' Previous philosophers assume the answer to these questions without providing an account (*logos*). These first philosophers were more engaged in questions of metaphysics, but epistemological questions, such as 'how do we know?' are prior questions to be addressed. Metaphysical assumptions, which Socrates addresses in the *Theaetetus*, require an account. Without an account, metaphysical assumptions ultimately lead to skepticism. The purpose of this section of the chapter is to provide the background to the characters, assumptions, and arguments of the first philosophers and the Sophists whom Socrates addresses in Plato's dialogue

---

8   A *logos* is a rational account, or what "ties down" a true belief. A *logos*, according to the *Theaetetus* and the *Meno* is what makes the difference between right opinion and knowledge. See Frances Cornford, *Plato's Theory of Knowledge: The Theaetetus and the Sophist of Plato* (Indianapolis: Bobbs-Merrill Educational Pub., 1957), 153, and *Meno* 98a in John Cooper, *Plato Complete Works* (Indianapolis: Hackett Pub., 1997), 895-96. The concept of *logos* will be fleshed out and defined further as the chapters proceed.

the *Theaetetus*. In this dialogue, Socrates seeks to address the philosophical problems of empiricism and skepticism, materialism, and resulting sophism.

To investigate the historical background of *Theaetetus*, we may begin with the main characters of the dialogue and the philosophical views that each appears to endorse. The main characters of the *Theaetetus* are Theodorus, a teacher of mathematics; Theaetetus, a student of Theodorus and said to be a "young Socrates;" and Protagoras, who is not present for the dialogue, but whose ideas inform a large portion of the dialogue. Catherine Zuckert claims that Theodorus' associating Theaetetus with Socrates is intended to show that Theaetetus has potential as a philosopher.[9] Socrates, the main character of the dialogue, proceeds to question Theaetetus, always trying to draw Theodorus into the conversation, with the goal of testing Theaetetus' potential as a philosopher. Socrates begins testing the young man by asking Theaetetus "what is knowledge?"[10] When Socrates questions Theaetetus, it becomes clear that Theaetetus has bought into the teachings of Protagoras, a Sophist, who is also a friend to Theodorus. Through the questioning of Socrates, it becomes apparent that Theaetetus has accepted the teachings of Protagoras, not by his understanding the views of Protagoras, but rather by the testimony of Theodorus.[11]

---

9   Zuckert, Catherine H. *Plato's Philosophers: The Coherence of the Dialogues* (Chicago: University of Chicago, 2009), 601.
10 Cornford, Francis M. *Plato's Theory of Knowledge* (New York: The Liberal Arts Press, 1957), 20. Cornford provides a translation of the *Theaetetus* with running commentary. Cornford will be cited both for the text of the dialogue and for his commentary. When using Cornford's commentary, the author will be referenced. When using the dialogue, Plato or to the characters in the dialogue will be referenced.
11 Zuckert, 607.

Specifically, Theaetetus has believed, following Protagoras, that "man is the measure." To be a philosopher, a "young Socrates," Theaetetus will need to engage in critical thinking regarding both the means and the content of knowledge. The means of knowing that Theaetetus employs at the beginning of the dialogue is testimony, including in the area of mathematics, rather than critical analysis that brings one to an understanding of what is true.[12]

The content of what Theaetetus "knows" — that "man is the measure" — is shown by Socrates to be a faulty assumption through the process of dialogue. Throughout the dialogue, Socrates helps Theaetetus, the "young Socrates," to move from making judgments on the basis of testimony to making judgments based on reason and understanding. In addition, Socrates delivers Theaetetus from his false assumption that "man is the measure" and all that is implied in this assumption. When Theaetetus goes through the process of critical analysis, he is in a better place to think philosophically and to arrive at knowledge. Specifically, he is ready to embark on a search for the definition of knowledge. Socrates sees the potential for this mathematician to think philosophically and shows him the method by which philosophers — lovers of wisdom — come to know.

Theodorus is associated with Protagoras[13] and has passed his teaching on to young Theaetetus, his student. Socrates draws Theodorus into the discussion to engage in understanding the meaning of Protagoras' teaching. The bulk of the dialogue is an analysis of the teaching that "man is the measure." This discussion touches upon the Heraclitian doctrine that "all is flux," and

---

12   Ibid., 607.
13   Ibid., 617.

Parmenides' assumption that "all is one." The *Theaetetus* is both an example of how Socratic philosophy is done, and an application of that philosophy towards philosophical assumptions that Socrates deems to be erroneous or fallacious. The function of the *Theaetetus* is to provide a method for engaging philosophically — in critical analysis — and for using that method to eliminate positions that are logically impossible or incoherent. The positions that Socrates scrutinizes demonstrating his method to Theaetetus, and disavowing Theaetetus of false beliefs in the process, include empiricism and skepticism, materialism and nominalism, and sophistry and relativism. These philosophical positions are rooted in pre-Socratic philosophy. The problematic nature of these assumptions becomes acute in Socrates' day. The problems related to these assumptions lead to an unhealthy skepticism, with unphilosophical consequences such as the rise of the Sophistry in Athens. In addition, Theaetetus and Theodorus ascribe to Protagoras' position by mere testimony rather than upon understanding.

Skepticism assumes that knowledge is not possible. Socrates refutes the claim that knowledge is not possible in the *Theaetetus* and provides an alternative model for approaching knowledge. Also, he provides a definition of knowledge and shows that empiricism, materialism, and relativism are mistaken assumptions. The next part of the chapter will show the roots of skepticism and empiricism through the words of the first philosophers and will show how Socrates engages with these historical positions in the *Theaetetus*.

II. Ancient Empiricism and Skepticism

In the process of answering the question "what is knowledge?", Theaetetus, early in the dialogue, says the following: "It seems to me that one who knows something is perceiving the thing he knows, and so far as I can see at present, knowledge is nothing but perception."[14] This perception is akin to seeing, or to common sense experience, and is a crude form of empiricism. Socrates replies: "The account you give of the nature of knowledge is not, by any means, to be despised. It is the same that was given by Protagoras, though he stated it in a somewhat different way. He says, you will remember, that 'man is the measure of all things — alike of the being of things that are and of the not-being of things that are not.'"[15] Socrates then goes on to suggest that Protagoras' view of the relativity of perception is based upon the metaphysical assumption that "all is flux." He says, according to this view:

> All the things we are pleased to say 'are,' really are in the process of becoming, as a result of movement and change and of blending one with another. We are wrong to speak of them as 'being,' for none of them ever is; they are always becoming. In this matter let us take it that, except Parmenides, the whole series of philosophers agree — Protagoras, Heracleitus, Empedocles ....[16]

The implications of the assumptions that Socrates names, and attributes to the first philosophers, is that if all is matter — all

---
14   Cornford, 29.
15   Ibid., 31.
16   Ibid., 37.

that exists is perceptible — then all is in the process of change, and there is nothing permanent and objective to be known. The epistemological assumption that knowledge is perception, combined with the metaphysical assumptions of the flux doctrine lead to the result that objective knowledge is not possible. Man is the measure of the subjective experiences he has, but there is no objectively shared experience among humans. If nothing is fixed, then there is no objective, permanent standpoint from which a "common" experience may be judged. There is no point of reference outside the "flux" of the material world. Furthermore, as natural beings that are also part of the material world in flux, we could never be sure that what we perceive is the same as what other humans perceive. This inability to know the world, or to be sure that others experience the world as we do leads to skepticism. The roots of this skepticism lie in the empirical method of some of the first philosophers. We will briefly explore the skeptical results of predominant empiricism in Xenophanes and Democritus.

One of the richest sources of the ideas of the first philosophers is to be found in Aristotle (384-322 BC). In Book IV, Section 5 of his *Metaphysics*, he addresses the skeptical implications of the empiricism of some of the first philosophers. In general, he notices that "Those who feel the difficulties have been led to this opinion by observation of the sensible world. They think that contradictions or contraries are true at the same time because they see contraries coming into existence out of the same thing."[17] Observation of the sensible world leads to contradictory appearances, and contradictions cannot lead to

---

17 Aristotle, and Jonathan Barnes. *The Complete Works of Aristotle: The Revised Oxford Translation*, Volume 2 (Princeton: Princeton University Press, 1984), 1593 (*Metaphysics* IV.5.1009a6).

knowledge. Aristotle continues his analysis of the problems of the first philosophers by noting that, "And similarly some have inferred from the sensible world the truth of appearances. For they think that the truth should not be determined by the large or small number of those who hold a belief and that the same thing is thought sweet by some who taste it, and bitter by others."[18] Again, this quote reveals the skeptical implications of following empirical observations that lead to the contradictory conclusions of some of the first philosophers. One of the first philosophers that Aristotle discusses in the context of skepticism is Xenophanes (570-475 BC).

Xenophanes is a Greek thinker who sharply critiqued the Homeric gods and argued that "God is one."[19] Whether this One is a monotheistic or pantheistic God is unclear, and scholars disagree over what he means. Although Xenophanes has some interesting metaphysical positions, his epistemology is of central importance for this chapter. Fragment 34 of what remains of Xenophanes' writings says: "Certain truth has no man seen, nor will there ever be a man who knows [from immediate experience] about the gods and about everything of which I speak; for even if he should fully succeed in saying what is true, even so, he himself does not *know* it, but in all things there is opinion."[20] From this quote, it seems that Xenophanes says that no one can be certain, or that certain knowledge is not possible, "from immediate experience." He then makes a distinction between knowledge and opinion. An implication is that objective

---

18   Aristotle, 193 (*Metaphysics* IV.5.1009b1).
19   Guthrie, W.K.C., *A History of Greek Philosophy: The Earlier Presocratics and the Pythagoreans, Vol. 1* (New York: Cambridge University Press; 1962), 375.
20   Ibid., 395.

knowledge is not possible, and all that men have are subjective opinions. Guthrie says of Xenophanes that:

> The Sceptics of the fourth century B.C. and later seized eagerly on these lines as anticipation of their view that knowledge was unattainable ... Xenophanes was thought to mean that everything is incomprehensible ... nobody knows the truth, for even if he should hit upon it by chance, he still does not know that he has hit upon it.[21]

This distinction between knowledge and belief, or opinion, is at the heart of the discussion in the *Theaetetus*. Socrates addresses the problem that Xenophanes recognizes by adding the necessity for a *logos*, or an account, which makes true belief (opinion) into knowledge. It is apparent that the addition of a rational *logos* was not an option for Xenophanes in the way that it was for Socrates, based upon Xenophanes' epistemological assumption that either knowledge is through the senses, or one cannot know at all. One might have knowledge by acquaintance of the direct objects of perception, according to Xenophanes, but that kind of subjective knowledge cannot be shared with others. In addition, the data provided by our senses may be deceptive. Guthrie says: "It has been accepted as evidence that Xenophanes drew a distinction between direct sensible experience, which gives certainty, and other objects of cognition about which none can be certain save God." Again, he notes that Xenophanes "was one of the first to suggest that the sense of sight may be deceptive."[22]

---

21 Ibid.
22 Ibid., 398.

Even if one were certain of the data of one's perception, one could still be deceived about appearances.

The results of Xenophanes' view is skepticism in epistemology, and resulting relativism with regards to truth. To make this point, Guthrie draws attention to Fragment 38: "'If God had not made yellow honey, men would think figs were much sweeter.'"[23] He then adds that: "This too is presumably intended to emphasize the limitations of human judgment, but introduces incidentally its *relative* character: men's assessment of a particular sensation depends on the sensations which they already happen to have experienced."[24] Guthrie says that Xenophanes is philosophically significant because his ideas regarding the distinction between belief and knowledge, his claim that the senses may be deceived, and his hitting upon the relativity of truth on the basis of sensory data are all the first hints of ideas that philosophers such as Democritus, Heraclitus, and Protagoras will develop further. Xenophanes is also philosophically significant because he raises challenges that Socrates addresses and finds means for overcoming in the *Theaetetus*.

Democritus (460-370 BC), influenced in some way by the epistemological problems recognized by Xenophanes, is also known for his metaphysics. He and Leucippus (5th century BC) developed materialism based upon atomic theory. Aristotle notes that Democritus:

> Says that either there is no truth or to us at least it is not evident. And in general it is because these thinkers suppose knowledge to be sensation, and this to be a physical alteration, that they say that what appears to our

---

23   Ibid., 401.
24   Ibid., 401.

senses must be true; for it is these reasons that Empedocles and Democritus and, one may almost say, all the others have fallen victims to opinions of this sort.[25]

Aristotle notices not only that philosophers such as Democritus do not think we can arrive at truth, not to speak of knowledge, but he also notices that this skepticism is a direct result of their empirical assumptions (that "knowledge is sensation"). He also notices that sensation is due to a "physical alteration." In the case of Democritus, this physical alteration in our sensory perception is due to atomic change both in the perceiver and in the thing perceived.

Though there have been philosophers before Democritus who were materialists — indeed almost all of the first philosophers are materialists — the atomists had become more consistent in their materialism. Guthrie says:

> … only now that the atomists have gone further in sharpening and making explicit the concept of materialism, have the problems of explaining intellection and knowledge in [material] terms become acute. Indeed they have come into sight for the first time. By the uncompromising clarity of their materialism, the atomists made it very difficult indeed for themselves to answer questions about the relation between sensation and thought.[26]

---

25 Aristotle, 1593 (*Metaphysics* IV.5.1009b 6-16).
26 Guthrie, W.K.C., *A History of Greek Philosophy: The Presocratic Tradition from Parmenides to Democritus, Vol. 2* (Cambridge: Cambridge University Press, 1965), 454.

Democritus has taken the assumptions of earlier materialists to the next level by developing a theory of knowledge based solely upon his theory of the atom. He explains all thought regarding the interaction of atoms. Guthrie recognizes Democritus' reductionism and its lack of success for attaining knowledge, but he adds, "We may still admire [his theories'] boldness and consistency."[27] Democritus' atomic theory is closely related to Heraclitus' flux doctrine. Socrates directly opposes the flux doctrine in *Theaetetus* by arguing that matter is always in motion and is thus always changing. Also, one's senses, as composed of matter in motion, are also always changing, therefore if all is matter, then there is nothing fixed that may be known. If nothing is fixed, there is no "nature of the thing" such that one can answer the question "what is x?." If all is becoming and there is no being, then there is no fixed nature that may be grasped and known by the mind. Instead, there is only matter in motion, and human beings are part of that ever-changing flow, of which there is no thing to be grasped as an object of knowledge. Socrates overcomes this problem by proposing that there is something beyond matter that is permanent.

In becoming more consistently materialist, the atomists make more apparent the problems for a theory of knowledge based upon matter as ultimate reality. Though the first philosophers were not primarily concerned with epistemological problems, the failure to find solutions to the problems arising from materialism bring to the surface the more fundamental epistemological issues which the *Theaetetus* addresses as the first self-consciously epistemological treatise. Though epistemology "which has bulked so large in later philosophical investigation,

---

27   Ibid.

occupied a much humbler place in the mind of a fifth-century thinker ... we must not expect to find it discussed for its own sake, or with the concentration and clarity bestowed on it in later centuries."[28] The *Theaetetus* is the first of many philosophical works in which epistemology is discussed, but it does not seem to be discussed merely "for its own sake,": but rather it is discussed with the goal of overcoming the skepticism that results from a lack of addressing epistemological assumptions. Aristotle, who is even more self-conscious than Socrates and Plato regarding epistemology, argues against the empiricism and skepticism of the first philosophers in a similar way that Socrates does. He asks for a *logos* or an account. He says: "And the starting-point in dealing with all such people is definition. Now the definition rests on the necessity of their meaning something; for the formula, of which the word is a sign, becomes its definition."[29] The challenges of skepticism at the end of the era of first philosophy lead to the necessity of a response by providing a more consistent *logos* to tie down true belief. Skepticism is a challenge because Socrates thinks that knowledge is possible, and it is the source of the Good for human beings. He does not think that the senses deliver knowledge and rejects empiricism in favor of a form of rationalism, where knowledge is a true belief with an account/*logos*. An account is akin to having rational justification by the elimination of contradictory positions.

---

28 Guthrie, Vol. 2, 454.
29 Aristotle, 1598 (*Metaphysics* IV.7.1012a 21-25).

III. Ancient Metaphysics and the Problems of Materialism

The assumption that all knowledge is through the senses is closely tied to the metaphysical assumption that all that exists is perceptible (materialism). The majority of the first philosophers, if not all of them, were materialists (material monists). We will explore the assumptions of some of these philosophers in connection with the *Theaetetus* to draw out the connection between materialism, skepticism, and the need for a *logos*. In the history of the first philosophers, especially towards the later part of their thinking, there is a development of the idea of being as one, and material. This would include Heraclitus' view that all is flux, or in motion and change, Parmenides' view that all is one and is permanence — he says that "Whatever is, is, and cannot not-be"[30] — and later to Gorgias' view that there is no being that may be known (being is non-being or nothing exists). The exploration of the assumption that all being is one and material is pressed to its logical conclusions, which, with Gorgias, results in radical skepticism and the promotion of Sophism.

Theaetetus 152C-153D addresses Heraclitus (535-475 BC) and the doctrine of flux concerning the impossibility of knowledge (if the doctrine were true). Plato attributes to Protagoras, the Sophist, a secret belief in the doctrine of flux. Cornford, in his introductory commentary on this section of the dialogue, says:

> Plato next introduces another element required for his theory of sense-perception. It is drawn from Heraclitus: 'All things are in motion.' The suggestion that

---

30 Guthrie, Vol. 2, 16.

> Protagoras taught this as a 'secret doctrine' to his 'pupils' would deceive no one ... Plato intends to accept from Heraclitus the doctrine that all sensible objects are perpetually changing — a fundamental principle of his philosophy. But to Plato sensible objects are not 'all things.' He will later point out that the unrestricted assertion, 'All things are always changing,' makes knowledge impossible.[31]

It is unclear why Plato attributes to Protagoras the "secret belief" in the doctrine of flux. Perhaps it is because both Protagoras and Heraclitus hold to a similar skepticism. Cornford points out that Plato himself subscribes to the idea that matter is always changing, sharing an assumption with Heraclitus. Plato differs from Heraclitus in the latter's assumption that all that *is* is the sensible world. Plato does not share the materialism of Heraclitus; and Socrates, by the end of the dialogue, argues that there must be a rational soul that perceives the unchanging world of thought.

Heraclitus is a fascinating character in the history of philosophy, whom Guthrie says is difficult to link to his predecessors and who "in all probability" was an "isolated thinker." Diogenes Laertes says of Heraclitus: "'He was no man's disciple' ... 'but said that he had searched himself and learned everything from himself.'"[32] While it may be challenging to connect Heraclitus to previous philosophers through direct teacher and pupil, it is clear from the fragments that remain of his writings that he is reflecting upon some of the same ideas as his predecessors. He is primarily concerned with the *logos*, and with grasping the na-

---

31 Cornford, 36.
32 Guthrie, Vol. 1, 416.

ture of being, and the implications of being. What is becoming apparent through the study of first philosophy is that the search for a *logos* (or account) is of primary importance, and is what distinguishes philosophers from other kinds of thinkers (such as poets or politicians). Heraclitus makes his search explicit, and this search may be what gives impetus to Socrates' pursuit of a *logos* in *Theaetetus*. The idea of a *logos* is not new with Socrates, and Heraclitus is one of the most explicit in his description of the *logos*; thus it would not be a stretch to think that Socrates is developing the notion of *logos* and seeing its further implications in connection with human knowing. Heraclitus says in Fragment 1:

> Although this Logos is eternally valid, yet men are unable to understand it — not only before hearing it but even after they have heard it for the first time. That is to say, although all things come to pass per this Logos, men seem to be quite without any experience of it — at least if they are judged in the light of such words and deeds as I am here setting forth. My method is to distinguish each thing according to its nature, and to specify how it behaves; other men, on the contrary, are as neglectful of what they do when awake as they are when asleep.[33]

What is interesting about this fragment is that Heraclitus seems to say that there is an eternal *logos* by which all things come to pass. In addition, he says the *logos* is common to all, as an objective reality, and a kind of common ground for human beings.[34]

---

33   Wheelwright, Philip, ed., *The Presocratics* (New York: The Odyssey Press: 1966), 69.
34   Ibid., 69.

Yet, most humans go by what is subjectively true for them. We see in these two fragments another contrast between what is true, and what appears, or opinion. This is the very contrast Socrates addresses in the *Theaetetus*. Guthrie has a wonderful analysis of the meaning of the Greek word *logos* in his section on Heraclitus and says that Heraclitus uses the term to mean " 'general principle, law, or rule' and 'the faculty of reason.'"[35] *Logos* as principle, and as the faculty of reason, is used by later philosophers. A problem for Heraclitus is how to rationally justify (or provide a *logos* for) the reality of the *logos* if all is flux? Can his doctrine of flux support an unchanging principle and a faculty of intelligence separate from the changing material world?

Heraclitus says, in Fragment 20, that "Everything flows and nothing abides; everything gives way, and nothing stays fixed."[36] Then he famously says, in Fragment 21: "You cannot step twice into the same river, for other waters, and yet others go ever flowing on."[37] In Fragment 29, he speaks of the universe, which is the same for all humans, as not being made but as eternal. The ever-changing material world is eternal. This is the heart of the flux doctrine. Socrates, in *Theaetetus* 159E, draws out three implications of this doctrine when he notes:

> It follows, then (1) that, on my side, I shall never become percipient in just this way of any other thing; for to a different object belongs a different perception, and in acting on its percipient it is acting on a person who is in a different condition and so a different person. Also (2) on its side, the thing which acts on me can

---

35 Guthrie, Vol. 1, 422.
36 Wheelwright, 70.
37 Ibid., 71.

> never meet with someone else and generate the same offspring and come to be of just this quality; for when it brings to birth another thing from another person, it will itself come to be of another quality ... Further (3) I shall not come to have this sensation *for myself*, nor will the object come to be of such a quality *for itself*."[38]

Socrates presses the implications of the flux doctrine to its skeptical limits, noting that no sensing being can perceive the same thing more than once, two people can never have the same perceptions (and so cannot have the same subjective experiences), and subject and object (both of which are changing) are dependent on one another.[39] Knowledge becomes impossible if the knower and the object to be known are continually changing. Some permanent being is necessary for knowledge.

Parmenides (born approx. 510 BC) is one such philosopher who argued for the permanence of being and that 'all is one.' He claims that it is impossible for nothing to be (i.e., non-being is impossible). Socrates mentions Parmenides in *Theaetetus* 180 D-E but treats of his position more fully in the *Sophist*. He says:

> ... I had almost forgotten, Theodorus, another school which teaches just the opposite, that reality 'is one, immovable: "Being" is the name of the All', and much else that men like Melissus and Parmenides maintain in opposition to all those people, telling us that all things are a Unity which stays still within itself, having no room to move in.[40]

---

38 Cornford, 56-57.
39 Ibid., 56.
40 Ibid, 94.

Plato is exploring the antinomies between the flux doctrine and the permanence doctrine. Both views share the common assumption that all is one, and this one is material. Socrates ultimately overcomes this antinomy by proposing another category of being, that of the soul, which is non-physical and intelligent. In addition, he will propose that the soul knows the Forms, which are non-corporeal, permanent, reality. This non-corporeal reality will be the source of being and the intelligibility of being. It will be the source of the *logoi*.

Parmenides is the founder of the Eleatic school in first philosophy. He wrote a poem in an epic meter that is composed of two halves. The first is called "The Way of Truth," and the second, "The Way of Seeming."[41] The title of the poem already reveals the theme of the contrast between truth and belief (or opinion, or seeming), which is at the heart of the *Theaetetus*. Parmenides too has a concern for *logos*. He says in Fragment 7: "For this shall never prevail, that things that are not are, but do thou keep thy thought from this way of inquiry; and let not habit born of much experience force thee along this way, to ply a heedless eye and sounding ear and a tongue, but judge by reason (logos) the much-contested refutation spoken by me."[42] Parmenides says that all is being because change is non-being, and non-being cannot be, and cannot be conceived to be. There is no such thing as non-being. Being is all that there is. Also, "If you give to it its full and proper force, you are precluded from saying that what is suffers any process of becoming or perishing, change or movement.'"[43] Parmenides opposes with the full force

---

41 Wheelwright, 92-100.
42 Guthrie, Vol. 2, 21.
43 Ibid., Vol. 2, 16.

of logic (a logic for which he may have no *logos* or account) the flux doctrine of Heraclitus.

Parmenides and Heraclitus share in the philosophical search for a *logos*. Yet both fail to ground the *logos* in being. Each of their positions results in skepticism regarding the possibility of knowing the physical world. They share a common monism but split over whether the material world is always changing or is fixed and unmovable. Socrates addresses both of these challenges[44] in *Theaetetus* by arguing for an unchanging, non-physical reality which is intelligible and is the ground for intelligibility.

IV. Ancient Sophism and Relativism

The apparent contradictoriness of the metaphysical assumptions of the first philosophers results in the skepticism of the Sophists. Gorgias presses the logic of the contradiction between those who argue that all is permanence, and those who argue all is change, resulting in a radical skepticism and nihilism. Protagoras, expressing a form of relativism, as a result of skepticism, concludes that "man is the measure of all things."[45] The era of first philosophy bottoms out in skepticism, relativism, and nihilism. The seemingly unresolvable challenges could have been the death of philosophy and the search for a *logos*. However, Socrates represents a fresh approach to these problems in the way he questions longstanding assumptions and points to their logical contradictions. He provides a new way forward by ask-

---

44 Socrates addresses Parmenides in more detail in the *Sophist*. Nevertheless, the solution to the problem of permanence and change is suggested in the *Theaetetus*.

45 Wheelwright, 239.

ing a more fundamental question: "what does that mean?" Or: "what is *x*?" He has made it one of his life's purposes to refute the Sophists. In the process of refutation, he will point towards a new avenue in the search for a *logos*.

Parmenides was concerned with explaining how all of nature was one. Gorgias (485-380), on the other hand, says: "Parodying the title *On Nature or the Existent* commonly given to works of the natural philosophers, he produced a treatise *On the Non-existent or on Nature*, in which he argued three theses: (a) that nothing exists, (b) that if anything existed we could have no knowledge of it, (c) that if anyone knew it he could not communicate his knowledge."[46] Gorgias begins with the metaphysical statement that "nothing exists." He is proposing a contrary to the view that "all exists," or everything that exists always exists.[47] Aristotle, commenting on this fragment, says:

> To prove that nothing exists he collects the statements of others, who in speaking about what is seem to assert contrary opinions (some try to prove that what is is one and not many, others that it is many and not one; and

---

46   Guthrie, Vol. 2, 17.
47   It should be noted that so far the first philosophers have assumed that all that exists has always existed, and this existence is material. If Gorgias means by "nothing exists" that nothing exists always, or eternally, he is offering a logical alternative. He does not provide any rational justification for this alternative; he does not provide a *logos*. Plato ultimately sides with the "all that exists has always existed" side of this antinomy. He escapes some of the issues of the materialists by bringing in the soul to ground the *logoi*. Yet, Plato does not provide rational justification for his dualism (all that exists is matter and spirit). In all of this discussion the idea that some existence has always existed, and some existence is temporal and created has not yet been considered. It will take another era of bottoming out in skepticism for Theism to be a viable philosophical option.

some that existents are ungenerated, others that they have come to be), and he argues against both sides. For he says that if anything exists, it must be either one or many, and either be ungenerated or have come to be. If therefore, it cannot be either one or many, ungenerated or having come to be, it would be nothing at all.[48]

The problem of the one and the many, and that of permanence and change have clearly contributed to Gorgias' skepticism. Guthrie says that "The Sophists seized on the forms of Eleatic logic to make all knowledge seem absurd, as Gorgias was doing with his defense of the thesis 'It is not.'"[49]

Gorgias, like other first philosophers, makes a distinction between truth and opinion. Based upon his metaphysical assumptions, he does not think that knowledge of the truth is possible. He says, "... if anything existed we could have no knowledge of it." And if we could have knowledge, we "could not communicate his knowledge."[50] According to Gorgias, all that is left are the opinions of men and the means of persuading through rhetorical skill, which usually means by appeal to emotion or use of threat. He says, "When persuasion joins with speech it can affect the soul in any way it wishes. Consider first how astronomers, using "speech and argument" (logos), manage to dispel men's former opinions ... and to implant, other opinions which had formerly seemed incredible and inconsistent with plain facts."[51] He goes on to say that "the power of speech over the disposition of the soul is comparable with the effect of

---

48   Aristotle, p. 1548, *Melissus, Xenophanes, and Gorgias*, 979a 11-20.
49   Guthrie, Vol. 2, 17.
50   Ibid., 17.
51   Wheelwright, 250.

drugs on the disposition of the body. As drugs can expel certain humors from the body and thereby make an end either of sickness or life, so likewise various words can produce grief, pleasure, or fear...."[52] Skepticism, which in Protagoras almost becomes the anti-*logos*, leads to relativism in epistemology. This relativism is the primary target of Socrates in the *Theaetetus*. The central theme of the dialogue is the definition of knowledge. To define knowledge, Socrates must dispel Theaetetus, the "young Socrates," of his erroneous belief, based upon Protagoras, that "man is the measure."

What we know of Protagoras (490-420 BC) historically, comes from several of Plato's dialogues, as well as from five fragments preserved by other authors. None of Protagoras' original written works survive, but we can glean the outlines of his philosophical stance from the fragments that we do have. Socrates, in the *Theaetetus*, is opposed to the skepticism that results from Protagoras' assumptions about knowing and being. Evaluation of three of the extant fragments attributed to Protagoras illuminates the skeptical implications of his statements. The first fragment is an epistemological statement. The second goes further than the first and extends beyond epistemological skepticism to include metaphysical skepticism. The third shows the relativity of truth based upon perception of the physical world.

The first fragment attributed to Protagoras states that "A human being is the measure of all things - of things that are, that they are, and of things that are not, that they are not."[53]

---

52 Ibid., 250.
53 Empiricus, Sextus. *Against the Mathematicians* 7.60=80B1. Quoted in S. Marc Cohen, Patricia Curd, and C.D.C. Reeve. *Readings in Ancient Greek Philosophy from Thales to Aristotle* (Indianapolis: Hackett Publishing Company; 1995), 75.

Socrates treats this statement as meaning that "knowledge is perception."[54] He proceeds to show that each man's perceptions are changeable, as are the objects of perception. Each man's judgment about what he perceives is not fixed and is subjective, thus making truth subjective to the individual. If truth is subjective to the individual, we do not arrive at knowledge, which knowledge both Theaetetus and Socrates agree would be certain, but instead, we arrive at uncertainty and skepticism. Socrates asks:

> If what every man believes as a result of perception is indeed true for him; if, just as no one is to be a better judge of what another experiences, so no one is better entitled to consider whether what another thinks is true or false, and (as we have said more than once) every man is to have his own beliefs for himself alone, and they are all right and true – then, my friend, where is the wisdom of Protagoras, to justify his setting up to teach others and to be handsomely paid for it, and where is our comparative ignorance or the need for us to go and sit at his feet, when each of us is himself the measure of his own wisdom?[55]

The implication is that Protagoras and the Sophists cannot teach others wisdom if 'knowledge is perception' and 'man is the measure' of each of his perceptions and what is true for him. There would be nothing to teach and no need for the Sophists as teachers. If knowledge is not possible, why are students paying Sophists to teach?

---

54   Cornford, 31-32.
55   Ibid., 60.

The second fragment from Protagoras, which has both epistemological and metaphysical skeptical implications, states: "Concerning the gods, I am unable to know either that they are or that they are not, or what their appearance is like. For many are the things that hinder knowledge: the obscurity of the matter and the shortness of human life."[56] In this quote, Protagoras implies that there are many things that "hinder knowledge" about the existence and nature of the gods. Human life is short and the subject matter, regarding the gods, is not clear. Knowledge about the gods is not possible, for Protagoras at least, given his epistemological starting point that "man is the measure." If man is the measure, then truth is relative to the individual. If truth is relative to the individual, then the individual subject may or may not have access to what is objective and real. The gods, as objectively existing external to my sensory perception, and beyond what appears, are beyond my ability to know.

The third fragment from Protagoras concerns the *logoi*. He says, "There are two opposing arguments (*logoi*) concerning everything."[57] Edward Schiappa, in his insightful analysis of the "two-*logoi*" fragment, says, "the important idea of the fragment is that there are two *logoi* in opposition about every "thing.""[58] He argues that Protagoras advances the Heraclitan flux doctrine with this "two-*logoi*" statement. He notes: "Sextus reports that Protagoras held that "the reasons [*logoi*] of all the appearances [phainomenon] subsist in the matter." The two-*logoi*, on Schiappa's interpretation, seem to make the statement more about metaphysics than about there being two sides to every argu-

---

56   Cohen, Curd, and Reeve, 75.
57   Ibid., 75.
58   Schiappa, Edward. *Protagoras and Logos: A Study in Greek Philosophy and Rhetoric* (Columbia: University of South Carolina; 1991), 89.

ment as in a debate. Schiappa makes the case that Plato in the *Theaetetus* must have had a similar understanding of Protagoras advancing a Heraclitan metaphysical position and says "when Plato discussed Protagoras' theory of knowledge in the *Theaetetus*, he cited Heraclitus (as well as Empedocles) as someone who would agree with the notion that 'if you speak of something as big, it will also appear small; if you speak of it as heavy, it will also appear light; and similarly everything.'"[59] Given the quote from Plato, and the connection Schiappa makes between the thinking of Heraclitus and that of Protagoras, the two-*logoi* fragment may be speaking of the relativity of our perception of the physical world. It is similar to "man is the measure." Man is the measure of what appears to him, which is the material world, and thus perception is relative to the perceiver. Put another way; all truth is relative to the perceiver. The two-*logoi* fragment speaks to the relativity of truth rather than to ethical relativism. Ethical relativism is a logical extension of the relativity of truth.

Protagoras' epistemological and metaphysical skepticism further leads to ethical relativism. If man is the measure of truth, then ethical truths are dependent upon the individual (or possibly upon the collective society). In addition, if the existence and nature of the gods are unknowable, then the gods cannot require anything of mankind, nor can they justly hold man accountable for his actions. Protagoras' view leads to deep skepticism, where moral accountability becomes arbitrary at best and impossible at worst. Sophism and ethical relativism are challenges in the *Theaetetus* because Socrates thinks there is some Good that is objective, knowable (has a *logos*), and is the ground of virtue.

---

59   Ibid., 94.

He thinks that philosophy is a means to pursue the Good. Also, if Theaetetus is a "young Socrates," then he must embody the philosophic spirit and desire to know. He must, like Socrates, pursue the *logos*.

V. The *Logos*

An understanding of the meaning and implications of Protagoras' philosophical assumptions is essential for us today because similar skeptical claims have resurfaced and there are similar implications for the relativity of truth, and ethical implications for how we live in our time. From the academy to popular culture, the dominant view is that man is the measure of truth, and that the existence and nature of ultimate reality is not clear.[60] Just as Socrates did not accept the skeptical claims of his day, but instead argued vigorously against skepticism, so too today Socrates may serve as a model for exposing faulty assumptions and their absurd implications.

We may be encouraged to renew pursuit of the definition and nature of knowledge, as well as exploring how to ground our knowledge in what *is*. Young philosophers, such as Theaetetus, must be rid of their Protagorean assumptions to pursue knowledge and to provide a *logos* for all that may be known.

Socrates argues that empiricism lacks a *logos* — sense perception cannot be "tied down" — thus it can never produce knowledge. A *logos* is an aspect of being that is grasped by virtue of understanding the nature of the thing in question. A *logos* is something that operates as an objective standard. All knowers may grasp it. When Socrates asks "what is *x*?" he is asking for

---

60   This view will be explored in depth in Chapter 4.

an account of the nature of *x*. He is asking about its nature, and oftentimes he is asking why someone thinks their answer to the question "what is *x*?" actually grasps the nature of *x*. He is asking for a reason, a *logos*, for the answer to the "what is *x*?" question. Additionally, Socrates argues that materialism lacks a *logos* because matter is always changing, whereas what is intelligible is permanent and objective. Lastly, Socrates argues that relativism concerning truth and relativism about ethics lacks a *logos*. He argues that man is not the measure of what is true but is only the measure of what he perceives through his senses, which may be mistaken. Socrates does not directly tell us what grounds a *logos*. But, using the Socratic method and the process of elimination that Socrates employs when asking for a definition, we may wonder what are we left with. It is clear, through the example of Socrates in the *Theaetetus*, that reason provides a *logos*; a *logos* requires non-physical mind; and that what "appears to me" is not the same as what is real. The real is known through a *logos*.

Knowledge is right opinion with an account/*logos*. Theaetetus does not have knowledge concerning accepting Protagoras' position that "man is the measure." Socrates shows that Protagoras' view lacks *logos*/ reason. He not only shows that Protagoras' view lacks reason but is contradictory and thus is not rational to believe. Knowledge requires a *logos*, which is more than a belief (based upon testimony, common sense appearance, or sensory data) or right opinion, which is not "tied down" by an account/*logos*. A *logos* goes deeper than the senses or the word of another and provides a reason such that the alternative view is impossible. This *logos* is what Socrates pursues, and what he demonstrates for Theaetetus in the dialogue.

Historically, the *Theaetetus* is more self-consciously focused upon questions of epistemology. This focus is driven by challenges raised during the era of first philosophy, which was focused primarily on metaphysics and the question of the eternality of material being. The first philosophers were searching for an explanatory ground (a *logos*) in the material world. They encountered problems, given the changeable nature of matter. The challenges that remained unanswered before Socrates were the problem of the one and the many, the problem of permanence and change, and the relativity of truth. These unanswered challenges resulted in a period of skepticism, giving rise to the Sophists. What could have been the end of philosophy and the search for a *logos* instead became a time of digging deeper to address more foundational assumptions. Socrates is more self-consciously addressing the challenges of the previous era, and he is more self-consciously pursuing knowledge based upon a *logos*. The next chapter consists of a close reading of the *Theaetetus* and an unfolding of Socrates' understanding of the *logos* that transforms true belief into knowledge.

Chapter 2

Socrates, *Logos*, and the Definition of Knowledge

The Greek culture of the Sophists had developed out of all the Greek instincts; it belongs to the culture of the Periclean age as necessarily as Plato does not: it has its predecessors in Heraclitus, in Democritus, in the scientific types of the old philosophy; it finds expression in, e.g., the high culture of two cities. And — it has ultimately shown itself to be right: every advance in epistemological and moral knowledge has reinstated the Sophists — Our contemporary way of thinking is to a great extent Heraclitean, Democritean, and

Protagorean: it suffices to say Protagorean, because Protagoras represented a synthesis of Heraclitus and Democritus.[1]

I. The Contemporary Problem of Skepticism

Everywhere around us, distinctions are being blurred. We hear claims such as "no one can really know," "there are no essential natures in things," "human beings are infinitely malleable," "there are no objective moral standards," "what's good for you is good for you, what's good for me is good for me," "there is no knowledge, only power."[2] These are popular skeptical claims. These popular claims are how skepticism is often expressed in contemporary public discourse. These popular skeptical claims are also conversation stoppers. They stem from much more profound philosophical skepticism that has gone unresolved since the modern British empirical philosophers of John Locke,[3] George Berkeley,[4] and David Hume.[5] Western philosophy

---

1 Nietzsche, Friedrich. *The Will to Power*, 428. https://archive.org/stream/TheWillToPower-Nietzsche/will_to_power-nietzsche#page/n55/mode/2up
2 Surrendra Gangadean addresses some of these popular skeptical claims in his work: *Philosophical Foundation: A Critical Analysis of Basic Beliefs.* (Lanham: University Press of America, 2008).
3 Uzgalis, William, "John Locke", *The Stanford Encyclopedia of Philosophy* (Spring 2016 Edition), Edward N. Zalta (ed.), forthcoming URL = http://plato.stanford.edu/archives/spr2016/entries/locke.
4 Downing, Lisa, "George Berkeley", *The Stanford Encyclopedia of Philosophy* (Spring 2013 Edition), Edward N. Zalta (ed.), URL = http://plato.stanford.edu/archives/spr2013/entries/berkeley.
5 Morris, William Edward and Brown, Charlotte R., "David Hume", *The Stanford Encyclopedia of Philosophy* (Spring 2016 Edition), Edward N. Zalta (ed.), forthcoming URL = http://plato.stanford.edu/archives/spr2016/entries/hume

has been dominated by empiricism,[6] which ultimately results in skepticism,[7] for at least the past 300 years. The dominance of empiricism, resulting in skepticism, has contributed to the breakdown of contemporary public discourse.

Presently there is no commonly held source of authority in the public sphere. Many of the sources that would claim authority for public discourse — such as common sense, intuition, science, and tradition — are based on experience, and each leads to skepticism. Empiricism, the view that all of our knowledge is through sense experience, is the dominant epistemology of our day. Empiricism always leads to skepticism. In the sciences, the scientific method only leads to a high probability of truth, not to certainty or indubitability. When scientists are honest, they cannot comment on philosophical questions, which are non-empirical. When not being entirely honest, some scientists go beyond what is empirically verifiable to make philosophical assumptions about the nature of ultimate reality (i.e., there is no God, or there is no soul that is separate from our brain), further contributing to skepticism. Philosophical skepticism is the view that knowledge is not possible. To put it another way, skepticism assumes that nothing is clear to reason. Nobody can really know for sure. Skepticism is the result of a lack of a common source of authority in the public realm.

Socrates position within the dialogue, *Theaetetus*, has predominantly been understood to be rationalist and foundational-

---

[6] Markie, Peter, "Rationalism vs. Empiricism", *The Stanford Encyclopedia of Philosophy* (Summer 2015 Edition), Edward N. Zalta (ed.), URL = http://plato.stanford.edu/archives/sum2015/entries/rationalism-empiricism

[7] Klein, Peter, "Skepticism", *The Stanford Encyclopedia of Philosophy* (Summer 2015 Edition), Edward N. Zalta (ed.), URL = http://plato.stanford.edu/archives/sum2015/entries/skepticism

ist concerning epistemology and realist in metaphysics. It is because of his rationalism, foundationalism, and realism that later Nietzschean and post-Nietzschean critiques from an empiricist, anti-foundationalist and anti-realist philosophy is so powerful. There are contemporary interpreters of the *Theaetetus* that suggest a moderate empiricist, and coherentist reading of the dialogue. Gail Fine, in her collection of essays: *Plato on Knowledge and Forms*,[8] argues that Plato supports both propositional knowledge and knowledge by acquaintance in the *Theaetetus*. She says:

> As I construe the argument, Plato is interested both in propositional knowledge and in knowledge of things. That he is interested in propositional knowledge is clear from the fact that he repeatedly emphasizes that knowledge but not belief implies truth. That he is interested in knowledge of things is clear from the fact that he argues that one can have knowledge only if one knows forms.[9]

Fine recognizes that some interpreters of Plato see only propositional knowledge, while others see only knowledge of things. She wants to account for both ways of knowing. To support her reading, Fine moves away from a traditional foundationalist reading of Plato to a coherentist reading that supports knowledge as holistic, which she thinks helps to avoid some errors associated with foundationalist accounts of knowledge. She says: "This replaces a linear infinite regress with a circle: accounts

---

[8] Fine, Gail. *Plato on Knowledge and Forms: Selected Essays.* (New York: Oxford University Press, 2003).
[9] Ibid., 12.

circle back on themselves. But, according to coherentists, if the circle is large enough and explanatorily powerful enough, it is virtuous, not vicious, and it constitutes the right sort of justification for knowledge."[10] Though seeing some of the value in Fine's allowing for knowledge by acquaintance in *Theaetetus*, this work ultimately sides on the rationalist, and knowledge as propositional, reading of the dialogue. In addition, this work favors a foundationalist understanding of Socrates' understanding of knowledge.

Like Fine, Dewey Hoitenga interprets the *Theaetetus* in a way that supports knowledge by acquaintance, but he also argues for a definition of knowledge justified on the basis of testimony and by inference from acquaintance and testimony. Hoitenga says in conclusion to a discussion about knowledge in the *Theaetetus*:

> In conclusion, our study of Plato has led us to a view of knowledge as justified, true belief. I know something whenever I believe it, it is true, and I can give an account of it. Unlike Plato, who narrows down such an account either to being acquainted with an object or to whatever can be inferred from what is known by such acquaintance, I have argued that an adequate justification of true belief can also include what comes to us on the testimony of others. In short, my true beliefs constitute knowledge when I can give an account of them in any one of three possible ways. If someone asks me, How do you know? I can answer by saying either "I

---

10   Ibid., 14.

saw it" (acquaintance), "I heard it" (testimony), or "It follows from what I saw or heard" (inference)[11]

Though admittedly not a view held entirely by Plato, Hoitenga thinks that seeing and hearing, as well as an inference from seeing and hearing are adequate sources of justification for knowledge. The argument of this chapter is in direct contradiction to Hoitenga's account of knowledge. Rather, the argument of the chapter follows Rosemary Desjardins' reading of the definition of knowledge within the *Theaetetus* as true opinion with an account by means of *logos*.[12] Desjardins says:

> As the senses are distinguished by the difference in their objects, so opinion (whether true or false) is differentiated from knowledge in being set over different objects (*Rep.* V, 477b3-8); cf. *Tim.* 37b3-c3; 51e6-52a7); again, opinion (whether true or false) comes through persuasion, whereas knowledge comes through teaching (Tim. 51e2-4); opinion can *happen* to be true, whereas knowledge properly claims infallibility (*Rep.* V, 477 e4-478a1; cf. *Gorg.* 454d1-8; even *Theaet.* 152c5-6; and for reiteration of the contrast in general, compare *Phaedr.* 247d1-e2; *Phil.* 58e5-59b8).[13]

Opinion is different from knowledge in that they consider different objects. The objects of opinion are changing, whereas the

---

11   Hoitenga, Jr., Dewey J. *Faith and Reason from Plato to Plantinga: An Introduction to Reformed Epistemology.* (New York: State University of New York, 1991), 32.
12   Desjardins, Rosemary. *The Rational Enterprise: Logos in Plato's Theaetetus.* (Albany: State University of New York Press, 1990), 2.
13   Ibid., 3.

objects of knowledge are unchanging. One may arrive at a correct opinion by accident, but knowledge requires a *logos* and is infallibly true.

Socrates addresses the assumptions of the first philosophers and the Sophists in Plato's dialogue, *Theaetetus*, and argues for a means for connecting *logos* and *ontos*. Socrates' conception of reason (rationalism) and being (realism) is one of the dominant positions in the history of philosophy until the Modern period when moderate empiricism slowly comes to replace Socrates' rationalism. Ours is not the first skeptical age resulting from a dominant empiricism and a loss of common authority. Plato, through the character of Socrates, dealt with related problems in his day. This chapter will provide an analysis of Plato's response to skepticism and resulting relativism, nominalism, and sophistry through a close reading of his dialogue the *Theaetetus*. The goal of the chapter is to explore the possibility of using Plato's responses to the challenges of skepticism in his day as an entry to addressing the skepticism of our day. Also, by examining how Socrates engages in dialogue, a method for public discourse and a common source of authority may be derived.

Before examining Plato, we should look at the problem of skepticism in more detail. Why is skepticism such a challenge? Why do so many think that knowledge is not possible? Empiricism is the view that all of our knowledge comes through sensory data. Sensory data is particular to the individual and is not shared. So, all the person may be sure of is what they receive through their senses. Your perception through the senses is unique to you. What is perceived by me is unique to me. These experiences are not shared, and so a shared body of knowledge beyond personal experience is probabilistic at best, and at worst is not possible.

Often naturalism (that all that exists is the material world)[14] and non-essentialism (that being has no essential qualities) in metaphysics are assumed by the empiricist. Since we cannot sense non-physical realities such as the soul or God, they are assumed to be unknowable or even not to exist. In addition, physical reality, which may be perceived by my senses, is assumed to have no essential properties that may be known. Matter is always changing, so there is nothing that is permanent in the world that my senses detect. Besides, my sense organs are also changing which makes grasping anything permanent very problematic.

When there is no objective way for knowing what reality is like, nature is all that exists, the physical world is ever-changing, and objects have no essential nature, there is no objective grounding for ethics. Thus, empiricism in epistemology results in relativism[15] in ethics. Relativism is the view that the individual determines the Good. Alternatively, relativism could be based on what a society determines. In either version of relativism (individual or social), there is no shared view of the Good for all human beings. A lack of common public authority results in a lack of a shared view of the common good for human beings. With the lack of a common source of authority in the public realm, the means of persuasion becomes propaganda and a will to power. This will to power is often played out by appeal to the legal system to enact new law or to change the existing law.

---

14 Papineau, David, "Naturalism", *The Stanford Encyclopedia of Philosophy* (Fall 2015 Edition), Edward N. Zalta (ed.), URL = http://plato.stanford.edu/archives/fall2015/entries/naturalism

15 Baghramian, Maria and Carter, J. Adam, "Relativism", *The Stanford Encyclopedia of Philosophy* (Spring 2016 Edition), Edward N. Zalta (ed.), forthcoming URL = http://plato.stanford.edu/archives/spr2016/entries/relativism

II. Socrates vs. Empiricism and its Skeptical Implications

In the dialogue the *Theaetetus*, Socrates responds to the challenges of Parmenides, a philosopher who believes all of reality is one and is permanence; and to Zeno and Heraclitus, philosophers who believe all of reality is one and is constantly changing and is in flux. The common assumption among these philosophers is that all of reality is one kind of thing. Plato also addresses the philosopher Protagoras, who claims that "man is the measure of all things." Protagoras' view about reality leads to relativism. Lastly, Plato addresses the Sophists[16] of his day, who claim that appearance is the sole reality. These Sophists are skeptical towards the possibility of knowledge and believe that persuasion is all that is left if one wants to get one's way in this world. In this dialogue, Socrates is searching for an explanation of what is unchanging in the world of particular, sensible, and changing appearances. He wants knowledge, but needs an "account," or a grounding in being, for true opinion. The *Theaetetus* is an attempt to find a definition of and an account for knowledge.

The common assumption among the philosophers that Socrates addresses in the *Theaetetus* is the view that all of our knowledge is through sensory experience. The goal of this dialogue is to find a definition of knowledge without resorting to the senses or what appears to me. He is concerned with whether knowledge is possible apart from recourse to a non-physical reality. The dialogue begins with the common sense assumption that knowledge is perception or appearance. Theaetetus, Socra-

---

16 See W.K.C. Guthrie. *The Sophists*. (New York: Cambridge University Press, 1971).

tes' primary interlocutor in the dialogue, claims the following: "Well, Socrates, with such encouragement from a person like you, it would be a shame not to do one's best to say what one can. It seems to me that one who knows something is perceiving the thing he knows, and, so far as I can see at present, knowledge is nothing but perception." Theaetetus attempts to defend the position that knowledge is perception and that one's perceptions are infallible, so, knowledge is infallible, against the questioning of Socrates. Socrates recognizes that this is a position also held by the philosopher Protagoras. Socrates says, "The account you give of the nature of knowledge is not, by any means, to be despised. It is the same that was given by Protagoras, though he stated it in a somewhat different way. He says, you will remember, that 'man is the measure of all things – alike of the being of things that are and of the not-being of things that are not.'"[17] Socrates recognizes in this quote that if knowledge is what appears to me, then knowledge becomes relative to me. An implication of knowledge being relative to the perception of the individual is that shared knowledge between perceivers is not possible. This skeptical implication is one that Socrates is ultimately going to reject.

The means by which Socrates rejects the position that "knowledge is perception" is important for this chapter because the very method that Socrates uses in dialogue with Theaetetus is the strongest argument against empiricism. Socrates does not directly present a positive argument for an alternative definition of knowledge (over and against "knowledge is perception"), at least not in this dialogue, but rather he reduces the position of Protagoras (conveyed by Theaetetus) to absurdity. The *reductio*

---

17   Cornford, 31.

ad absurdum argument is a rational argument, not an empirical argument. Socrates counters empiricism with reason and argument. To show Socrates' approach to gaining knowledge, we will engage in a careful examination of the dialogue to explicate his method for approaching knowledge and the implications for employing a similar method in contemporary public discourse.

Socrates attributes the Heraclitan belief that all is change and in flux to Protagoras. Socrates goes on to show that if all sensible things are continually changing then knowledge of the material world is not possible. Socrates shows that if "the universe is motion and nothing else,"[18] then there are really two kinds of motion: "One kind has the power of acting, and the other of being acted upon."[19] One source of motion and change is our perceptions. We perceive what appears to us which we call "'seeing', 'hearing', 'smelling', 'feeling cold', 'feeling hot' and again pleasures and pains and desires and fears, as they are called, and so on…."[20] Another source of motion and change is the physical world in which "all these things are … in motion."[21] Francis M. Cornford, in his commentary on the *Theaetetus*, says the following:

> When perception is not taking place, we are finally told, one cannot have any 'firm notion' of either agent or patient as 'having any being' or 'being any definite thing'. The last words are ambiguous. 'Being any definite thing' means having any definite quality, such as white. 'Having any being' means that there is strictly

---

18   Ibid., 46.
19   Ibid., 46.
20   Ibid., 46.
21   Ibid., 46.

no such thing as an agent or a patient as such: there is nothing that is acting or being acted upon, but only two things or changes with the capacity of acting and being acted upon.[22]

The bizarre consequence of this view, which is a form of nominalism — the view that there are no essential natures (non-essentialism) — seems to be that there is no permanent self that is perceiving and there is no permanent object of perception. One can easily see how this view leads to skepticism. Socrates shows that Protagoras' position is absurd by drawing out the logical implications of the view. He argues that there are three implications of these two kinds of change. First, each person will not have the same sensation two times because our sense organs will be different every time we perceive something. Secondly, no two people can have the same sensations from the same object. And thirdly, it would seem that the object of perception and the perceiver of the object would not exist independently of one another.[23] At this point in the dialogue, Socrates has connected the doctrine of "all is flux" with the assumption that "man is the measure" and the view that "perception is knowledge."[24] These assumptions imply that knowledge is relative to the individual. Socrates asks:

> If what every man believes as a result of perception is indeed true for him; if, just as no one is to be a better judge of what another experiences, so no one is better entitled to consider whether what another thinks

---
22 Ibid., 50.
23 Ibid., 56.
24 Ibid., 58.

> is true or false, and (as we have said more than once) every man is to have his own beliefs for himself alone and they are all right and true – then, my friend, where is the wisdom of Protagoras, to justify his setting up to teach others and to be handsomely paid for it, and where is our comparative ignorance or the need for us to go and sit at his feet, when each of us is himself the measure of his own wisdom?[25]

How can Protagoras and the Sophists teach others wisdom if "knowledge is perception" and "man is the measure" of each of his own perceptions and what is true for him?

Socrates leads by example in his arguments against these assumptions. His example is one of asking what statements mean and asking for arguments for the truth of judgments that are made by his interlocutors. Socrates says to Theaetetus, "You go entirely by what looks probable, without a word of argument or proof. If a mathematician like Theodorus elected to argue from probability in geometry, he wouldn't be worth an ace. So, you and Theodorus might consider whether you were going to allow questions of this importance to be settled by plausible appeals to mere likelihood."[26] What Socrates is saying is that in a dialogue mere appearances are never acceptable, but what is acceptable are reasons and argumentation, and he is asking for such of his interlocutors.

At this point in the dialogue, Socrates shows that remembering is different from perception, and therefore knowing must be more than mere perceiving since memory is not perception. Based upon the fact that perception may not be equated with

---

25   Ibid., 60.
26   Ibid., 62.

memory, Socrates concludes that knowledge cannot be equated with mere perceiving. He says to Theaetetus, "...if you say that knowledge and perception are the same thing, it leads to an impossibility."[27] If I perceive my dog lying on the floor at one moment, and then at a later moment I remember my dog lying on the floor, I both know my dog lies on the floor because I perceived it at the time, and I do not know my dog lies on the floor because by remembering I am not directly perceiving and so I do not know. Socrates shows that it is impossible that I both know and do not know that my dog lies on the floor. And thus, he concludes that since I have memories, and memories are not perception, and I know the content of my memories, then perception is not knowledge.

Socrates once again reduces the assumptions of his interlocutors to absurdity by means of reason. He models an alternative to empiricism in the art of his questioning. He says to Theaetetus, "I have encountered many heroes in debate, and times without number a Heracles or a Theseus has broken my head: but I have so deep a passion for exercise of this sort that I stick to it all the same. So, don't deny me the pleasure of a trial, for your own benefit as well as mine."[28] The method of common dialogue, searching for and exchanging reasons and arguments for positions, is an alternative means for knowledge that Socrates models for us in this dialogue. He never explicitly says that reason and argument gain knowledge, but by his probing questions, he models a method for knowing reality for the reader.

In the next section of the dialogue, Socrates attacks the claims that "man is the measure" and that "perception is knowl-

---

27 Ibid., 65.
28 Ibid., 76.

edge." In doing so, the question of judgment comes up, and he asks what the difference is between a judgment and perception. Judgments may be either true or false, whereas perceptions are immediate appearances to me, which are infallible (they are neither true nor false, they just *are*). Protagoras believes that one can have perceptions, but one can also have beliefs arising from perception. Beliefs, or propositions, are judgments that are either true or false. Socrates asks how men can have differences in judgments and disagree about what is true or false if each man is the measure of what is true or false. Socrates also explores the possibility that man, understood collectively, is the measure of truth. In this context, he questions how it is that States may have different judgments about laws and practices of other States if each State is the measure of truth. In both cases, Socrates implies that if man (understood individually or collectively) is the measure of truth, then individuals or States are not justified in objecting to the judgments of others. Put another way; if truth is relative to the individual or the community, then an external critique is always unjustified.

Socrates notes that the Sophists claim to teach wisdom. He asks, "And they hold that wisdom lies in thinking truly, and ignorance in false belief?"[29] So the Sophists make a distinction between wisdom which leads to truth, and ignorance which leads to falsehood. The categories of 'true' and 'false' are beyond perception and sensation. Socrates wonders how we can justify differences in our judgments about true and false if man is the measure of what is 'true' and 'false.' He asks:

---

29   Ibid., 78.

> When you have formed a judgment on some matter in your own mind and express an opinion about it to me, let us grant that, as Protagoras' theory says, it is true for you: but are we to understand that it is impossible for us, the rest of the company, to pronounce any judgment upon your judgment: or, if we can, that we always pronounce your opinion to be true, do you not rather find thousands of opponents who set their opinion against yours on every occasion and hold that your judgment and belief are false?[30]

The consequences of Protagoras' position would be that the judgment that is true for me is false to thousands of other people. So, a judgment can be both true and not true at the same time. Socrates says this is absurd. Socrates shows the self-referentially absurd consequence of Protagoras' view and asks:

> What is the consequence for Protagoras himself? Is it not this: supposing that not even he believed in man being the measure and the world in general did not believe it either – as in fact it doesn't – then this Truth which he wrote would not be true for anyone? If on the other hand, he did believe it, but the mass of mankind does not agree with him, then, you see, it is more false than true by just so much as the unbelievers outnumber the believers.[31]

The strange results of Protagoras' view that "man is the measure" is that his view may be true for him and false for the mass of mankind who may judge otherwise. Protagoras' assumption

---

30   Ibid., 78.
31   Cornford, 78.

leads to the interpretation that truth may not be reserved to the individual but may be based upon the opinions of a society. If society deems something to be true, then it is true for that society. But if the individual deems something to be true, it may be false according to society because the majority do not agree with it. For example, it may be true for one individual that marriage is the union between one man and one woman, but society may deem that statement to be false. So, the claim is both true for the individual, and it is false for society which deems it so. Socrates considers the possibility that the statement "man is the measure" may mean that man as a collective is the measure of what is true. The view that ethical categories, such as justice, are conventions of the State is a view that Plato explores further in his *Republic*.

What is of note from Socrates' dealings with what the statement "man is the measure" might mean, and his wondering whether it might be true or not, is that we see how Socrates himself approaches Truth. First, he asks what a statement means: he asks what it means for knowledge to be perception, and for man to be the measure, and for society to be the measure. Second, he proposes logical options for what these statements might mean. Third, he critically examines each logical option put forward. Fourth, he eliminates any option that leads to an absurdity, where absurdity is a contradiction (a violation of reason as the laws of thought). Fifth, he requires an argument for any judgment (which may be true or false) made by one of his interlocutors. Though Socrates himself does not seem adequately satisfied with the definition of knowledge provided within the dialogue, he does give the reader a roadmap for pursuing knowledge.

Retrieving Knowledge

The next section of the dialogue, on first reading, appears to be a diversion from the original task of defining knowledge. In this section, Socrates explores the contrast between the Philosopher and the Orator (understood to be a Sophist). Socrates is drawing our attention to the difference in epistemology between the Philosopher (one involved in identifying and distinguishing among what *is* by means of reason) and the Orator (who is concerned with what is immediately perceptible). He also shows us that the Philosopher is concerned with ultimate explanations, with the whole of reality, and with things in themselves. Whereas the Orator is concerned with politics, law, and what is pragmatic, Socrates says:

> The free man always has time at his disposal to converse in peace at his leisure. He will pass as we are doing now, from one argument to another ... like us, he will leave the old for a fresh one which takes his fancy more; and he does not care how long or short the discussion may be, if only it attains truth. The Orator is always talking against time, hurried on by the clock; there is no time to enlarge upon any subject he chooses, but the adversary stands over him ready to recite a schedule of the points to which he must confine himself. He is a slave disputing about a fellow-slave before a master sitting in judgment....[32]

Socrates describes the Philosopher as a free man, a man of leisure, whereas the Orator is a slave and is hurried; he has no time for discussion. Socrates contrasts the Philosopher, who is concerned with knowing ultimate reality, with the Orator who is

---

32   Cornford, 84.

concerned with practical things such as politics or law or "meetings, and dinners, and merrymakings."[33]

Socrates says the Philosopher "spends all his pains on the question, what man *is*, and what powers and properties distinguish such a nature from any other."[34] He repeatedly says that the Philosopher is concerned with the whole, and with understanding the whole of reality. However, it is just at this point that others mock the Philosopher. It is the job of the Philosopher to identify properly and distinguish what *is*. Socrates says the Philosopher thinks "about the meaning of kingship and the whole question of human happiness and misery, what their nature is, and how humanity can gain the one and escape the other – in all this field, when that small, shrewd, legal mind has to render an account, then the situation is reversed,"[35] and the Orator becomes the object of mockery. He explains that the common man often mocks the Philosopher for his questioning and his searching for answers to the question of what *is*. But when it comes to dialogue about what *is* it is the Orator, or the Sophist, that is now the object of mockery because he knows not how to argue and discuss these things.

In a side discussion, Socrates encourages Theodorus, a follower of the Sophist, Protagoras, to take flight from this world to the other — that is from this world of the senses to the world of the intelligible. He also says, "for to know [that righteousness is a reflection of the divine] is wisdom and excellence of the genuine sort; not to know it is to be manifestly blind and base."[36] In saying this, Socrates implies that knowledge of the

---

33 Ibid., 84-85.
34 Ibid., 85.
35 Ibid., 86.
36 Ibid., 87.

Good will result in a righteous life, whereas failing to know what is the Good will have negative consequences in this life and beyond. He further says:

> There are two patterns, my friend, in the unchangeable nature of things, one of divine happiness, the other of godless misery – a truth to which their folly makes them utterly blind, unaware that in doing injustice they are governing less like one of these patterns and more like the other. The penalty they pay is the life they lead, answering to the pattern they resemble. But if we tell them that, unless they rid themselves of their superior cunning, that other region which is free from all evil will not receive them after death, but here on earth they will do well for a time in some form of life resembling their own and in the society of things as evil in themselves....[37]

The context of this quote seems out of place in a dialogue that is pursuing the question, "what is knowledge?" But here Socrates is teaching us what is most worthy to know. He is saying that knowledge of the Good is the most important pursuit in life and it is the Philosopher who has the proper method for obtaining this knowledge. Whereas the Orator or the Sophist, beginning with sense perception, will ultimately fail to know what is truly the Good. To have knowledge of the Good, we must first understand what knowledge is in itself. So, Socrates returns to the question, "what is knowledge?" in the next section of the *Theaetetus*.

---

37   Ibid., 88.

Socrates takes up again the question of whether 'man is the measure' as Protagoras asserts. He also continues with the consideration that man as a collective may be the measure of what is true and of what is good for the State. He considers a claim made by Theaetetus that what is good for the State is what is "advantageous" for the state. Socrates notes, what is "advantageous" is a judgment (which is either objectively true or false) and requires a standard outside of the majority opinion of the State. So, the claim that what is good for the State is what is "advantageous" for the State is not itself a claim that may be proved by the consent of the community. Therefore, Socrates argues, man as a collective unity is not the measure of what is true. Socrates shows the impossibility of the interpretation (man, collective, is the measure of truth) and that we must look for another interpretation that is more meaningful. Socrates demonstrates to the reader that meaningless statements cannot be true.

With his refutation of Protagoras' view that 'man is the measure,' Socrates moves next to a discussion of Heraclitus' view that 'all is flux' or 'all is in change.' Socrates describes the flux doctrine in the following way:

> That which affects is neither hotness nor whiteness, but it becomes hot and white — and so for all the rest. You surely remember we were speaking in this way previously, that as nothing is itself one by itself, so neither is that which affects or is affected, but from both of them becoming mutually together, the perceptions and the things perceived come to be and give birth to some as certain sorts and some as perceiving?[38]

---

[38] Plato, and Seth Benardete. *The Being of the Beautiful: Plato's Theaetetus, Sophist, and Statesman.* (Chicago: University of Chicago Press, 1984)

There is no permanent being; things "become" by mutual interaction, and so, perceptions and things perceived come to be as these mutual interactions occur and are perceived. Socrates goes on to explore the claim that 'all moves and alters.' He notes that if there is only local motion but not alteration, then there is some being of which to speak. If all is flowing, then there is no being. Then he asks: If there is no being, then what is perception? There would be no perception (if all is flowing). If all is flowing, there is no being to perceive. But perception, according to Theaetetus, is knowledge. So, knowledge is non-knowledge and every answer is correct, including contradictory answers.[39]

However, if we say "so" and "not-so" we say something. If all is in motion, we could not even say this. If we could not even say this, then there would be no words (we would be left with silence). But we are saying something right now, so this is another instance of the *reductio ad absurdum* argument that Socrates so frequently employs.[40] At this point, Socrates and Theaetetus reject the claim that knowledge is perception. In addition, they reject that all is in motion and affirm that there must be something permanent — there must be being. We are left to infer that if matter is in motion, matter is not permanent being. Therefore, the permanent being that exists must be non-material. The non-material is the mind or soul.[41] Socrates gets to this "soul" by an analysis of perception. The senses are the tools of

---

Theaetetus, 182b. For an analysis of the "flux doctrine" the Benardete translation is clearer than Cornford's translation.
39   *Theaetetus*, 183a.
40   Ibid., 183b.
41   Mind and soul are used synonymously here to mean the conscious, rational, self.

perception, but "we" perceive. Socrates brings in the soul as that part of us which "sees" what is perceived.[42]

Socrates observes that the senses are part of the body, and we have multiple sense organs. He asks, what is it that perceives these various sensations? He wonders what organ perceives 'exists' and" not exists,' which are non-empirical categories. Theaetetus says: "I think there is no special organ at all for these things, as there is for the others. It is clear to me that the mind in itself is its own instrument for contemplating the common terms that apply to everything."[43] At this point in the dialogue, Socrates and his interlocutors are pressed to go beyond sense perception to the activity of the soul to make sense of non-empirical categories. Socrates does not assume that there is a soul, but he infers that there must be a soul given the problems he encountered with analysis of the claim that 'knowledge is perception.' It is impossible for knowledge to be equated with perception, so we must go beyond perception to the soul to get to the objects of knowledge.

Socrates claims that 'existence,' or being, is what the soul apprehends by itself. Being is considered by the soul, not by the senses.[44] He argues that sensations of the body come easily and naturally, whereas reflection about being comes with difficulty and must be through a process of education. Perception of sensory objects requires interpretation. He says, "Knowledge does not reside in the impressions, but in our reflection upon them. It is there, seemingly, and not in the impressions, that it is possible to grasp existence and truth."[45] A summary of Socrates' argu-

---

42 Ibid., 184d.
43 Cornford, 104.
44 Ibid., 106-107.
45 Ibid., 107.

ment may be stated in this way: Perceptions cannot apprehend existence (being); existence is necessary for truth; truth is necessary for knowledge; therefore, perception is not knowledge.

The inference to be made from Socrates' argument is that reasoning gets to truth and being, so reason gives us knowledge. Socrates demonstrates the elimination of possibilities as the path to gaining truth: "...it certainly wasn't at all for this purpose that we began conversing, in order that we may find whatever knowledge is not, but what it is. But still and all, we've advanced so far at least, so altogether not to seek it in perception but in that name, whatever the soul has, whenever it alone by itself deals with the things which are."[46] By the end of his argument against the flux doctrine, what we can glean from Socrates' careful analysis is that if all is change and our perceptions are constantly changing then knowledge is not possible. Knowledge is not possible because nothing in nature is permanent, and there are no fixed natures. Therefore, there is nothing permanent to be known (i.e., there is no permanent being). In addition, because knowledge is not possible, discourse becomes impossible. Cornford states that "all discourse will be impossible since there will be no fixed and stable things for our words to refer to."[47] There must be permanent being if words are to have any meaning. Furthermore, there must be a fit between our soul, permanent being, and the words that express being. In other words, Socrates shows that there must be an isomorphism between reason and being.

Socrates presses Heraclitus' position to its logical conclusion and claims that if knowledge is perception and all is

---

46 *Theaetetus*, 187a
47 Cornford, 97.

change, then perception is not stable, and knowledge is not knowledge.[48] To say that 'knowledge is not knowledge' is contradictory and absurd. Socrates provides another *reductio ad absurdum* argument, modeling how knowledge may be obtained by process of elimination. He is showing us the path to knowledge by eliminating what cannot possibly be true. Ultimately, Socrates shows us that equating reality with the sensible world leads to skepticism and that no knowledge is possible without some fixed being. The theory that 'all is flux' is self-referentially absurd. So far in the argument Socrates has shown that man is not the measure of truth, that knowledge is not perception, that all is not flux, that some non-material and permanent being must exist, that we perceive being with the soul, and that there is an isomorphism between reason and being. In each case, he reduces the opposite position to absurdity by showing the contradictory nature of each claim.

Next, Socrates and his interlocutors consider the possibility that knowledge is true opinion. They consider that knowledge is passed on to the student by a teacher through persuasion. They ultimately conclude that 'true opinion' is not knowledge and that something more than persuasion is necessary for knowledge. Socrates and Theaetetus then consider the possibility that *logos* converts beliefs into knowledge, where *logos* is 'giving an account.' Theaetetus says that he had heard from another that "true belief[49] with the addition of an account (*logos*) was knowledge, while belief without an account was outside its

---

48   Ibid., 98.
49   Cornford translates the Greek "*aletheia doxa*" as true belief, Benardete translates it "true opinion", and Fowler translates it "true opinion". "True opinion" seems closer to the original Greek and will be used for the remainder of the chapter.

range. Where no account could be given of a thing, it was not knowable – that was the word he used – where it could, it was knowable."[50] Socrates thinks the suggestion that 'true opinion with an account' is knowledge may be fruitful. He then pursues what knowledge as 'true opinion with an account' might mean and what this definition might entail.

Socrates' questions now center on the meaning of *logos* or what it is to give an account. Problems with understanding the meaning of what it is to 'give an account' soon surface. Cornford summarizes the problems that Socrates draws attention to when he says that "it has now been established that knowledge cannot be gained, as the theory holds, by analyzing a concrete thing, presented in a complex notion, into a simple part, each presented in a simple perception which is not knowledge."[51] Analysis of a concrete thing is still an object of perception, and breaking down this perception into simpler parts is still problematic because we are looking for an account in the process of perception — which perception, Socrates has already determined, will not yield knowledge. Socrates further explores the meaning of *logos* or 'account': Maybe *logos* is an utterance or speech act. Maybe *logos* is an enumeration of elementary parts. Lastly, *logos* may be distinguishing one thing from another thing.[52] Cornford summarizes Socrates' refutation of each of these senses of *logos* when he says:

> The point is that we cannot get 'knowledge,' supposed to be somehow superior to mere beliefs or notions, by adding a *logos* in any of these senses considered. These

---

50 Ibid., 142.
51 Ibid., 153.
52 Ibid., 155-158.

senses appear to exhaust the possible ways in which an 'account' can be given of an individual thing. (1) we may name it (express our notion of it in speech); (2) we may enumerate the material parts of which it is composed; or (3) we may point it out by a description which will serve to distinguish the thing we indicate from other things. But none of these 'accounts' will yield any 'clearer' or more certain kind of cognition than we started with.

The Platonist will draw the necessary inference. True knowledge has for its object things of a different order – not sensible things, but intelligible Forms and truths about them.[53]

The end of the dialogue leaves us knowing that knowledge is not through the senses, but we have no positive definition of knowledge. We have no 'account' of what knowledge is. True opinion with an account sounds like a good definition of knowledge, and what some contemporary analytic philosophers have called 'justified true belief.' Yet the problem with this definition has always been what counts as justification or what counts as an 'account' (*logos*) for knowledge.

By the end of the *Theaetetus* Protagoras' view that 'man is the measure' is refuted, implying that there is another standard for Truth outside of our perceptions. Heraclitus' view that 'all is flux' is also refuted, implying that there must be some being that is eternal and unchangeable, and that there is more to reality than the mere physical world of our perceptions; that our soul grasps the reality behind the objects of sense percep-

---

53   Ibid., 162.

tion. If there is a soul in addition to our bodies and this soul is non-physical then Socrates gets us to a non-physical reality, or what may be called 'spirit' (something that is non-physical and conscious). The dialogue, then, is an argument against materialism (or physicalism), which is an assumption of Protagoras and the Sophists. Through dialogue and argumentation with his interlocutors Socrates proves that man is not the measure, all is not flux, and knowledge is not perception. If all is not flux, then there must be something that is permanent, existing in addition to the physical realm that is continually changing. In addition, if knowledge is not perception, then knowledge must be something else.

Though Socrates does not directly answer the question, 'what is knowledge?' in the *Theaetetus*, he does demonstrate to the reader how to obtain knowledge. Knowledge may turn out to be true opinion with an account, but the 'account' is not grounded in sense perception but in something other than the senses. Socrates models what this knowledge looks like in his Socratic Method of questioning, and of refuting positions that lead to absurdities or contradictions. He shows us that knowledge is obtained by reason and argument (rather than by sense perception) such that the opposite position is impossible. Instead of relying upon sensory data, which at best yields a high probability of truth, Socrates uses a deductive approach to knowledge, arguing to a necessary conclusion by the elimination of what is logically impossible. What is a necessary truth is also indubitable, or certain. Early in the dialogue, Socrates and Theaetetus agree that knowledge is infallible. At the time, they were discussing sensory perceptions and agreed that our sensory perceptions were not infallible. Socrates shows that though

I cannot doubt the content of my perceptions, what I perceive through my senses is not reality, but appearances. If we want to maintain that knowledge is infallible, then there must be a surer grounding (or 'account,' or *logos*) for our judgments. The account that Socrates and Theaetetus are looking for when they say that 'knowledge is true judgment with an account' is the *logos*, where *logos* is interpreted as reason in the strong deductive sense (proof of necessity by showing the impossibility of the opposite).

The term *logos* is used in at least 111 locations within the *Theaetetus*, with multiple uses of the term in each location.[54] Cornford translates *logos* (and its various forms) in the following ways: saying, speaking, speech, argument, account, grounds, proof, telling, word, discourse, conversation, description, name, call, reason, explanation, defense, discussion, theory, and definition. The most common uses of *logos* in the *Theaetetus* are "saying" and "account." Theaetetus suggests that it is a *logos* that converts true opinion into knowledge.[55] Socrates and Theaetetus only explore the possibility that the *logos*, translated "account" by Cornford, is grounded in sensory perception. Socrates determines that grounding an "account" in sensory data, which is particular to the perception of the individual perceiver, and is constantly changing, will not ground the *logos* in being, which is unchanging and universal, and thus will not yield infallible knowledge.

The *logos*, we may infer, is an aspect of all being; it is intelligible, grasped by the reasoning soul, but not grasped by perception through sensory data; and it is universal and unchanging. When we communicate, we are exchanging *logoi*. "Discourse,"

---

54 By 'location' is meant within a section of Stephanus Numbers for the dialogue.
55 Cornford, 142-143.

"conversation," and "dialogue" are exchanges of reasons between the souls of intelligent beings. Socrates suggests, in the midst of exploring what this 'account' (*logos*) might be, that thinking is "discourse (*logos*) that the soul carries on with itself about any subject it is considering."[56] He adds that "I should describe thinking as discourse, and judgment as a statement pronounced, not aloud to someone else, but silently to oneself."[57] Cornford, in his commentary on the *Theaetetus*, assumes that the 'account' that Socrates is looking for will be found only in the Theory of the Forms, which theory is expounded in other Platonic Dialogues. Many have objected to the Theory of Forms, most notably Aristotle, and there is not space to explicate and analyze the Theory within the context of this work, but one may argue that Socrates provides enough in the present dialogue for a workable theory of knowledge without recourse to the Forms.

III. Plato and the TOA Definition of Knowledge

We are used to saying that the contemporary definition of knowledge as justified true belief goes back to Plato's dialogues *Meno* and *Theaetetus*. For instance, Gail Fine, in her work, *Plato on Knowledge and Forms*, says "At *Meno* 98A, Plato offers just one definition of knowledge – as justified true belief...."[58] Dewey Hoitenga, in his *Faith and Reason from Plato to Plantinga*, says, "knowledge is true belief accompanied by an account, as Plato puts it, or, in the language of contemporary philosophers,

---

56 Ibid., 118.
57 Ibid.
58 Fine, Gail. *Plato on Knowledge and Forms: Selected Essays*. (New York: Oxford University Press, 2003), 50.

knowledge is *justified true belief.*"⁵⁹ A third and more lengthy quote, from Alvin Plantinga, shows the contemporary conflation of Plato's definition of knowledge with justified true belief (JTB):

> It would be colossal understatement to say that Anglo-American epistemology of this century has made much of the notion of epistemic justification. First, of course, there is the widely celebrated "justified true belief" JTB account or analysis of knowledge, and analysis we imbibed with our mothers milk. According to the inherited lore of the epistemological tribe, the JTB account enjoyed the status of epistemological orthodoxy until 1963, when it was shattered by Edmund Gettier with his three page paper "Is Justified True Belief Knowledge?" After 1963 the justified true belief account of knowledge was seen to be defective and lost its exalted status; but even those convinced by Gettier that justification (along with truth) is not *sufficient* for knowledge still mostly think it *necessary* and *nearly* sufficient for knowledge: the basic shape or contour of the concept of knowledge is given by justified true belief, even if a quasi-technical fillip or addendum ("the fourth condition") is needed to appease Gettier. Of course there is an interesting historical irony here: it isn't easy to find many really explicit statements of a JTB analysis of knowledge prior to Gettier. It's almost

---

59 Hoitenga, Jr., Dewey J. *Faith and Reason from Plato to Plantinga: An Introduction to Reformed Epistemology.* (New York: State University of New York, 1991), 1.

as if a distinguished critic created a tradition in the very act of destroying it.[60]

The purpose of these quotes is to show that the contemporary or post-Nietzschean[61] assumption about Plato's definition of knowledge is that it is the same as contemporary JTB formulations. However, Plantinga does acknowledge that prior to Gettier there are not many formulations of knowledge. It is almost as if Plato provided a definition of knowledge, which was taken for granted for a couple thousand years, and then Gettier re-formulated the definition as JTB, and contemporary epistemologists accepted that they are the same. The question to be raised here is: is it really the case that Plato's definition is the same as contemporary JTB formulations of knowledge?

Plato's definition is not the same as contemporary JTB formulations. We are doing philosophy in a post-Nietzsche era. Nietzsche has rejected Plato's vision of epistemology, has proposed a radical revaluation of all values, and subsequent philosophers have carried out the implications this revaluation. It wouldn't be surprising to find that the post-Nietzschean formulation of the definition of knowledge is the exact opposite of how Plato would define knowledge. Post-Nietzschean philosophy is a revaluation of Platonic philosophy, and so post-Nietzschean definitions of knowledge are either revaluations of the definition of knowledge or reactions to the revaluation of the defini-

---

60 Plantinga, Alvin. *Warrant: The Current Debate*. (New York: Oxford University Press, 1993), 6.
61 "Post-Nietzschean" is a term that will be used to describe philosophy after Nietzsche and is intended to include the analytic, pragmatic, and continental traditions in philosophy. That these traditions may be joined through reference to Nietzsche will be argued for in Chapter 4.

tion of knowledge, as in the case of Plantinga and Hoitenga.[62] This section of the chapter will argue that Plato's formulation of knowledge is not equivalent to a post-Nietzschean formulation

---

62   Rather than question whether the received JTB formulation of knowledge is the definition of knowledge that Plato actually gives, Plantinga addresses contemporary post-Nietzschean definitions of knowledge as they pose a threat to religious belief. Plantinga does not address the empirical assumptions of Gettier's formulation of justification, rather Plantinga rejects the necessity of justification altogether. Plantinga offers an alternative to many post-Nietzschean formulations of JTB by proposing that knowledge is "warranted true belief," where a belief is warranted if it is formed by cognitive faculties functioning properly, in an appropriate environment, and according to a good design plan. Plantinga's epistemology is externalist, and essentially empiricist with a religious twist. He allows that when a person has cognitive faculties that are functioning properly according to a good design plan, she will form the belief that "God exists." The warranted belief that "God exists" is a spontaneously arising belief that is something akin to John Calvin's *Sensus Divinitatus* — a sense of the divine — that is an immediate and intuitive awareness. A problem for the person who forms the belief "God exists" in this immediate way is that when she meets someone with a contradictory belief (a defeater), she loses her warrant. When faced with a defeater, one must provide a defeater-defeater, which is very much like providing a reason, or a Platonic account, for true belief. So, Plantinga may talk a lot about warrant as sufficient to ground true belief, warrant only grounds a true belief until that belief is met with a defeater, or counter-argument. The person holding to belief on the basis of warrant who encounters a Socrates will be forced into providing a *logos* very quickly. Plantinga may have done a lot for bringing the religious believer to the table of philosophical discussion in a post-Nietzschean world, even carving out a space in the academy where metaphysics is ordinarily verboten, in the study of philosophy of religion, he does not get the believer out of the position of having to provide a reason for belief in the face of contradictory positions. To put it another way, the believer must still show the eternal power and divine nature of God in the face of unbelief. Warrant does not dissolve the need for providing a rational account. For a more detailed discussion of these issues, see: Fitzsimmons, Kelly. *Plantinga on Justification, Warrant, and the Proper Function of our Rational Faculties.* (Master's Thesis, Arizona State University, 2000).

of knowledge as JTB. A comparison between Plato's formulation of knowledge in the *Meno* and the *Theaetetus* and the contemporary discussion of JTB with its associated Gettier problems will be explored. Finally, an argument will be made that for the survival of meaning, philosophy, the West, and public discourse regarding our most cherished values, we must return to a Platonic and Socratic method, definition, and application of knowledge.

The previous section engaged in a detailed analysis of the *Theaetetus*, and how Plato, through Socrates, addresses empiricism, materialism, skepticism, and sophism. It is in the context of these assumptions that he formulates a definition of knowledge as a true opinion with an account (TOA). In contrast to the contemporary JTB formulation, we will call the Socratic-Platonic definition the TOA account of knowledge. The TOA account is decidedly anti-empiricist and anti-materialist, which must be kept in mind for doing post-Nietzschean analysis. As we shall discover in the next chapter, the post-Nietzschean world assumes the empiricism-materialism-skepticism-sophism worldview that Socrates opposes; it is the exact opposite of the Socratic-Platonic worldview.

In *Theaetetus*, knowledge is defined as true opinion with an account. This formulation is essential to distinguish JTB and TOA. A transliteration of the Greek is: "*logou aletheia doxan epistemen,*"[63] which is translated by H.N. Fowler as: knowledge is "true opinion accompanied by reason."[64] The previous chapter provided a lengthy analysis of the Greek term *"logos."* We should also explore *aletheia* and *doxa* to understand how Plato's

---

63 Plato, and H.N. Fowler. *Plato VII Theaetetus and Sophist*. (Cambridge: Harvard University Press, 1977), 201.
64 Ibid., 202.

formulation is different from the contemporary JTB definition of knowledge. Liddell and Scott[65] define *aletheia* as "truth" or "reality." *Aletheia* is contrasted with appearance or put another way; truth is not appearance; appearance is not reality. *Doxa* is often interpreted as "opinion," but also means the following: to appear, to seem, to think, or to accept, and often has the sense of belief or popular opinion.[66] *Doxa* in Plato's dialogues is like holding to a popular view or basing an opinion upon what appears to be the case. This "appearing" to be the case could be like saying "it seems to me," or it could be based on one's sense perceptions, what appears to my senses. *Doxa* may be construed as what the majority of people think or believe based upon common sense perception or based upon the collective common sense of tradition passed on from one generation to another. If *doxa* is to become knowledge — from seeming to *is* — it must be tied down with a *logos*, and it must be based in reality (*aletheia*). It is important to note that the Socratic-Platonic TOA formulation of knowledge assumes that there is an isomorphism between reason/*logos* and being/*ontos*. *Aletheia* is connected to reality, or being, and *logos* grasps the reality of being. A post-Nietzschean philosophy does not recognize the isomorphism between reason and being; thus a post-Nietzschean formulation of knowledge, such as the JTB formulation, may also fail to recognize the isomorphism between reason and being. To better understand the TOA formulation of knowledge, and to see the distinctions that Plato draws between knowledge, opinion, and true opinion, we will explore a few passages from the *Republic* and the *Meno*, and then we will return to the *Theaetetus*.

---

65 Liddell and Scott. *An Intermediate Greek-English Lexicon*. (Oxford: Clarendon Press, 1995), 34.
66 Ibid., 207-208.

As was discovered in the *Theaetetus*, Socrates argues that there must be a conscious soul that grasps the *logoi*. In the *Republic*, Plato describes the soul as tripartite: the rational part, the spirited part (*thumos*), and the appetitive part. These parts seem to equate to intellect, will (*thumos*), and emotion. Just as Plato sees the soul as having different functions, he sees reality as having different levels. The functions of the soul are somewhat connected to the different levels of reality as we attempt to move from images that appear to the five senses, to opinions about those images, to thoughts we make through empirical investigation (calculation and measurement), to knowledge of the intelligible realm. Socrates has the following to say to Glaucon about the division between opinion (*doxa*), which is connected to sensation, and knowledge, which is connected to reason: "Haven't you noticed that opinions without knowledge are shameful and ugly things? The best of them are blind — or do you think that those who express a true opinion without understanding are any different from blind people who happened to travel the right road?"[67] The distinction between opinion and knowledge makes the difference between "blindly" holding to what is possibly false and harmful to human beings, or "virtuously" attaining to truth and what is good for human beings.

In attempting to talk about knowledge of the good in the *Republic*, Socrates uses three allegories: that of the Sun, the Line, and the Cave. Each of these allegories brings out something different in the relationship between the visible world and the invisible world; the relationship between opinion and knowledge; and between what is harmful and what is good for human beings. Socrates says that he is unable to speak about the

---

67 Plato, *Republic* 506c5.

good — the highest reality — directly, but that "I am willing to tell you about what is apparently an offspring of the good and most like it."[68]

Socrates begins to talk about the offspring of the good with the allegory of the sun. He says that "beauty itself and the good itself and all the things that we thereby set down as many, reversing ourselves, we set down according to a single form of each, believing that there is but one, and call it 'the being' of each."[69] Socrates is saying that the many things that appear to us through the senses have their being from the form of each thing. He adds further: "And we say that the many beautiful things and the rest are visible but not intelligible, while the forms are intelligible but not visible."[70] The many visible things we perceive with our eyes and other senses, but the form of each is intelligible and cannot be perceived by the senses. "And with what part of ourselves do we see visible things?" Socrates asks. "With our sight," says Glaucon. Socrates responds, "and so audible things are heard by hearing, and with our other senses we perceive all the other perceptible things."[71] Sensible things are perceived by our senses. More is needed for perception besides physical objects and sensory perception. Socrates adds that:

> Sight may be present in the eyes, and the one who has it may try to use it, and colors may be present in things, but unless a third kind of thing is present, which is naturally adapted for this very purpose, you know that

---

68 Ibid., 506e1.
69 Ibid., 507b4-6.
70 Ibid., 507b8-9.
71 Ibid., 507c1–5.

> sight will see nothing, and the colors will remain unseen … I mean what you call light.[72]

What is necessary for "seeing" with the eye are physical objects, a sense of sight, and light by which we can see. Socrates observes, "Then it isn't an insignificant kind of link that connects the sense of sight and the power to be seen — it is a more valuable link than any other link things have got, if indeed light is something valuable …."[73] The valuable link that Socrates speaks of is the sun.

Although sight is the most "sunlike of the senses" and it receives from the sun the power it has, the sun is not sight, but the sun is one of the necessary conditions for sight. The sun is that by which we see physical things in the world. Socrates goes on to make an analogy to the good, saying, "This is what I call the offspring of the good, which the good begot as its analog. What the good itself is in the intelligible realm, in relation to understanding and intelligible things, the sun is in the visible realm, in relation to sight and visible things."[74] Socrates shows that the good is to reason what the sun is to our eyesight. He continues:

> … Understand the soul in the same way: When it focuses on something illuminated by truth and what is, it understands, knows, and apparently possesses understanding, but when it focuses on what is mixed with obscurity, on what comes to be and passes away, it

---

72 Ibid., 507d7-e3.
73 Ibid., 508a1-3.
74 Ibid., 508b8-9.

opines and is dimmed, changes its opinions this way and that, and seems bereft of understanding.[75]

In this quote Socrates makes a connection between understanding what is true (presumably by reason) and lack of understanding (mixture and obscurity) and opinion (presumably by sensation). As the sun sheds light on the physical world, and gives the power of sight, "So that what gives truth to the things known and the power to know to the knower is the form of the good."[76] The good is both an object of knowledge and is the cause of knowledge. The good is the source of being and the intelligibility of being; thus, the good is highest. Socrates says, "Not only do the objects of knowledge owe their being known to the good, but their being is also due to it, although the good is not being, but superior to it in rank and power."[77] As the sun gives life and light to all that lives on earth, the good is the source of life to the rational soul. Socrates thus distinguishes between the physical and visible world of the senses, and the non-physical invisible realm of the forms, the highest of which is the good. Knowledge of the good is what is most desirable for human beings.

The second allegory that Socrates uses to describe these two different realities and how they are known is the allegory of the line. He says that reality:

> … Is like a line divided into two unequal sections. Then divide each section — namely, that of the visible and that of the intelligible — in the same ratio as the line

---

75 Ibid., 508d2–7.
76 Ibid., 508e3-4.
77 Ibid., 509b7-8.

> in terms now of relative clarity and opacity, one subsection of the visible consists of images. And by images I mean, first, shadows, then reflections in water and in all close-packed, smooth, and shiny materials, and everything of that sort, if you understand…In the other subsection of the visible, put the originals of these images, namely, the animals around us, all the plants, and whole class of manufactured things.… Would you be willing to say that, as regards truth and untruth, the division is in this proportion: as the opinable is to the knowable, so the likeness is to the thing that it is like?[78]

Imagine a vertical line divided in two. The top half represents the intelligible realm. The bottom half represents the visible realm. At the very bottom of the bottom half are images, or copies, of the physical world. The next portion up the vertical line represents objects in the physical world. Socrates then has us consider the section of the top half of the vertical line, which represents the intelligible realm, and how it is divided. He says:

> In one subsection, the soul using as images the things that were imitated before, is forced to investigate from hypotheses, proceeding not to a first principle but to a conclusion. In the other subsection, however, it makes its way to a first principle that is not a hypothesis, proceeding from a hypothesis but without the images used in the previous subsection, using forms themselves and making its investigation through them.[79]

---

78 Ibid., 509d6-510a5.
79 Ibid., 510b1-6.

The lower subsection of the top half of the divided line is involved with calculations and observations, making hypotheses and inferences from what is observed in the physical world to some conclusions about those observations, much like what we would call the empirical sciences and mathematics. There is one level higher on the divided line which has to do with understanding without the aid of sensation. Socrates says: "By the other subsection of the intelligible, I mean that which reason itself grasps by the power of dialectic."[80] Reason alone, apart from the senses, grasps the highest being of the intelligible realm.

Socrates makes a distinction between what may be known by reason and what may be known by scientific inquiry, though they are both on the upper portion of the vertical line. Glaucon says to Socrates:

> I understand ... that you want to distinguish the intelligible part of that which is, the part studied by the science of dialectic, as clearer than the part studied by the so-called sciences, for which their hypotheses are first principles. And although those who study the objects of the sciences are forced to do so by means of thought rather than sense perception, still, because they do not go back to a genuine first principle, but proceed from hypotheses, you don't think that they understand them, even though, given such a principle, they are intelligible. And you seem to me to call the state of the geometers thought but not understanding, though being intermediate between opinion and understanding.[81]

---

80 Ibid., 511b2-3.
81 Ibid., 511d7-9.

Socrates affirms what Glaucon is asking and says that "there are four such conditions in the soul, corresponding to the four subsections of our line: understanding for the highest, thought for the second, belief [*doxa*] for the third, and imaging for the last."[82] Imagination is the power that grasps images, is the least like knowledge and is at the lowest portion of the divided line. Moving up the line, belief or opinion (*doxa*) is the power that grasps the objects of sensation. What is implied is that opinion is based upon perception. Moving up the line to the intelligible realm, thought is the power that makes conclusions about particulars based upon measuring and calculating and is closest to mathematical and scientific reasoning (true opinion). In contrast to the physical sciences is the "science of dialectic," the power of understanding, which grasps reality. Whereas science infers from particulars to first principles, reason, and the science of dialectic, grasps the first principles in a non-empirical way.

In the allegory of the cave, Socrates has us imagine a cave with people chained facing the wall of the cave, upon which are cast shadows, and which these people take to be reality, producing something like a show on the wall of the cave. These prisoners hear sounds and see sights that are produced by others, but they take these images and sounds to be real. They then go on to form judgments and make predictions about the appearances they have observed since their youth. At some point, one of these prisoners is forced from the cave to the light of day and has to reorient his sight. He moves in stages from the firelight, then he is forced into daylight, and then he is temporarily blinded by the brightness of the sun. As he ascends from the cave to the light of day, he not only has to adjust how he sees,

---

82   Ibid., 511d10.

he has to rethink his entire view of reality. What he thought was true was a mistake based on shadows. As his eyes adjust, he can see the "real" world. He can see the source of the shadows, which he previously took to be reality, and he can see things like trees, birds, and heavenly bodies. Eventually, he can look at the sun, the source of all life. When he sees the sun, he has grasped the truth of the source of all being. In due time, he goes back into the cave out of compassion for his fellow man, undergoing the painful, blinding transition back into the darkness. Yet, he is ultimately rejected by his fellow humans who think he has ruined his eyesight and brought back dangerous teachings.[83]

The cave represents the physical world in which we human beings find ourselves. We are the prisoners, and we are held captive to the false images by means of our senses. What comes to us through sensory perception we take to be reality, but in fact, sensory perceptions give us images, opinion, often false judgment, and even ignorance. We are taking copies for reality when we think we know through the senses. We are chasing shadows on the cave wall. The one who leaves the cave and looks upon reality, represented by trees, birds, and heavenly bodies, is the one who transcends the realm of appearances using reason to contemplate reality — the forms. The sun, which represents the source of all light and life, represents the beatific vision, or the form of all forms, the good itself. All the other forms, in so far as they are ideals, partake of the form of the good. The form of beauty partakes in the good as well. Socrates says that:

> In the knowable realm, the form of the good is the last thing to be seen, and it is reached only with difficul-

---

83 Ibid., 514a-518b2.

ty. Once one has seen it, however, one must conclude that it is the cause of all that is correct and beautiful in anything, that it produces both light and its source in the visible realm, and that in the intelligible realm it controls and provides truth and understanding, so that anyone who is to act sensibly in private or public must see it.[84]

In this journey from opinion to knowledge, the good is the universal ground of all things, or the metaphysical ground of beauty and all things correct (ethics). The good is that by which we see, and the light of the good is in human beings as reason, the power by which men act rationally in public and private life. Reason is the source of right action. In this allegory we see Plato's epistemology: knowledge is of true being, not mere sensory impressions and opinion. True being gets its reality from the good. As highest reality, the good is the source of beauty itself, and the reflection of beautiful and correct things in the world. Knowledge of the good would be most important.

    Plato again makes the distinction between knowledge and opinion in the *Meno*. As in the allegory of the Line from the *Republic*, Socrates holds that there may be degrees of belief and understanding. At one point in the *Meno* Socrates questions a slave boy concerning geometry. He has the slave boy work out a geometrical problem, and Socrates concludes that the slave boy, being ignorant of geometry, must have *a priori* knowledge of geometry to have worked out the problem as he did. In the example of the slave boy, Socrates attempts to show that knowledge is not acquired but may be innate. The slave boy is not

---

84   Ibid., 517b7-c3.

entirely ignorant but may have some innate ideas within him that enable him to solve the geometry problem. If he has innate ideas within him, he has the possibility of growth now that he is aware of himself and his capacities. W.K.C. Guthrie notes that:

> One of the most important lessons of the *anamnesis* [recollection] doctrine was that learning was a continuous process, with several stages between (apparent) blank ignorance and knowledge — important because it invalidated the Sophist's favourite method of attack by the crude 'either-or' question....[85]

Guthrie notes that if all we had were the stark contrast between complete ignorance or knowledge, there would be no way to explain the prevalence of false opinion and no way to account for growth in understanding, which are empirical facts. Some people have false opinions, such as many of the interlocutors with whom Socrates engages; and we witness some people who grow in understanding, such as the slave boy.

Meno and Socrates discuss true opinions that lead to right action, particularly when it comes to the statesman. Socrates asks:

> What if someone had had a correct opinion as to which was the way but had not gone there nor indeed had knowledge of it, would he not also lead correctly?... And as long as he has had the right opinion about that of which the other has knowledge, he will not be a

---

[85] Guthrie, W.K.C., *A History of Greek Philosophy: Plato: The Man and His Dialogues Earlier Period, Vol. IV* (Cambridge: Cambridge University Press; 1975), 257. It seems reasonable to hold to the possibility of *a priori* knowledge without being committed to Plato's theory of recollection.

worse guide than the one who knows, as he has a true opinion, though not knowledge ... So true opinion is in no way a worst guide to correct action than knowledge.[86]

True opinions are sufficient for right action for the statesman. When it comes to action, the person who has a true opinion and the person who knows will both act in the right way. Yet Meno observes that "the man who has knowledge will always succeed, where he who has true opinion will only succeed at times."[87] Knowledge is more prized than true opinion because knowledge gets us to certainty that true opinion lacks. Guthrie says that: "Knowing the essence of the unchanging *Forms* of just, brave and the rest, he would no longer rely on an empirical guess as to the probable outcome of his actions ... His former right *doxa* [opinion] would have become knowledge 'by working out the reason', for the Form of the Good, if he only knew it, is the cause of a good act."[88]

What Guthrie calls "working out the reason," is what Socrates calls "tying down," or *logos*, in the *Meno*. He suggests that knowledge is true opinion that is "tied down" with an account. He says that true opinions "run away and escape if one does not tie them down" and that they will "remain in place if tied down."[89] True opinions are not worth much until one provides a reason for them. Socrates says, "After they are tied down, in the first place they become knowledge, and then they remain in place. That is why knowledge is prized higher than correct

---

86 Plato, *Meno* 96e8-97c1.
87 Ibid., 97c4-5.
88 Guthrie, Vol IV, 263.
89 Plato, *Meno* 97d8.

opinion, and knowledge differs from correct opinion in being tied down."[90] Once a true opinion is tied down with a reason, it becomes knowledge. What does it mean to be "tied down" with an account, or a reason? At the end of the *Meno*, Socrates reveals that he does not know whether virtue may be taught because Meno has asked the wrong question. How can they know whether virtue may be taught when they have neither defined virtue nor knowledge? What is virtue? What is knowledge? Both of these terms need to be defined. The *Theaetetus* picks up with the question that the *Meno* leaves off with, namely the question, "what is knowledge?"

To summarize the TOA definition of knowlege: Plato's dialogue the *Theaetetus* contains a search for a definition of knowledge in the face of empiricism and epistemological relativism. Socrates, among several others, addresses the philosopher Protagoras, who claims that "man is the measure of all things." Protagoras' view about reality leads to relativism with regards to knowledge. In this dialogue, Socrates also addresses the sophists of his day who claim that appearance is the sole reality. These philosophers are skeptical towards the possibility of knowledge and believe that persuasion is the appropriate means if one wants to get one's way in this world. In the *Theaetetus*, Socrates searches for an explanation of what is unchanging in the world of particular, sensible, and changing appearances. He wants to know if knowledge of the world of appearance is possible, and searches for an 'account' or a grounding in being for true belief. The *Theaetetus* is an attempt to find an account for knowledge.

---

90 Ibid., 98a1-6.

Retrieving Knowledge

The common assumption among the philosophers that Socrates addresses in the *Theaetetus* is the view that all of our knowledge is through sensory experience. The goal of this dialogue is to find a definition of knowledge without resorting to the senses or what appears to me. In addition, Socrates does not rely upon the theory of the forms in this dialogue. He is concerned with whether knowledge of this world, the world of appearance, is possible apart from recourse to a non-physical reality.

Socrates and his interlocutors consider the possibility that knowledge is true judgment. They consider the possibility of knowledge being passed on to the student by a teacher through the means of persuasion. They ultimately conclude that 'true opinion' is not knowledge and that something more than persuasion is necessary for knowledge. Socrates and Theaetetus next consider the possibility that *logos* converts true opinion into knowledge, where *logos* is 'giving an account.' Theaetetus says that he had heard from another that "true belief with the addition of an account (*logos*) was knowledge, while belief without an account was outside its range. Where no account could be given of a thing, it was not knowable – that was the word he used – where it could, it was knowable."[91] Socrates thinks the suggestion that 'true opinion with an account' is knowledge may be fruitful. Though at the end of the *Theaetetus*, it seems that Socrates is second-guessing whether they have arrived at an adequate definition. By looking at what Socrates does in the dialogues, one may argue that Socrates provides a method for knowing, as well as an adequate definition of what knowledge *is*.

---

91   Cornford, 142.

Much of post-Nietzschean epistemology discusses knowledge in the context of language, particularly in the context of propositions, which are linguistic conventions that may carry truth value. For post-Nietzschean philosophers, propositions may or may not refer to a reality outside of a language game.[92] Some pose the question: do we know propositions (linguistic devices), or do we know reality? Within a Socratic-Platonic-Aristotelian context we may think of the relationship between concepts, judgments, and propositions in the following way: "(A) First we have concepts. (B) These concepts are expressed in terms. (C) Terms, and thereby concepts, are united by us in *enunciative* propositions. (D) Our assent to this union of terms takes place, and this *is* the judgment. (E) We express this assent verbally in a *judicative* proposition."[93] Judicative propositions are a means of verbally expressing our judgments about reality, or at least what seems (*doxa*) to be reality. Propositions are either true or false. Propositions may be thought, spoken, written, or signed (as in American Sign Language). So, it is not propositions that are known, but reality that is known. Propositions are a verbal expression of our thoughts — judgments — about reality and are either true or false because they either match reality or they do not.

We grasp reality first through concepts — 'what is x?' Then propositions are about x — 'x is y' — which either match reality, and are true, or do not match reality and are false. A *logos* is added to show how/that a proposition actually does match reality — that the proposition is true. A *logos* is an argument — a

---

92 The linguistic turn in philosophy, which deals with propositions, will be discussed in Chapter 4.
93 McCall, Raymond J. *Basic Logic: The Fundamental Principles of Formal Deductive Reasoning.* (New York, Barnes and Noble Books, 1952), 39.

syllogism, perhaps — that links the proposition to reality in a necessary way. Necessity and impossibility are the categories of knowledge, whereas possibility and probability are the categories of true opinion (science and mathematics). Possibly 'x is y.' Probably 'x is y.' We can try to make observations to either verify or falsify whether 'x is y.' This is the realm of science in Plato's epistemology. On the Line, it is the second highest level, just below knowledge. The physical sciences do not hold the same status as knowledge for Plato because knowledge does not depend upon the senses and true opinion (*doxa*). Instead, knowledge is true opinion with an account, and this account brings about certainty. The only categories that can bring about certainty are necessity and impossibility. Socrates demonstrates the method of gaining knowledge when he rules out possibilities brought up in dialogue because they are logically impossible. He uses the *reductio ad absurdum* argument time and time again. By ruling out some possibilities, we are left with others until all impossibilities are eliminated, and we are left with the last position standing, and this last position is necessarily the true opinion because it has been "tied down" by the argument. The *logos* eliminates impossibility. This is the force of reason — the laws of thought — particularly the law of non-contradiction (LNC). If one were to denounce or deny LNC in any way, then knowledge, true opinion with an account, would not be possible because a *logos*, by means of the LNC would not be possible. This is why Nietzsche, in his revaluation of values, takes aim at LNC as ontological. He intentionally sets himself up against reason, Plato, philosophy as it has been done since the Pre-Platonic philosophers, and the West in general by denying LNC applies to being.

Let us reexamine what Socrates is doing in the dialogues that brings about knowledge. First, he asks 'what is x?' In doing so, he applies the law of identity (LI) to identify what a thing or idea *is* properly and to distinguish it from all other things or ideas. In Aristotelian terms, he is involved with the first act of the mind in concept formation. This is the most basic application of reason (the laws of thought) and is the most fundamental for gaining knowledge. If we do not properly identify a thing or idea, then we cannot make a true proposition about it. Much of the Socratic method is spent in interrogating the meaning of a word (i.e., piety, virtue, knowledge, wisdom, beauty, etc.). Socrates and his interlocutors are involved in trying to understand the reality — the meaning — of the thing or idea that the word stands for. Words express concepts, and concept formation involves the engagement of the mind with reality. 'What is x?' is the same as 'what is the reality or meaning of x?' Once the reality or meaning of a word has been grasped, a judgment may be made, and a proposition stated.

For Aristotle, a judgement is the second act of the mind and takes the form 'x is y.' Judgments contain quantification (universal or particular) and two concepts that are joined by affirmation or are separated by negation. Judgments are either true or false. Propositions represent judgments (as words represent concepts). It seems that the law of non-contradiction (LNC) and the law of excluded middle (EM) become very important with judgments because a judgement is not both a and non-a in the same respect and at the same time (i.e. 'knowledge is perception' and 'knowledge is non-perception' cannot both be true in the same respect and at the same time). The second step that Socrates takes in the pursuit of knowledge is that he interrogates judgments by using these laws and either eliminates or affirms judgments based upon whether a law of thought is violated or not. This is where he uses the *reductio ad absurdum* so masterfully. The third aspect of Socrates' pursuit of knowledge is his use of arguments, usually in the form of a syllogism, to support the truth claim of a judgment via a *logos*, or an account. Again, these arguments employ LNC and EM by excluding impossible claims and arriving at necessary conclusions.[94] The fourth way Socrates pursues knowledge is by establishing the truth claim of a judgment with a *logos* such that a necessary truth is concluded, and then he uses reason deductively to argue for the truth of other claims. He proceeds from more basic to less basic — concepts, then judgments, and lastly arguments — and uses the same method to build a system of truth.[95] This deductive system building has been the downfall of many rationalist philosophers and seems to be due more to the failure to critically analyze starting assumptions upon which the system is built, than a problem of reason, the laws of thought. In this sense, some rationalists claim to use reason, but in fact, fail to use reason completely. Reason may be used by these philosophers to test the coherence of a set of assumptions without using reason to test the foundation upon which the set of assumptions rests. Knowledge is systematic and does rest upon foundations, but foundational assumptions must also undergo the same rational scrutiny that less basic assumptions in the system undergo. For example, Socrates may get us to a definition of knowledge — true opinion with an account — but does

---

94 For an example of how Socrates uses the laws of thought to reduce the "flux doctrine" to absurdity see *Theaetetus* 182b-183b.

95 Whether Socrates/Plato applies his method consistently to his own set of assumptions as he applied it to others is a question for another time.

he provide us with an argument that knowledge is ultimately of the non-physical forms? Or does he uncritically assume the reality of the forms? So, it is possible to get some things about reality right, such as the definition of knowledge and the role of reason in knowing, while getting other things wrong, such as that ultimate reality consists in the forms, and the form of the Good.[96] We can learn from the method of Socrates, and take the definition of knowledge, and now apply it to the fundamental philosophical questions: 'What is real?' 'Is matter real?' 'Is the soul real?' 'Is God real?' 'Is everything, something, nothing real?' These are the fundamental philosophical questions that have largely been abandoned post-Nietzsche because reason — the laws of thought — as ontological has been abandoned.

The rationalism of Socrates-Plato led to a false conception of reality (and Aristotle does not do much better), and the method for knowing gets tied to the conclusions arrived at through the method, so Nietzsche and post-Nietzschean philosophers reject both the method and the conclusions. This rejection is a mistake. This book is a call to reexamine the definition and method for knowing that Socrates demonstrates in the dialogues. Furthermore, it is a call to re-apply the method of Socrates to the original questions of philosophy: what is being? Post-Nietzschean philosophers claim to have abandoned metaphysics and claim to abandon the question of being, when in fact they unquestioningly assume an answer to the question 'what is real/being?' They assume matter is all that there is. Matter is the only reality, and then they systematically (using reason, which cannot be avoided) build an entire rationally coherent system of belief based upon that assumption and press it to its

---

96 Assuming that there is an argument against the existence of forms.

logical, rational conclusions. While denying that reason is ontological, they assume it in the act of constructing a system of belief.[97] The materialist juggernaut is proving itself to be a false god in our day, promising prosperity and delivering meaninglessness. The madness of post-Nietzschean philosophy and the meaninglessness of contemporary public discourse is a direct result of the assumed materialism of Nietzsche and his progeny.

There will be resistance against reviving Socrates' definition of knowledge, and a reaffirmation of reason as ontological because it will press all of us to rethink our easy skepticism and comfortable fideism. It will be difficult for believers and unbelievers alike. It will be rejected by current philosophers who prosper from skepticism, like the Sophists of Socrates' day, and who push a political agenda from positions of authority within the academy. A re-examination of the definition of knowledge is necessary for human dignity. We need meaning, which can only be gained through exercising our rational nature over and against the current emotivism and will to power exercised in the public sphere. We need to re-examine the definition of knowledge for the sake of the discipline of philosophy, which is dying quickly. And lastly, we must reexamine the definition of knowledge for the survival of the West, which is built upon principles that assume reason and rationality. Reason as a shared source of authority is necessary for a global community that differs over basic philosophical assumptions yet seeks to be united. In short, reason is necessary for public discourse regarding our most cherished beliefs and values.

---

97 See Seth Meyers work for an explication of Nietzsche's world and life view. Nietzsche's consistency is perhaps what drove him mad.

To conclude this section, the TOA definition of knowledge appears to be what Plato actually thinks knowledge *is*, even though we might be left wondering at the end of the *Theaetetus* when Socrates says to young Theaetetus:

> And it is utterly silly, when we are looking for a definition of knowledge, to say that it is right opinion with knowledge, whether of difference or of anything else whatsoever. So neither perception, Theaetetus, nor true opinion, nor reason or explanation combined with true opinion could be knowledge.[98]

Theaetetus responds, "Apparently not."[99] Cornford says in his commentary on this passage that:

> The point is that we cannot get 'knowledge', supposed to be somehow superior to mere beliefs or notions, by adding a *logos* in any of the senses considered ... The Platonist will draw the necessary inference. True knowledge has for its objects things of a different order — not sensible things, but intelligible Forms and truths about them ... Hence we can know them and eternal truths about them. The *Theaetetus* leads to this old conclusion by demonstrating the failure of all attempts to extract knowledge from sensible objects.[100]

Knowledge is by reason and grasps eternal truths. In summary, the TOA formulation of knowledge can be stated in the following way: S TOA-knows that P *IFF*:

---

98 Plato and Fowler, *Theaetetus* 210 a, 255.
99 Ibid., 255.
100 Cornford, 162-163.

1) S presupposes (*a priori*) that reason is the laws of thought, and that reason is ontological.[101]
2) P is true, based on reality (not mere appearances).
3) S has an opinion that P.
4) S has a true opinion about P because his opinion is accompanied by reasons, grounded in being such that certainty is the result (not mere psychological certainty, but the certainty of logical necessity). By the end of the *Theaetetus*, both Socrates and young Theaetetus are convinced that knowledge is not perception. Now we should explore the JTB formulation of knowledge to see how it is similar and how it is dissimilar to the TOA formulation.

IV. Gettier and the JTB Definition of Knowledge

To set the context for analysis of the JTB formulation of knowledge, let us return to Alvin Plantinga's quote:

> It would be colossal understatement to say that Anglo-American epistemology of this century has made much of the notion of epistemic justification. First, of course, there is the widely celebrated "justified true belief" JTB account or analysis of knowledge, and analysis we imbibed with our mothers milk. According to the inherited lore of the epistemological tribe, the JTB account enjoyed the status of epistemological orthodoxy until 1963, when it was shattered by Ed-

---

[101] That reason is ontological may be presupposed *a priori* will be discussed in the next chapter.

mund Gettier with his three page paper "Is Justified True Belief Knowledge?" After 1963 the justified true belief account of knowledge was seen to be defective and lost its exalted status; but even those convinced by Gettier that justification (along with truth) is not *sufficient* for knowledge still mostly think it *necessary* and *nearly* sufficient for knowledge: the basic shape or contour of the concept of knowledge is given by justified true belief, even if a quasi-technical fillip or addendum ("the fourth condition") is needed to appease Gettier. Of course there is an interesting historical irony here: it isn't easy to find many really explicit statements of a JTB analysis of knowledge prior to Gettier. It's almost as if a distinguished critic created a tradition in the very act of destroying it.[102]

Earlier this quote was used to show the conflation of Plato's definition of knowledge with the JTB account. Plantinga says, "... the JTB account enjoyed the status of epistemological orthodoxy until 1963, when it was shattered by Edmund Gettier...." And then he says, "...it isn't easy to find many really explicit statements of a JTB analysis of knowledge prior to Gettier. It's almost as if a distinguished critic created a tradition in the very act of destroying it." How can JTB enjoy the status of orthodoxy until 1963, if Gettier is one of the first to make JTB explicit in 1963? The only way to make sense of these seemingly conflicting statements is that contemporary epistemologists assume that Plato held to a JTB version of knowledge. If we look at Gettier's formulation of JTB and his objections to the formulation, by

---

102 Plantinga, Alvin. *Warrant: The Current Debate*. (New York: Oxford University Press, 1993), 6.

which he "destroyed" the tradition, we will see that JTB is not equivalent to TOA, and in fact may be the exact reverse of what Plato says about knowledge. Suggesting that Gettier's definition is the opposite of Plato's definition may seem controversial on the face of it, but given the philosophical context, Gettier's place in history, and his inherited epistemological assumptions, Gettier's definition is a revaluation of Plato's definition. The next chapter will detail the process of the revaluation of Plato by Friedrich Nietzsche, but for now, a quote from Richard Rorty will provide us with a bit of the philosophical context within which Gettier does epistemology. Gettier is working within an analytic philosophical tradition of which Rorty says:

> ...I think the following is a good way of bringing together the upshot of both the Quine-Putnam-Davidson tradition in analytic philosophy of language and the Heidegger-Derrida tradition of post-Nietzschean thought. Consider sentences as strings of marks and noises emitted by organisms, strings capable of being paired off with the strings we ourselves utter (in the way we call "translating"). Consider beliefs, desires, intentions — sentential attitudes generally — as entities posited to help predict the behavior of these organisms. Now think of those organisms as gradually evolving as a result of producing longer and more complicated strings, strings which enable them to do things they had been unable to do with the aid of shorter and simpler strings. Now think of *us* as examples of such highly evolved organisms....[103]

---

103 Rorty, Richard. *Essays on Heidegger and Others: Philosophical Papers Volume 2*. (New York, Cambridge University Press, 1991), 6.

All of philosophy is couched in naturalistic terms and strings of marks and noises for (most of) the analytic and continental post-Nietzschean philosophers. This is undoubtedly not the same view of reality as the Socrates-Plato-Aristotle view outlined above concerning thought and language. Rorty argues that both the analytic and continental traditions of philosophy share common assumptions when one sees "post-Nietzschean European philosophy and postpositivistic analytic philosophy converging to a single, pragmatist account of inquiry"[104] that assumes Darwinian naturalism, empiricism, and resulting skepticism. Pragmatism is the end product of both the analytic and continental traditions of philosophy because of the materialist-empiricist-skepticism worldview assumed post-Nietzsche. Although the next chapter will detail Nietzsche's revaluation of Plato and his subsequent influence on both traditions, it is essential to bring to mind the post-Nietzschean philosophy in the discussion of JTB, because Gettier's formulation of the JTB account of knowledge occurs within the historical and philosophical context of materialism-empiricism-skepticism. The formulation of the definition of knowledge as JTB and the framing of the Gettier problem are couched within an empiricist framework, the very position Plato argues against in *Theaetetus*. We will find that if we change the framework of the definition of knowledge, the Gettier problem dissolves.[105]

---

104 Ibid., 3.
105 As do many other post-Nietzschean epistemological problems such as the internalism vs. externalism, fallibilism vs. infallibilism, and realism vs. anti-realism debates.

In his now infamous three-page paper, "Is Justified True Belief Knowledge?"[106] Edmund Gettier says that:

"(a) S knows that P *IFF*

(i) P is true,

(ii) S believes that P, and

(iii) S is justified in believing that P."

Then he goes on to say, "I shall argue that (a) is false in that the conditions stated therein do not constitute a *sufficient* condition for the truth of the proposition that S knows that P."[107] Before examining Gettier's objections to "(a)," we should attempt to understand what each of the conditions of "(a)" means. Gettier does not tell us what he means by "true" in his short paper, and in a post-Nietzschean context truth may not mean "what corresponds with reality," but may mean something like "adheres to the conventions of a particular language game." But let's take Gettier to be assuming a correspondence view of truth — as Plato also assumes about truth — that the proposition in my mind corresponds with reality. Again, Gettier does not help us to understand what he means by "S believes that P."

In the TOA version of the definition of knowledge, we could say "S opines that P," which means something like "it seems to S that P" or "it appears to S that P." Should we take Gettier to be saying something similar? Or is Gettier saying something more like "S gives assent to P"? Either way, this condition has some ambiguity, and it is unclear as to whether Gettier and Plato

---

106 Gettier, Edmund J. "Is Justified True Belief Knowledge?" *Analysis*. Vol. 23 No. 6 (Jun. 1963), 121-123.
107 Ibid., 121.

are saying the same thing. The reality of the difference between the two is made clear in the third condition: "S is justified in believing that P." Gettier does not tell us what he means by "justified," but he does give some clues within the paper. The first clue comes from his quoting a previous formulation of the definition of knowledge by Roderick Chisholm who states this condition in the following way: "S has adequate evidence for P." And again, he notes that A.J. Ayer states the condition in this way: "S has the right to be sure that P is true." Here we see justification being associated with "adequate evidence" and conferring a "right to be sure." Gettier adheres to the view that justification is evidence of some sort. He then goes on to critique his original formulation of the definition of knowledge in an attempt to show that justification, or some form of evidence, is not sufficient for knowledge. He argues that one can have JTB and yet lack knowledge.

He provides two counterexamples that he thinks are sufficient to overthrow the JTB formulation. In case 1 he says:

> Suppose that Smith and Jones have applied for a certain job. And suppose that Smith has strong evidence for the following conjunctive proposition:
>
> (d) Jones is the man who will get the job, and Jones has ten coins in his pocket.
>
> Smith's evidence for (d) might be that the president of the company assured him that Jones would in the end be selected, and that he, Smith, had counted the coins in Jones's pocket ten minutes ago.
>
> Proposition (d) entails:

(e) The man who will get the job has ten coins in his pocket.

Let us suppose that Smith sees the entailment from (d) to (e) and accepts (e) on the grounds of (d), for which he has strong evidence. In this case, Smith is clearly justified in believing that (e) is true.[108]

But as it turns out it is not Jones who gets the job, but Smith gets the job because he also has ten coins in his pocket of which he was not aware. So now (e) is true, but (d) is false, and Smith formed his belief about (e) on the basis of (d). So here is a case where "(i) (e) is true, (ii) Smith believes that (e) is true, and (iii) Smith is justified in believing that (e) is true"[109] But this is obviously not a case of knowledge. The point of this and all Gettier-type examples (and there are many)[110] is to show that one may have justified true belief and still lack knowledge. The effect of the Gettier problem is to show either that justification is not sufficient for knowledge, or that knowledge is not possible, and we are stuck in skepticism. There is something that all Gettier-type problems generally have in common. The "strong evidence" for belief or the justification one has for belief, in each case is either based on empirical data or testimony (empirical data of another). In the Smith and Jones case above, Smith's "strong evidence" for believing that Jones would get the job was based upon the testimony of his boss, and the empirical evidence of counting the ten coins. The statement of the JTB definition of knowledge is already set within the analytic tra-

---

108 Ibid., 122.
109 Ibid., 122.
110 See Plantinga, *Warrant the Current Debate*.

dition's empiricist framework, so the concerns of the JTB are about the empirical world. However, the empirical world was not the source of knowledge for Plato. On the contrary, at best we could only arrive at probability with regards to "knowing" the empirical world for Plato. It was of non-empirical eternal truths that we could have knowledge. Whereas Gettier equates justification with strong empirical evidence, Plato would equate justification, if we want to apply that term anachronistically to Plato, with giving an account, or a *logos*, that provides certainty. Gettier justification could never provide certainty, so the JTB formulation of knowledge could never provide knowledge. It is more like non-knowledge. As Socrates shows us in the *Theaetetus*, perception is not knowledge, and one could never have certainty about the changing physical world of flux. It is only of permanent things that one could have knowledge. What Gettier calls "strong evidence," perceptual evidence, in Plato's formulation is very weak evidence. Strong evidence for Plato is that which gives an account, or a *logos*, and provides certainty.

In a 50-year anniversary retrospective piece on Gettier's original paper, Fred Dretske[111] reflects upon the Gettier counterexamples and what exactly was wrong with Gettier's formulation. He says that:

> Gettier's counterexamples are constructed from two assumptions about justification ... (1) The justification one needs to know that P is true is a justification one can have for a false proposition ... (2) If you are justi-

---

111 Dretske, Fred. "Gettier and Justified True Belief: 50 Years On." Accessed 2/18/2017. http://www.philosophersmag.com/index.php/tpm-mag-articles/11-essays/10-gettier-and-justified-true-belief-50-years-on

fied in believing P, and you know that P entails Q and accept Q as a result, you are justified in believing Q.[112]

He then says "almost all philosophers who aren't skeptics accept 1 without hesitation. After all, if one can, as we all believe we can — sometimes at least — come to know (just by looking) that there are bananas in the fruit bowl," but then again we could be tricked by wax bananas, "the justification, the kind of evidence, needed to know is clearly less than conclusive. It is something one can have for a *false* proposition."[113] He then says that by accepting (2) one is just making a deductive inference, which is unproblematic. The problem comes in when one believes both (1) and (2). Dretske locates the problematic nature of the Gettier problem with (1). He thinks "the kind of justification one needs to know is not the kind one can have for a false proposition."[114] So, one cannot have justification for a false belief. However, notice what counts as justification in Dretske's example: "just by looking" at the bananas, I can know that there are bananas in the bowl. But wax bananas are counterexamples to my "looking" as justification. Why is perceiving bananas good enough for knowing there are bananas in the bowl? Why is perceiving knowledge? Socrates argues the exact opposite; perception is not knowledge. Justification for Gettier and Dretske is akin to Plato's *doxa*/seeming/appearing. Gettier's justification is a seeming, not a knowing. JTB can more accurately be defined in the following way given the empirical assumptions of Gettier and Dretske-type justification:

---

112 Ibid., 2.
113 Ibid., 2.
114 Ibid., 6.

S knows that P *IFF*   (a) S believes (*doxa*) P

(b) P is true

(C) S has justification (*doxa*) for believing that P

This is like saying "it seems to S that P is true because for S it seems like P." Seeming/appearance is not reality in Plato's formulation, and perception is not knowledge. Therefore, the Gettier formulation of knowledge is not a recipe for knowledge at all. This formulation does not get us to the top of Plato's Line where knowledge is achieved. It is not clear that Gettier's formula even gets us on the upper half of the Line above mere opinion.

Dretske does see a problem with saying that one can have justification for a false belief, but he does not recognize the empirical assumptions latent in Gettier's formulation of justification. Dretske backs away from what he takes to be skeptical implications in the quote above when he says that "almost all philosophers who aren't skeptics accept 1 without hesitation."[115] However, Plato would not accept "(1) The justification one needs to know that P is true is a justification one can have for a false proposition"[116] and yet he is not a skeptic. Plato would say that one cannot have an account for a false opinion. Having an account for false opinion is not possible because false opinions do not match reality — they are not true — so no *logos* can be provided. We do not need to fall into skepticism either. Remember that true opinion for Plato was akin to thinking and scientific reasoning and was enough to motivate right action.

---

115 Dretske, 2.
116 Ibid., 2.

So, for most of our everyday activity, true opinion is sufficient. We do not need philosophical certainty for everything, not even for most things, just for the most important things. Dretske concludes by saying that "Gettier 1 has to go," and then says:

> Resistance to this conclusion might come from a misunderstanding of what is required for a "conclusive" justification, a justification that one cannot have for a false proposition. If one thinks of a conclusive justification, a justification one cannot have for a false proposition, as something like a logical proof, then, of course, this conclusion will sound absurd. It would be a way of saying that to know P one must be able to prove that it is true. Sceptics may believe that, but no one else does ... That would set the standard for knowledge much too high.[117]

Logical proof is precisely what Socrates demonstrates for us in *Theaetetus* and is precisely what he thinks will counter the skepticism of his day. Dretske's so-called "conclusive justification" is only a standard that is too high within an empiricist framework. Of course, we could not have something like logical proof within the context where justification is based upon appearance and sense perception. However, if we change the framework from one of empiricism to one where reason grasps truths, then it becomes possible to have logical proof and the certainty that follows. To dissolve the Gettier problem, we do not need to find a fourth condition (JTB plus some other condition). Instead, we should return to knowledge as defined for us in the *Theaetetus*: true opinion with an account.

---

117 Ibid., 5.

It is significant that the definition of knowledge, allegedly passed down from Plato to contemporary analytic philosophers, is not questioned until a post-Nietzschean, materialist-empiricist-skeptical era. It is in the context of empiricism that the definition is reformulated and questioned by Gettier. It is almost as if the original context of Plato's definition of knowledge has been forgotten in a post-Nietzschean world that is guilty of semanticide. The rectification of names requires that we ask, "what is knowledge?" and try to name it correctly again. We should not assume that we cannot have knowledge when we do not even know what knowledge is. Even the skeptic in *Theaetetus* recognizes the need to define the word knowledge before discussion of whether we can know or not know. Empiricism has killed the discussion of knowledge because empiricism always leads to skepticism, the view that knowledge is not possible. *Theaetetus* is an argument against empiricism and skepticism. In a classic case of emptying a word of meaning, empiricism has emptied "knowledge" of meaning. We need to return to the *Theaetetus* to understand "knowledge" and what Socrates shows us about knowledge. He certainly does not think that knowledge is empirical. The concept of knowledge needs re-examination, and the term "knowledge" needs rectification. Empiricism changes the meaning of knowledge based on its empirical assumptions, the very thing that Socrates calls into question.

Empiricism is not the only challenge that we face in a post-Nietzschean era. The post-Nietzschean worldview denies the isomorphism between reason and being, effectually cutting off the upper half of the Line and access to truth (*aletheia*),[118]

---

118 We are also cut off from the Good and the Beautiful, left to adore and/or abhor the shadows.

thus trapping humanity within the cave, where *doxa* reigns. The post-Nietzschean life in the cave is described in detail by Charles Taylor in his tome, *A Secular Age*.[119] He calls this reality the "immanent frame." In the chapter titled "The Immanent Frame," Taylor says the following:

> So my contention is that the power of materialism today comes not from the scientific "facts", but has rather to be explained in terms of the power of a certain package uniting materialism with a moral outlook, the package we could call "atheist humanism", or exclusive humanism. What gives the package its power? I have been trying to answer this above in terms of certain values which are implicit in the immanent frame, such as disengaged reason, which pushed to the limit, generate the science-driven "death of God" story.[120]

The immanent frame is just the empiricism-materialism-skepticism-sophism worldview that Socrates opposes. The immanent frame is life without God in the world. Nietzsche is the most explicit to state that God is dead, and it is we who have killed him. It is to the immanent frame that we turn in the next few chapters. It begins with the death of reason, carried to the death of God, and then to the death of the West and all else associated with a transcendent outlook.

---

119 Taylor, Charles. *A Secular Age*. (Cambridge: The Belknap Press of Harvard University Press, 2007). The secular age that Taylor describes includes the Modern period as well as the post-Modern/post-Nietzschean period being discussed in this paper.
120 Ibid., 569.

Chapter 3

Logos and Anti-*Logos*: Epistemology after Nietzsche

"'Reason" in language — oh, what an old deceptive female she is! I am afraid we are not rid of God because we still have faith in Grammar."[1]

IN A CLOSE analysis of the tragic worldview of Friedrich Nietzsche, Matthew Meyer, in *Reading Nietzsche through the Ancients: An Analysis of Becoming, Perspectivism, and the Principle of Non-Contradiction*, details the philosophical assumptions that

---

1 Nietzsche, Friedrich Wilhelm. *The Anti-Christ, Ecce Homo, Twilight of the Idols, and Other Writings* (New York: Cambridge University Press, 2005), 483.

Nietzsche affirms through his reading of the ancient (pre-Platonic) philosophers. The philosophical doctrines that Meyer draws out of Nietzsche's writings include Nietzsche's affirmation of the Heraclitan "flux doctrine," or what Meyer later terms "ontological structural realism,"[2] where all is becoming, and this becoming is a relation of force; Nietzsche's empiricism that leads to his perspectivism;[3] and lastly Nietzsche's understanding of the will to power. These assumptions comprise a "tragic worldview" because in them we see Nietzsche's metaphysics, epistemology, and ethics, which when put together lead to a radical (tragic) skepticism.

Whereas Meyer emphasizes Nietzsche's embrace of a Heraclitan-Protagorean philosophy, the purpose of this chapter is to emphasize Nietzsche's rejection of the philosophy of Parmenides; particularly his affirmation of being, and the logical and ontological implications of such a rejection. Nietzsche's rejection of Parmenidean 'being' results in his rejection of a grounding of a *Logos*. This chapter will argue that the *Logos* is the key idea of the Western philosophical tradition.[4] Nietzsche rejects the *Logos* in its ontological form, and by implication its logical form. Therefore, Nietzsche rejects the Western philosophical tradition. In his rejection of the *Logos*, Nietzsche represents a break with the Modern period in philosophy and

---

2   Myers argues that the opposition of forces gives rise to "something" even if momentarily.
3   Perspectivism is the view that one only has access to one's own "perspective" or what appears to be the case for the individual. It is equivalent to Theaetetus' first definition "knowledge is perception."
4   An argument that is made by Eva Brann, and which will be developed further in this chapter and in the Epilogue. Brann, Eva. *The Logos of Heraclitus: The First Philosopher of the West on Its Most Interesting Term* (Philadelphia: Paul Dry Books, 2011).

is in the vanguard of Postmodern thinking. Breaking with the Western search for the *Logos* results in skepticism, meaninglessness, madness, and ultimately silence. Where Meyer highlights the positive philosophy of Nietzsche, this chapter will highlight the anti-*logos* anti-philosophy of Nietzsche.

Meyer observes:

> ... Nietzsche's critique of logic is really an attack on ontologies that arose from what he thinks is the misguided application of logical principles to reality ... Nietzsche's criticism of logic ... should be construed as an attack not on logical consistency, but on the Parmenidean presupposition that there is an isomorphism between thinking and being.[5]

What Meyer describes as an isomorphism between thinking and being will be referred to as 'reason is ontological.' Reason is ontological implies that the laws of thought are also the laws of being. Reason as ontological will be described and assessed in the first part of the chapter in which we explore the meaning of *Logos* in the thinking of Heraclitus, Parmenides, Plato, and Aristotle. The second section of the chapter will explore Nietzsche's rejection of Parmenidean 'being' and consequently the isomorphism between thinking and being, or 'reason is ontological' and the full implications of this rejection. The third section of the chapter will demonstrate Nietzsche's break with the Western philosophical tradition, and his leading the way for Postmodern thinking concerning the relationship between reason and being.

---

5   Meyer, Matthew. *Reading Nietzsche through the Ancients: An Analysis of Becoming, Perspectivism, and the Principle of Non-contradiction* (Boston: De Gruyter, 2014), 78.

Meyer conjectures, "If it is correct that Nietzsche's critique of logic or what I have called his denial of the isomorphism between thinking and being lies at the heart of his *break with the Western metaphysical tradition* and his attempt to revive what I have called a tragic worldview, it is rather surprising that the issue has not played a more prominent role in Nietzsche scholarship...."[6] The unique contribution of this chapter is to draw attention to Nietzsche's critique of logic and his rejection of 'reason as ontological,' and the subsequent implications for Western philosophy. Post-Nietzschean philosophers assume a rejection of the isomorphism between reason and being. The goal of this and the next chapter is to make explicit this uncritically held assumption.

I. *Logos* and Reason

The first section of the chapter aims to define *logos* for the early Greek philosophers. It aims to connect *Logos* and reason, and reason with being. To connect *Logos*/reason with being is to establish that reason is ontological, or as Meyer states: to show an isomorphism between thinking and being. Eva Brann begins her work: *The Logos of Heraclitus: The First Philosopher of the West on Its Most Interesting Term*, with this powerful insight:

> *Logos* is, I think, not only Heraclitus's key word, but that of the Western Philosophical tradition, which acts as a tradition because its moments are both bound together and driven apart by dialogue: the back-and-forth of the *logos*. This dialogue had its first great episode, mentioned above, between Heraclitus and Par-

---

6   Meyer, 79 (italics added)

menides, no matter who spoke first or whether they literally spoke to each other.[7]

Logos is the key idea of the Western philosophical tradition, yet Nietzsche in his anti-*logos* breaks with this tradition. According to Brann, philosophy begins, historically and conceptually, with the *Logos*. Historically, she argues, the Western tradition of philosophy begins with Heraclitus. Conceptually, it begins with his introduction of the *Logos* into the nascent philosophical dialogue going back to Thales of Miletus and his claim that all is one, and this one is water. Philosophy begins with reasoning about being. Brann thinks the dialogue between Heraclitus, regarding *Logos*, and Parmenides, regarding being (*ontos*), is at the heart of subsequent philosophical dialogue. She asks:

> Can anyone deny that these two are about the same search, the search pursued of old and now and ever, even though the one — to return them to their proper order — thinks as a logologist (so to speak), the other as an ontologist? And that they set out for the future for us, the two perennial, yet ever-evolving terms of that inquiry, *Logos* and Being and its one paramount and never resolved perplexity: One and/or Many?[8]

What is *Logos*, and what is being? What happens to the tradition of Western philosophy if the two objects of perennial pursuit are denied having any reality? If the search is terminated, does the tradition also terminate? Nietzsche, who claims "I

---

[7] Brann, 9.
[8] Ibid., 106.

am dynamite,"[9] and a prophet of a new philosophy to come,[10] proposes that both *Logos* and being are fictions of a flawed philosophical tradition.

Brann says that *Logos* in the context of the first philosophers, such as Heraclitus, means "collecting and laying down, tale-telling and relating, counting and account-giving, arguing, and, so, speaking, saying, and above all, the thinking, the reasoning, that is behind uttering — and finally also writing."[11] *Logos* begins in thought and is expressed with words — either orally or written — particularly in giving an account. Giving an account is the exchange of reasons. W.K.C. Guthrie, in his discussion of the history of Heraclitus, uses six pages to define *logos*. Some of the highlights of his careful analysis of *logos* in-

---

9   Nietzsche not only seems to want to terminate the Western tradition, he wants to demolish it. He says in *Ecce Homo*, an autobiography of sorts, written just before the onset of his madness, in a chapter "Why I am a Destiny": "I know my lot. One day my name will be connected with something tremendous, — a crisis such as the earth has never seen, the deepest collision of conscience, a decision made *against* everything that has been believed, demanded, held sacred so far. I am not a human being, I am dynamite." Friedrich Wilhelm Nietzsche. *The Anti-Christ, Ecce Homo, Twilight of the Idols, and Other Writings* (New York: Cambridge University Press, 2005), 143.

10 Nietzsche says in a somewhat prescient passage: "It could even be possible that whatever gives value to those good and honorable things has an incriminating link, bond, or tie to the very things that look like their evil opposites; perhaps they are even essentially the same. Perhaps! — But who is willing to take charge of such a dangerous Perhaps! For this we must await the arrival of a new breed of philosophers, ones whose taste and inclination are somehow the reverse of those we have seen so far — philosophers of the dangerous Perhaps in every sense. — And in all seriousness: I see these new philosophers approaching." Friedrich Wilhelm Nietzsche. *Beyond Good and Evil: Prelude to a Philosophy of the Future* (Cambridge: Cambridge University Press, 2002), 6.

11 Brann, 10.

clude: "an account of anything, explanation;" "a speech;" "taking thought ... holding conversation with oneself;" "words;" "cause, reason or argument;" "the truth of the matter; "general principle or rule;" "the faculty of reason; and lastly, "definition, or formula expressing the essential nature of anything."[12] Guthrie's careful analysis links *logos* with reason and giving an account. From Brann and Guthrie, we get a sense of the meaning of *logos* for the first philosophers.

Rosemary Desjardins gives us a sense of *logos* in Plato's dialogue *Theaetetus* when she explains:

> *Logos* is one of those tricky words that do not translate easily, because to translate it is to do just what this dialogue will warn us against; that is, the Englishing of it tends to reduce it to just one of its aspects. For *logos* in Greek captures the comprehensive sense of rational structure as it applies either to product (hence can mean speech, a statement, a definition, a rational account or explanation, an argument, or simply discourse as such), or to the power of reason which produces the structure.[13]

The primary word used for "reason" in Ancient Greek is *logos*. *Logos* can mean *word*, but it also means account or explanation. The term has the sense of reason as grounds, theory, law, principles or formulas. *Logos* connotes the laws by which the mind operates. Liddell and Scott define the Classical Greek use of *logos* as "*the word*" or "*that by which the inward thought is ex-*

---

12 Guthrie, W.K.C. *A History of Greek Philosophy* (Cambridge: University Press, 1962) 419-424.
13 Desjardins, Rosemary. *The Rational Enterprise: Logos in Plato's Theaetetus* (Albany: State University of New York Press, 1990) footnote 4, 200.

pressed."[14] *Logos,* as defined by the ancient Greeks, is the inward account that gets expressed by words or speech or writing. The Latin word for reason is *ratio*. According to Charlton T. Lewis and Charles Short's *Latin Dictionary, ratio* can have the following meanings: "a reckoning, account, calculation, computation; that faculty of the mind which forms the basis of computation and calculation, and hence of mental action in general, i.e., judgment, understanding, reason."[15] By defining *logos*, we have established a connection between reason/thinking and the expression of thought through words and giving an account. Though the connection between *logos* and being may be inferred from *logos* as law, we must now make more explicit the connection between *logos*/reason and being.

Though Heraclitus introduces the search for the *Logos* in the West, Parmenides seems to be the first philosopher to make the explicit connection between *logos* and being in his discussion about the impossibility of non-being. He says in Fragment 2: "Never shall it be proven that not-being is ... let reason be your judge when you consider this much disputed question."[16] Parmenides is saying that it is logically and ontologically impossible for "not-being" to exist. Whatever does exist *is*, not-being *is not. A* is not *non-a*. This is a statement of the law of identity (LI), elucidated later by Aristotle, applied to being. Again, Parmenides says in Fragment 5: "I will tell you of the two roads

---

14   Liddell and Scott. *An Intermediate Greek-English Lexicon,* based upon the 7th ed. (Oxford: Clarendon Press; Impression 1995, First Edition 1889), 477.

15   Charlton T. Lewis, and Charles Short. *A Latin Dictionary.* Founded on Andrews' edition of Freund's Latin dictionary. Revised and enlarged. (Oxford. Clarendon Press. 1879).

16   Wheelwright, Philip Ellis. *The Presocratics* (New York: Odyssey Press, 1966), 96.

of inquiry which offer themselves to the mind. The one way, that It Is and cannot not-be, is the way of credibility based on truth. The other way, that It Is Not and that not-being must be, cannot be grasped by the mind: for you cannot know not-being and cannot express it."[17] There are either two ways: the way of *Is*, or the way of *not-Is*. To state it another way, being is being, being is not non-being. *A* is *A* (*A* is not *non-A*). Clearly, these fragments link reason to being by applying the laws of thought to what exists in the world. But Parmenides makes the connection between reason and being even more explicit when he says in Fragment 7d: "Thinking and the object of thought are the same. For you will not find thought apart from being, nor either of them apart from utterance."[18] Thinking is the product of thinking beings, and thought is about being. *A* is *A* applies to thinking and to being. Thought and being cannot be separated; reason and being cannot be separated. Finally, Parmenides says in Fragment 8: "Thought and being are the same."[19] There is an isomorphism between thinking and being; reason is ontological. Brann says that Heraclitus and Parmenides are "about the same search," but that each puts the emphasis on a different aspect of the search — Heraclitus on *Logos*, and Parmenides on Being — yet she thinks that they are similar in that they are thinking about being. In this sense, both affirm that reason is ontological.[20]

---

17 Ibid., 96.
18 Ibid., 98.
19 Ibid., 98.
20 It is interesting to note that Brann denies that the Heraclitan "flux doctrine," that Nietzsche so enthusiastically endorses, originates with Heraclitus. Rather, it is a notion brought in by later philosophers, namely Plato and Aristotle (Brann, 104). Even if Nietzsche misreads Heraclitus (and Plato), we must still come to terms with how he understands the

In his affirmation of reason as that which grasps the nature of being, Parmenides thinks that our senses may be deceived by the appearance of change and "not being." Thus, his view leads to skepticism regarding the deliverances of the senses. Nietzsche, an empiricist, begins his critique of a *logos*-driven philosophy of the West with Parmenides when he says in his *Pre-Platonic Philosophers* that:

> As a critique of epistemological faculties, however, this raw distinction [between spirit and body] is of the greatest worth; it is the original source first of dialectic (though there is no philosophy from a combination of concepts), and later of logic (in other words, we discover the mechanism of our abstraction in concepts, judgments, and conclusions). Add to this the explanation, as a partisan of the immovable whole ... of the entire world as a deception — an astounding and fruitful boldness.[21]

Nietzsche begins his critique of the Western philosophical tradition with these observations: Parmenides is mistaken in his "rationalism" — in his dialectic and logic — especially in applying concepts, judgments, and conclusions to the realm of being. This observation turned critique will be one of the most persistent themes in all of Nietzsche's work. In this critique, we

---

"flux doctrine" as it is the doctrine that underwrites his rejection of reason as ontological. Meyer is helpful in drawing out Nietzsche's understanding of Heraclitus and his own development of the "flux doctrine" in his *Reading Nietzsche through the Ages*, and in his chapter "Nietzsche's Ontic Structural Realism." (Metaphysics of Entanglement. Accessed 7/7/2016. http://www.metaphysics-of-entanglement.ox.ac.uk/).

21 Nietzsche, Friedrich Wilhelm, and Greg Whitlock. *The Pre-Platonic Philosophers* (Urbana: University of Illinois Press, 2001), 86.

can already see Nietzsche's latent empirical assumptions as well as his partisanship concerning a (distorted) Heraclitan view. Again, we can sense Nietzsche's partisan views when he states that Heraclitus has:

> An aesthetic view of the world. Here with Parmenides, everything aesthetic ends; hate and love are not a game but rather effects of the same daimon. We see in this genius the struggle to overcome dualism, yet it transpires in only a mythical manner — the notion of reducing Becoming and passing away to a love struggle between Being and Not-Being. What a colossal abstraction![22]

Parmenides' "colossal abstraction" in applying reason/*logos* to being is the error that Plato and subsequent Western philosophy will continue, until Nietzsche's "philosophizing with a hammer"[23] brings it to a halt. Before going further into Nietzsche's critique of reason as ontological, it is necessary to define reason as ontological as developed by Plato and Aristotle.

Plato links reason/*logos* with being in the *Theaetetus* in his definition of knowledge as true opinion with an account. The dialogue is an argument against empiricism, skepticism, and the Heraclitan-Protagorean "flux doctrine,"[24] Plato has an overarching goal of overcoming the problem of the One/Many and Being/Becoming antinomies of the first philosophers, as well

---

22 Nietzsche, *PPP*, 83.
23 Nietzsche, Friedrich Wilhelm, and Walter Arnold Kaufmann. *Twilight of the Idols: Or How One Philosophizes with a Hammer* in *The Portable Nietzsche* (New York: Viking Press, 1954), 463.
24 All of which are assumptions that Nietzsche holds. The *Theaetetus* then serves as a powerful argument against the "tragic worldview" of Nietzsche.

as the skepticism posed by the Sophists who see these problems as interminable, but the desire to interact in public life pragmatically.[25] Plato must ground the *Logos* in being, following Parmenides, so that there is an isomorphism between thinking and being, but he must also explain the world of change and appearance, following Heraclitus. Plato will ultimately ground the *logos* in the being of the unchanging forms that are accessible only to reason while acknowledging that the world of perception, though less reliable, is not entirely unknowable.[26] Knowledge is about being and is obtained by thinking about the meaning of the words that we use through a process of dialectic, which Socrates demonstrates in the dialogues. In the *Theaetetus*, Socrates not only demonstrates how to understand the nature of things; he demonstrates how the knowledge of these things is obtained. Knowledge is attained when one has a true opinion and can give an account by "tying" true opinion down with a *logos*. Both Socrates' method for knowing, through dialectic, and his definition of knowledge, assume that reason is ontological.

Dialectic assumes that through a process of asking "what is *x*?" we can arrive at the true nature, or being, of *x*. Our minds can understand the being of *x* by grasping its essential qualities. Knowledge as "true opinion" with an account assumes the following: a) opinions are about propositions, and propositions express being; b) truth is what corresponds to reality, and; c) an account is what "ties down" or guarantees true opinion, and an account is what guarantees that the proposition that I have grasped with my mind, in my understanding, by means of reason, corresponds with reality. In a dialogue, words express con-

---

25 Through an almost Nietzschean will to power.
26 Plato acknowledges that the world of appearances may yield true opinion.

cepts, which are either meaningful or lack meaning. If a concept is meaningful, then the one who has grasped the concept has understood, by an activity of the mind, the nature of some aspect of being/reality. Judgments, or propositions, are either true or they are false (*A* or non-*A*, by the law of excluded middle LEM). True judgments are those propositions that accurately report reality. We know that we have made a true judgment when we can give an account, or a *logos*, for the judgment being made. A *logos* is a reason that makes the proposition indubitable.[27] A *logos* links my true opinion to reality. When one possesses knowledge, there is a fit between one's mind and the world of being through the *logos* in one's mind (reason) and the logos in the world (law/order). It is because Plato so firmly held to the fit between thinking and being that he thought that knowledge was possible.

Reason, minimally, may be defined as the laws of thought: 1) The law of identity (LI), which states that *a* is *a*; a thing is what it is. 2) The law of non-contradiction sometimes referred to as the principle of non-contradiction (LNC or PNC), which states that something is not both *a* and *non-a* in the same respect and at the same time. 3) The law of excluded middle (LEM), which states that something is either *a* or *non-a*. Already, in stating these laws, we can observe that they apply to being. For example: 'some thing *a* is *a*.' The is here signifies existence. Existence is being. Even if one were to say, 'some thought *a* is *a*,' one could not escape the is that implies being. Thoughts do not exist apart from a being that thinks them; thus, thoughts are the product of being and are about being.

---

27 Socrates and Theaetetus agree that knowledge is infallible. In other words, knowledge is certain.

Heraclitus and Parmenides assume the laws of thought in their search for a *logos* (rational account). These laws are assumed by Socrates and his interlocutors in Plato's *Theaetetus*, in the search for a *logos* to "tie down" a true belief. Yet these laws are made explicit and defended in Aristotle's *Metaphysics* IV 1005b15-1012b30.[28] Meyer makes a point to draw attention to the fact that these laws are discussed in the *Metaphysics*, within the context of the exploration of being *qua* being, rather than in the *Organon*, where Aristotle outlines his Logic.[29] That Aristotle discusses the laws of thought in a book about being gives us the context for the laws of thought as the laws of being. Thinking is about being, and the laws of thinking are also the laws of being. *Logos* puts a restriction on what can *be* or *not be*. For example, reason tells us that there can be no square circles. One knows by the definition of a square (a plane geometrical figure with four equal sides and four right angles) and the definition of a circle (a plane geometrical figure with all points on the radius equidistant from the center) that they do not share the same qualities. A square is a square (*a* is *a*), a circle is a circle, and a square is not a circle (*a* is not *non-a*). I cannot think of a square circle (it is logically impossible), and a square circle cannot exist in reality (it is ontologically impossible). Reason applies to thinking and being.

Aristotle's logic assumes the laws of thought in forming concepts, the first act of thinking/reason. In forming concepts, the mind identifies and distinguishes some thing. The law of identity is assumed in concept formation. The second act of reason is in making a judgment: x is y. Judgments are proposi-

---

28 Aristotle, and Jonathan Barnes. *The Complete Works of Aristotle: The Revised Oxford Translation* (Princeton: Princeton University Press, 1984).
29 Meyer, 84.

tions which are either true or false (true or non-true). The law of excluded middle is at work in assessing judgments. Finally, once a thing is identified (its properties named), it cannot both be what it is (have certain properties) and not be what it is in the same respect and at the same time, according to the law of non-contradiction. The third act of the mind is argument, in the form of deductive reasoning, which assumes both concept and judgment in addition to the laws of thought. Aristotle explains the principles of deductive reasoning in his logical works. The laws of thought are explained in the *Metaphysics* because the laws are intended not only to apply to logical thinking, but the laws apply to being. The *logos* is in the mind as reason, and the *logos* is in being as laws/natures that may be grasped by the mind. Because there is a fit between mind and world, it is possible to have knowledge of the world through giving an account (through deductive reasoning), and less certain, but still a legitimate means of understanding, through a process of induction (science).

It is just this notion of reason as ontological, or that reason can grasp being, that Nietzsche denies in his affirmation of the Heraclitan-Protagorean flux doctrine. Aristotle argues against the Heraclitan-Protagorean flux in *Metaphysics* IV in the context of his discussion of the laws of thought. In chapter 2 of *Reading Nietzsche through the Ancients*, Meyer provides a detailed explication of this section of the *Metaphysics*. The most significant aspect of Meyer's discussion for this chapter is the distinction that he draws out between what he calls "PNC-ontological" and "PNC-logical" in Aristotle's discussion of the law of non-contradiction.[30] Meyer notes that "Aristotle's defense

---

30 What Meyer calls "principle of non-contradiction" or PNC, will be called the law of non-contradiction or LNC.

of PNC-ontological is not an attempt to point out an isolated mistake made by a pre-Socratic like Heraclitus. Instead, it is an attack on an entire ontology that Aristotle thinks is the ultimate consequence of the naturalist and empiricist commitment of the pre-Socratics."[31] It is this same naturalist and empiricist commitment that Socrates argues against in *Theaetetus*, and which Nietzsche affirms when he rejects reason as ontological, and it is the same naturalist and empiricist commitment that underwrites much of the rejection of reason in the postmodern post-Nietzschean thinkers. Thus, it seems that establishing that reason is ontological will be an essential first step as an argument against naturalism and empiricism.

We turn now to a close reading of *Metaphysics IV*. Meyer's explication of *Metaphysics IV* in chapter 2 of his *Reading Nietzsche through the Ancients* is pointed and elegant, and it would be a challenge to provide a better interpretation, yet it is useful for this chapter to directly examine the text of *Metaphysics IV* 3-7 in order to follow Aristotle's reasoning regarding the ontological aspect of the laws of thought.[32] Aristotle begins section 3 with a discussion of the philosopher as the person most suited to the study of being: "The philosopher, who is studying the nature of all substance, must inquire also into the principles of deduction."[33] Principles of deduction (reason) apply to the nature of all substance (being). He goes on to say that "he whose subject is being *qua* being must be able to state the most certain

---

31 Meyer, 82.
32 This section is an independent reading of Aristotle, but it is inspired by Meyer's chapter "Aristotle's Defense of the Principle of Non-Contradiction in *Metaphysics IV*." Anyone interested in this topic should consult Meyer's work.
33 Aristotle, *Metaphysics* 1005b6-7.

principles of all things ... this is the philosopher, and the most certain principle of all is that regarding which it is impossible to be mistaken."[34] The philosopher's subject matter is being as such, and his tools are those principles (of all that is/being) that are indubitable. It seems as though Aristotle is saying that the tools of reasoning, in the area of epistemology, are before the study of being, the area of metaphysics. In the laws of thought, we will see a connection between these laws and being such that to separate the two would be a mistake in both epistemology (empiricism) and metaphysics (ontological naturalism). Aristotle proceeds to say that "for a principle which every one must have who knows anything about being, is not a hypothesis; and that which every one must know who knows anything, he must already have when he comes to a special study."[35] It seems that Aristotle is saying that for us to know anything about being we must already have prior knowledge of principles by which we know being. These principles are not hypothetical, so they must be indubitable. They are not derived from being since they are before knowing being. We can infer that these are *a priori*, self-evident, first principles. As *a priori*, our knowledge of these principles is before our knowledge of being, and as self-evident,[36] they cannot be doubted without losing meaning.

Aristotle goes on to state these *a priori*, self-evident, first principles, beginning with the law of non-contradiction (LNC):

---

34 Ibid., 1005b10-12.
35 Ibid., 1005b14-17.
36 "Self-evident" here is used in its logical sense, not in its psychological sense. Psychological self-evidence is the condition in which something seems self-evident to me (i.e., it seems self-evident that I had eggs for breakfast this morning). What is logically self-evident cannot be doubted without losing significant meaning.

> Evidently then such a principle is the most certain of all; which principle this is, we proceed to say. It is, that the same attribute cannot at the same time belong and not belong to the same subject in the same respect; we must presuppose, in fact of dialectical objections, any further qualifications which might be added. This, then, is the most certain of all principles, since it answers to the definitions given above. For it is impossible for any one to believe the same thing to be and not to be, as some think Heraclitus says; for what a man says he does not necessarily believe.[37]

Meyer says Aristotle's statement "that the same attribute cannot at the same time belong and not belong to the same subject in the same respect" is the PNC-ontological.[38] What Meyer terms PNC-ontological will be extended to include all three laws of thought and be termed 'reason is ontological,' though in this section of the argument Aristotle is focused primarily on LNC/PNC. PNC-ontological means that the book cannot be both red and non-red in the same respect and at the same time. The same attribute cannot both be affirmed and denied of a subject in the same respect and at the same time. Aristotle claims that this is "the most certain of all principles." PNC-ontological is the most logically and objectively certain, but not necessarily psychologically and subjectively certain, as it is possible for a person to fail to grasp and understand the principle. In the above passage, we also see that Aristotle affirms that it is "impossible for anyone to believe the same thing to be and not be" in the same respect and at the same time. From PNC-ontological, that the laws of

---

37 Aristotle, *Metaphysics*, 1005b17-25.
38 Meyer, 86.

reason are the laws of being, we can derive PNC-logical, that the laws of reason are the laws of thought. PNC-logical says that it cannot be *true* that the same predicate at the same time belongs and does not belong to the same subject in the same respect.[39] Put another way; the proposition is necessarily false that 'the book is both red and non-red in the same respect and at the same time.' PNC-ontological is an application of reason to being, and PNC-logical is an application of reason to thinking. PNC-logical assumes PNC-ontological.[40]

Aristotle points out that some may demand proof for LNC, the most certain of all principles. He responds by saying: "For it is impossible that there should be demonstration of absolutely everything; there would be an infinite regress so that there would still be no demonstration. But if there are things of which one should not demand demonstration, these persons cannot say what principles they regard as more indemonstrable than the present one."[41] LNC is *a priori*, self-evident, and the necessary starting point of all demonstration. It is a first principle of being and thinking. In this respect, the laws of thought are foundational to all other thinking. Aristotle does not think positive demonstration may prove LNC without begging the question, but he does provide a negative demonstration for LNC, and for reason as ontological in *Metaphysics* 1006a12-1009a3.

---

39   Meyer, 86.
40   That PNC-logical assumes PNC-ontological is essential because Nietzsche and subsequent post-Nietzschean thinkers attempt to uphold PNC-logical (ordinary rules of thinking) while denying PNC-ontological. This move to retain the ordinary rules of thinking, while denying that reason applies to being underwrites much of contemporary practical reason and pragmatism and will be explored in Chapter 4.
41   Aristotle, *Metaphysics*, 1006a8-10.

Aristotle's negative demonstration is to show that the person who objects to LNC either begins with silence or that he ends up in meaninglessness and should be silent. Either way, his demonstration aims to show that the one who denies LNC should remain silent because without LNC words lack significant meaning. Meyer says that PNC-ontological is assumed in all significant speech. Aristotle begins, "We can, however, demonstrate negatively even that this view is impossible if our opponent will only say something; and if he says nothing, it is absurd to attempt to reason with one who will not reason about anything, in so far as he refuses to reason."[42] For the person who is not silent and demands demonstration, Aristotle says that the starting point for discussion is:

> That he shall say something which is significant both for himself and for another; for this is necessary, if he really is to say anything. For, if he means nothing, such a man will not be capable of reasoning, either with himself or with another. But if he grants this, demonstration will be possible; for we shall already have something definite. The person responsible for the proof, however, is not he who demonstrates but he who listens; for while disowning reason he listens to reason.[43]

In this passage, we see that a person who wants to dispute LNC either says something significant (meaningful) or he does not. If he does not, then there is no dispute (silence). If the person who disputes LNC says something significant (meaningful)

---

42   Ibid., 1006a13-15.
43   Ibid., 1006a19-27.

then they are the person whom both denies reason (in demanding proof for LNC) and affirms reason by affirming significant speech and the process of argumentation. In asking for demonstration, this person has already affirmed reason: "And again he who admits this has admitted that something is true apart from demonstration [so that not everything will be 'so and not so']."[44] This person has assumed the thing they are asking to be proven in affirming significant speech.

Aristotle next goes into an intricate discussion regarding significant speech and its application for reason as ontological. He says, "...this at least is obviously true, that the word 'be' or 'not be' has a definite meaning, so that not everything will be so and not so."[45] If words have a definite meaning, then words correspond to some being. For he says, "if such and such is a man, then if anything is a man, that will be what *being* a man is."[46] The meaning of words is limited; for example, "man" may be a "two footed animal,"[47] or he may be a featherless biped or a rational animal. Though there be several meanings for the term "man" there are still a limited number of meanings. He goes on to argue:

> If, however, they were not limited, but one was to say that the word has an infinite number of meanings, obviously reasoning would be impossible; for not to have one meaning is to have no meaning, and if words have no meaning reasoning with other people, and indeed with oneself has been annihilated; for it is impossible

---

44   Ibid., 1006a27-28.
45   Ibid., 1006a29.
46   Ibid., 1006a32-33, emphasis added.
47   Ibid., 1006a33.

to think of anything if we do not think of one thing; but if this *is* possible, one name might be assigned to this thing.⁴⁸

If words had an infinite number of meanings, then we never get to what a thing is; we never *identify* a thing. Words would have no meaning, and if there is no meaning, then there is no thought and no communication. But if we do "think of one thing" then we can name this one thing. Naming is identifying. It is saying "man" is "two legged," or the being that we use the word "man" to describe is identical to the being that is "two legged." This is an application of the law of identity (LI), *a* is *a*. Words are about thoughts, and thoughts are about being. To deny LI is to deny that words have meaning. Aristotle notes that "in general those who use this argument do away with substance and essence. For they must say that all attributes are accidents, and that there is no such thing as being essentially man or animal."⁴⁹ Thus Aristotle seems to have in mind in this passage, those who deny substance and essence, are those who hold to the "flux doctrine." The denial of "substance and essence" also applies to Nietzsche. If there are no substance or essences, then words do not apply to being (at least not to essential properties), which means all words apply to accidental properties (if they apply to properties at all).

> If all statements are accidental, there will be nothing primary about which they are made, if the accidental always implies predication about a subject. The predication, then, must go on *ad infinitum*. But this

---

48   Ibid., 1006b5-14.
49   Ibid., 1007a21-23.

is impossible; for not even more than two terms can be combined. For an accident is not an accident of an accident, unless it be because both are accidents of the same subject.[50]

Accidental qualities require a subject. A subject has essential qualities. Without a subject (being), there are qualities of qualities *ad infinitum*[51]

Meyer observes that: "what Aristotle has provided here is a negative demonstration of [the impossibility of affirming and denying the same thing of a subject] by arguing that this ontological fact is a necessary condition for significant speech, dialectics, demonstration, and even the attempt to deny PNC-ontological."[52] Aristotle provides a self-referentially absurd argument to show that if one denies that reason is ontological, then that person should remain silent. To assert anything, one must assume the very laws of thought that they aim to deny; doing so ends up in self-contradiction and the lack of significant speech. Aristotle argues that "not all terms will be accidental" or everything would be everything, or all being is one thing without distinction. Thus, there must "be something which denotes substance. And it has been shown that, if this is so, contradictories cannot be predicated at the same time."[53] If everything is everything, then our discussion with the person who denies

---

50 Ibid., 1007a35-1007b4.
51 This seems to be something like the post-Nietzschean position that there are only signs, and nothing signified. Words are about other words. These words have no intrinsic meaning outside the meaning that we assign to them. Yet, are we beings that have the essential feature of assigning meaning to words?
52 Meyer, 94.
53 Aristotle, *Metaphysics*, 1007a16-18.

that reason applies to being "is evidently about nothing at all."[54] To affirm anything is to say something definite about it. It is to identify and distinguish. It is to affirm one thing and to deny its opposite. The one who denies the laws of thought as ontological cannot identify or distinguish anything. They can neither affirm nor deny anything. To be consistent with the denial of reason as ontological, they should remain silent. This ends Aristotle's negative demonstration of the ontological status of reason (as the laws of thought and being).

The next section of *Metaphysics IV* is an argument, based on the premise that reason is ontological, against empiricism and related perspectivism and skepticism. The purpose of this lengthy examination of Aristotle's defense of reason as ontological is to show that the laws of thought apply to being as well as to thought, and that to deny such is to relinquish significant speech. Denying that reason is ontological is associated with Heraclitus' "flux doctrine," as well as empiricism that leads to perspectivism and deep skepticism. In short, the Heraclitan-Protagorean worldview is in direct opposition to the Platonic-Aristotelian worldview, which affirms reason is ontological, the primacy of reason in knowing, that there is a human nature that is rational (the *logos* in us), and there is a non-physical substance in which the *logoi* are grounded (the Forms). Plato and Aristotle are foundational to the Western philosophical tradition of *Logos* and being, and the isomorphism between thinking and being prevails until the postmodern period, spearheaded by Friedrich Nietzsche. Friedrich Nietzsche calls into question the Platonic-Aristotelian conjunction of *logos*-being as well as the consequent history of philosophy and its contribution to

---

54 Ibid., 1008a31.

the West. It is to Nietzsche's critique, and ultimate rejection of reason, that we now turn.

II. Nietzsche and Anti-*Logos*

Nietzsche begins his career as a philologist — literally, a lover of *logos* — and his first lectures, recently published in English as *The Pre-Platonic Philosophers*, are his first attempts to return to the beginning of philosophy to find a basis for a new direction in philosophy at the end of the Modern period. The title, *Pre-Platonic Philosophers*, is significant because Nietzsche thinks that with Plato the tradition of philosophy takes a wrong turn. In fact, Nietzsche thinks that he is the philosopher to return philosophy to its rightful course, which he sees in the thinking of the pre-Platonic philosophers, especially in Heraclitus. Plato, according to Nietzsche, promulgates the error of associating *logos*/reason and being. Compounding this error, Plato and subsequent philosophers, including the whole Christian tradition, connect being with the Good, "legislating" morality and instituting an illegitimate will to power indicative of a culture in a state of decline and decadence. Nietzsche's intention in going back to the pre-Platonic philosophers is to return to a period of philosophy before the coupling of *logos* and being. Nietzsche thinks that Heraclitus defends a radical flux doctrine in which there is no permanent being, only becoming through the relation of force.[55] Nietzsche's endorsement of a Heraclitan flux doctrine marks the beginning of his rejection of reason as ontological. He denies that reason is ontological from his first works through his last. Though Nietzsche changes some of his views

---

[55] See Meyer for an explication of Nietzsche's Heraclitan-Protagorean metaphysical commitments.

as his thinking progresses over the years, the rejection of reason remains consistent and one from which he does not swerve. His consistency in the rejection of reason may have been his ultimate undoing, leading him into madness. The last of Nietzsche's writings, published just prior to his madness, reveal the extent to which he has gone in his rejection of reason in his associating himself with the anti-Christ; explicitly making himself the anti-*Logos*.[56] The next section of the chapter aims to provide a sampling of quotes that demonstrate Nietzsche's rejection of reason — the laws of thought — and their application to concepts, judgments, arguments, and words/language.

To put the significance of Nietzsche's rejection of reason into perspective, let us return to the broader argument of the chapter. Meyer claims that "Nietzsche's rejection of the isomorphism of thinking and being is not an isolated point but forms the basis for his attack on an entire conception of reality which holds that there are substances endowed with intrinsic properties out there waiting to be known by the philosopher. In short, it forms the basis for his attack on the metaphysical tradition."[57] The broader argument of this chapter is that *Logos* is the driving concept of the Western philosophical tradition. Yet, this *Logos* is the very concept that Nietzsche rejects. Thus, Nietzsche

---

56   In section 7 of *Ecce Homo*, Nietzsche says that: "One way of *measuring* the strength of an attacker is by looking at the sort of opponents he needs; you can always tell when something is growing because it will go looking for powerful adversaries — or problems; since a warlike philosopher will challenge problems to a single combat. The task is *not* to conquer all obstacles in general but instead to conquer the ones where you can apply your whole strength, suppleness, and skill with weapons, — to conquer opponents that are your *equals* … Equality among enemies — first presupposition of an *honest* duel" (*EH* p. 82-83). Then he goes on to name Christianity as his opponent.

57   Meyer, 82.

rejects the Western philosophical tradition. In the first part of the chapter, we saw the importance for philosophy that *logos/* reason applies to being. In this next section of the chapter, we will see Nietzsche's rejection of *logos* and reason as ontological. In fact, an intentionally anti-*logos* philosophy emerges when we explore the works of Nietzsche.

Nietzsche's lectures from his days as a philologist at the University of Basel around 1871 have been translated into English and published as *The Pre-Platonic Philosophers*. This work is a survey of the first philosophers, in which Nietzsche gives the most time and attention to a discussion of Heraclitus. Through this discussion we see Nietzsche's own interpretation and approval of Heraclitus's flux doctrine. He states:

> Well, this is the intuitive perception of Heraclitus; there is no thing of which we may say, "it is." He rejects *Being*. He knows only Becoming, the flowing. He considers belief in something persistent as error and foolishness. To this he adds this thought: that which becomes is one thing in eternal transformation, and the law of this eternal transformation, the Logos[58] in

---

[58] Nietzsche self-identifies with Heraclitus. Scholars such as Brann and Guthrie take pains to point out that most fundamental feature of Heraclitus' thinking is the *Logos*. Yet, in his discussion of Heraclitus, Nietzsche hardly mentions his *Logos*. This passage represents one of Nietzsche's rare mentions of Heraclitus's *Logos*. Here it seems that Nietzsche identifies Heraclitus's *Logos* with a law of eternal transformation. Nietzsche, in order to remain consistent with his rejection of reason as ontological, has to change the meaning of Heraclitan *Logos* as rational mind. Greg Whitlock, in his commentary on *PPP* says: "Heraclitus comprehended the Logos, the all-pervasive intelligence. This Logos is intelligence or mind, which would later be called nous by the pre-Platonic philosophers. Nietzsche insists that logos is an intelligence, which he further

all things, is precisely this One, fire. Thus, the one overall Becoming is itself law; *that* it becomes and *how* it becomes is its work.[59][60]

In this passage we see Nietzsche identifying Heraclitan epistemology as an "intuitive perception," a theme he will return to often in later works. This "intuitive perception" will be an alternative to rational analysis. Based upon this intuitive perception, according to Nietzsche, Heraclitus rejects Being in favor of Becoming. It is important to note that the preference of Becoming over Being is not on the basis of rational insight. Affirmation of the Heraclitan flux doctrine, and consequent judgment that "something persistent exists" is false, are judgments based upon intuitive appearances — how things seem to the perceiver. These intuitive appearances yield rational judgments: "All is Becoming/flux;" "There is no Being." These statements are ul-

---

    identifies as *will*. This is an especially poignant moment in the lecture series. Heraclitan Logos becomes identified with a notion of will ... Nietzsche's own conceptual modifications of the will are already underway here, informed in part by the pre-Platonics and in part by his scientific readings" (*PPP*, p. 209-210). Whitlock sees in Nietzsche's identification of Logos with will the beginning of his thinking about the will to power that will be the causal force that undergirds his version of the "flux doctrine" in his later thinking (*PPP*, p. 218). To change *Logos* to Will is a radical re-valuation indeed, and Nietzsche's program of the revaluation of values is present from his first works.

59 Nietzsche, *PPP*, 63.
60 It must be kept in mind that this is how Nietzsche understands Heraclitus. Eva Brann does not understand Heraclitus in this way and says of Nietzsche, who so closely identifies himself with Heraclitus, "He takes his co-opted predecessor to deny both the separation between thought and nature and the being of Being. He explains Heraclitus's paradoxes as the splendid result of the intuitive anti-rationalism that guides his representation of a force-replete world," and she later remarks, "Talk of willful misconstrual!" Brann, 118-119.

timately true or false and may only be judged as such in light of the laws of thought. The very doctrine that Nietzsche begins with — namely, "all is flux" — to deny the laws of thought, relies upon the laws of thought to affirm the truth of the position.

Nietzsche never provides a reason beyond Heraclitus's "intuitive perception" as to why Heraclitus's position should be affirmed as the truth about reality. He goes on to draw out the epistemological implications of the affirmation of the flux doctrine when he asserts: "If everything is in Becoming, then, accordingly, predicates cannot adhere to a thing but rather likewise must be in the flow of Becoming."[61] According to Aristotle, predicates are always predicated of a subject. If all is Becoming, there is no permanent subject, and thus by implication, there are only predicates of predicates, the very thing that Aristotle points out is impossible when he argues that LNC applies to being as well as to thought. Here we see the origin and root of Nietzsche's denial of reason as ontological. He begins with an "intuitive perception" that all is Becoming, and then on that basis denies there are things, and thus predicates do not adhere to subjects. Since words express subject and predicate (in the form of judgments), words do not express being. There is not an isomorphism between being and thinking, and by implication, between being, thinking and words.

In speaking about Parmenides, in contrast with Heraclitus, Nietzsche explains that Parmenides concludes: "We can conceive only Being. Of Not-Being we can have no idea. Possessing ideas and believing in Being merge together."[62] In this merging together, we see Nietzsche's recognition of Parmenides' contri-

---

61   Nietzsche, *PPP*, 65.
62   Ibid., 85.

bution to the stage in philosophical development where reason applies to being. Nietzsche goes on to observe of Parmenides' thought: "Thus Logos recognizes the true essence of things; in other words, the abstractions and the perceptions of sensation are only deceptions."[63] In his discussion of Parmenides, Nietzsche identifies a distinction between the Parmenidean pursuit of truth through *Logos*, and that of the "perception of sensation." He goes on to say that:

> [In the thought of Parmenides] we have an unnatural tearing apart of the intellect. The consequence must finally be [a dichotomy between] spirit (the faculty of abstraction) and bodies (lower sensory apparatus), and we recognize the ethical consequences already in Plato: the philosopher's task to liberate himself from the bodily, meaning from the senses. [This is] the most dangerous of false paths, for no true philosophy can construct itself from this empty hull….[64]

Whereas Heraclitus's "intuitive perception" saw reality immediately through the senses, Parmenides is caught in an unnatural rational abstraction that separates the faculties of sensation from that of reason, which leads to a "dangerous" metaphysic that separates body from soul in all subsequent philosophy. Nietzsche infers that Platonic dialectic and the subsequent development of logic stem from the Parmenidean conflation of reason and being. He then launches a lifelong attack on this perceived conflation.

---

63 Ibid., 86.
64 Ibid., 86.

Nietzsche's first published work, *The Birth of Tragedy* (1872), was not well-received within the scholarly community of Basel because in this work he moves away from philology to developing his philosophy. *BT* develops some of the assumptions of *PPP* and is an attempt to show that the ancient Greek philosophy was part of a tragic Dionysian worldview out of which an optimistic Socratic philosophy developed in response to the need to make sense of a chaotic world of flux. Nietzsche is opposed to the philosophical optimism of Socrates and says that:

> ...We find a type of deep-seated illusion, first manifested in Socrates: the illusion that thought, guided by the thread of causation, might plumb the farthest abysses of being and even *correct* it. This grand metaphysical illusion has become integrated to the scientific endeavor and again and again leads science to those far limits of its inquiry where it becomes art — *which, in this mechanism, is what is really intended.*[65]

The primary error of Socratic optimism is the mistake that "thought, guided by the thread of causation," which seems to be the causal implications of a chain of reasoning, "might plumb ... being ... and even *correct* it." Socrates' mistake is to link reason to being, and then to think that reason may improve being. The improvement of being is by science and through morality. Nietzsche does not think that there is any being, so science does not discover and improve the world, and morality does not improve human beings. These attempts by optimistic philosophers

---

65 Nietzsche, Friedrich Wilhelm, and Francis Golffing. *The Birth of Tragedy and the Genealogy of Morals* (New York: Anchor Books, Doubleday; 1956), 93.

are but a "grand metaphysical illusion," the creation of which makes philosophers artists. In referring to art here, Nietzsche seems to mean that the optimistic philosophers are the creators of myth. Socrates and most of the sciences create myths in the propagation of the illusion that thought can "plumb the farthest abysses of being." The optimistic Socratic philosophers do not *see* the reality of the isomorphism between thinking and being, rather, they *create* the myth that there is an isomorphism between thinking and being. Nietzsche sets out to expose this "myth" that all of philosophy since Heraclitus has taken to be reality.

In his 1873 essay, "On Truth and Lying in an Extra-Moral Sense,"[66] Nietzsche further develops the notion that philosophers convey myths/illusions (or lies) regarding the connection between thinking and being. "On Truth and Lying" shows Nietzsche's rejection of reason as ontological in a more explicit way as he further develops his philosophy, as opposed to his previous philological work. "On Truth and Lying" is a direct revaluation of Aristotle's connection of being in the world (subject) to concept in the mind and its expression by means of word/language. Instead, Nietzsche sees the process of conception as originating in sensation (intuitive perception), which gives rise to nerve stimuli, which produces an image (where?), which in turn is expressed in sound (words). From these words we create concepts. Words are the lies we make up in the form of "metaphors of things." These words do not correspond to things in themselves. We have forgotten that words are just metaphors for "things." We do not grasp concepts from our contact with being (the

---

66 Nietzsche, Friedrich Wilhelm, Sander L. Gilman, Carole Blair, and David J. Parent. *Friedrich Nietzsche on Rhetoric and Language* (New York: Oxford University Press; 1989), 246-257.

thing-in-itself), because, "The thing-in-itself (which would be pure, disinterested truth) is also absolutely incomprehensible to the creator of language and not worth seeking."[67] Knowledge of the thing-in-itself would be knowledge of truth — reality, being — which Nietzsche thinks is impossible because there is no being. He rhetorically asks, "what is truth?" and responds:

> A mobile army of metaphors, metonyms, anthropomorphisms, in short, a sum of human relations which were poetically and rhetorically heightened, transferred, and adorned, and after long use seem solid, canonical, and binding to a nation. Truths are illusions about which it has been forgotten that they *are* illusions, worn-out metaphors without sensory impact ....[68]

Language expresses "truths" of a particular society. Language is conventional, the rules of which we all tacitly agree to follow. A "liar" in society, then, is one who does not go along with the linguistic conventions of the group. The one who speaks the "truth" (of the philosophers) is, in fact, the real liar, whereas the one who goes against the linguistic conventions of the group and "lies" may, in fact, be a truth teller, such as Nietzsche conceives himself. So, the truth is a lie, and a lie the truth. A revaluation indeed! It is:

> Only by forgetting that primitive metaphor-world, only by the hardening and rigidification of the mass of images that originally gushed forth as hot magma out of the primeval faculty of human fantasy, only by the invincible belief that *this* sun, *this* window, this table is

---

67 Nietzsche, "On Truth and Lying", 248.
68 Ibid., 250.

a truth-in-itself, in short, only insofar as man forgets himself as a subject, indeed as an *artistically creative* subject, does he live with some calm, security, and consistency.[69]

Man, as artist, creates the metaphor-world that is language and conception and then forgets that he has created the world which he takes to be reality. As artist, a constructor of the world that is not real, man lies to himself about the nature of reality and calls it "truth." Lastly, Nietzsche makes the bold claim that "The word 'appearance' contains many seductions; and so I avoid it as much as possible. For it is not true that the essence of things appears in the empirical world."[70] Nietzsche refuses to divide the world into the Modern categories of "thing-in-itself," referring to being, and to the world of appearance, or that which the senses deliver. Instead, he thinks that all is becoming, and appearances confirm this. Thus, all we have are senses and appearances. The senses tell us that all is becoming. The isomorphism between thinking and being is a fiction created by philosophers and propagated through the vehicle of language for millennia. This is fiction that we have forgotten that we have made. Nietzsche is here to remind us.

In his *Human, All Too Human* (1878), Nietzsche offers an alternative to the optimistic Socratic philosophy, which he calls "historical philosophy" and which seems to be the beginning of his genealogical approach to exposing human constructs that we have taken to be "truth." Nietzsche states that:

---

69 Ibid., 252.
70 Ibid.

> Lack of historical sense is the family failing of all philosophers; many, without being aware of it, even take the most recent manifestation of man, such as has arisen under the impress of certain religions, even certain political events, as the fixed form which one has to start out … But everything has become: there are no eternal facts, just as there are no absolute truths. Consequently what is needed from now on is *historical philosophizing*, and with it the virtue of modesty.[71]

Because philosophers of the past have forgotten that they are myth-makers and artistic creators of what we call reality, a new form of philosophy is needed to bring us to the truth that "everything has become;" therefore, "there are no absolute truths." Nietzsche's new historical philosophizing sets out to expose the fiction of the isomorphism between thinking (truths) and being. If all is becoming, then our thoughts do not grasp and express reality. The new philosophy is meant to deconstruct these hardened "truths" of previous philosophical myth-making. To drive home this error of philosophy, Nietzsche says:

> To the extent that man has for long ages believed in the concepts and names of things as in *aeternae veritates* he has appropriated to himself that pride by which he raised himself above the animal: he really thought that in language he possessed knowledge of the world … only now — it dawns on men that in their belief in language they have propagated a tremendous error. Happily, it is too late for the evolution of reason, which

---

[71] Nietzsche, Friedrich Wilhelm, and Richard Schacht. *Human, All Too Human* (Cambridge: Cambridge University Press, 1996), 13.

> depends on this belief, to be again put back. — Logic too depends on presuppositions with which nothing in the real world corresponds, for example on the presupposition that there are identical things, that the same thing is identical at different points of time ....[72]

Nietzsche says that logic "depends on presuppositions with which nothing in the real world corresponds" and then goes on to deny that the law of identity applies to being. Instead of recognizing that logic is the necessary precondition to having any presuppositions and is a first principle necessary for any subsequent presuppositions, Nietzsche assumes that logic itself is a fiction of philosophy. Nietzsche cannot make his critique of the optimistic philosophy without the use of the tools of logic. By divorcing reason as the laws of being from reason as the laws of thought, he makes use of the fiction that is logic to critique logic. In his mind, logic "depends on presuppositions with which nothing in the world corresponds," such as the law of identity, yet given the "evolution of reason" we are at a point in history where we can see that logic is a fiction, but it is a fiction that may be turned back on itself. Philosophy becomes a fiction that exposes itself as a fiction. Philosophy becomes critique.

Why was it necessary for philosophers to invent the fiction of logic? Nietzsche answers this question in *Beyond Good and Evil: Prelude to a Philosophy of the Future* (1886), by saying that:

> We are fundamentally inclined to claim that the falsest judgments (which include synthetic judgments a priori) are the most indispensable to us, and that without accepting the fictions of logic, without measuring real-

---

72 Ibid., 16.

ity against the wholly invented world of the unconditioned and self-identical, without a constant falsification of the world through numbers, people could not live — that a renunciation of false judgments would be a renunciation of life, a negation of life.[73]

Our "falsest judgments," regarding the isomorphism between thinking and being, are the most "indispensable to us" because without these "fictions of logic" we would not be able to live. The laws of thought are a survival mechanism for the kinds of changing beings (becomings?) that we are, in the face of a chaotic and becoming world. Without our invention of logic and our imposition of order on the world of becoming, life would be nihilistic. Yet it is important for us to realize that our descriptions of the world are fictions and do not in any sense approximate reality. Hence, the philosopher is an artist, a myth maker. The only problem is that we have forgotten this fact about the philosopher.

In his *Twilight of the Idols, Or How One Philosophizes with a Hammer* (1888), written in one of his most prolific years, just prior to his madness, Nietzsche wants to be sure that we are aware, that not only is logic, language, and philosophy a myth that we have created, but so is every other aspect of human cultural production. He says:

> Today we possess science precisely to the extent to which we have decided to accept the testimony of the senses — to the extent to which we sharpen them further, arm them, and have learned to think them through. The rest is miscarriage and not-yet-science — in other

---

[73] Nietzsche, *BGE*, 7.

words, metaphysics, theology, psychology, epistemology — or formal science, a doctrine of signs, such as logic and that applied logic which is called mathematics. In them reality is not encountered at all, not even as a problem — no more than the question of the value of such a sign-convention as logic.[74]

Science, insofar as we accept the testimony of the senses and "have learned to think them through," seems to be the only discipline that does not come under the hammer that metaphysics, theology, psychology, epistemology, logic, and mathematics do. Each of these fields falls under Nietzsche's crushing blows due to the claim that they get to reality, not through the senses, but by reason. Nietzsche, ever consistent in his claims, persists in the view that there is no isomorphism between thinking and being, that reason is *not* ontological. All of the cultural productions that affirm that reason is ontological that affirm the *Logos* are dangerous fictions that must be exposed to the hammer of the new philosophy.

Having destroyed human cultural productions based upon the *Logos*, Nietzsche presses the limits of the denial of reason further, even to the point of denying the existence of a thinking subject, or a self:

> Everywhere [reason] sees a doer and doing; it believes in will as *the* cause; it believes in the ego, in the ego as being, in the ego as substance, and it projects this faith in the ego-substance upon all things — only thereby does it first *create* the concept of "thing." Everywhere "being" is projected by thought, pushed underneath, as

---

74 Nietzsche, *TI*, in *The Portable Nietzsche*, 482.

the cause; the concept of being follows, and is a derivative of, the concept of ego. In the beginning there is that great calamity of an error that the will is something which is effective, that will is a capacity. Today we know that it is only a word.[75]

Reason sees a self as a cause, as a substance, as a subject. This reasoning subject then projects the concept of subjects — things — out upon the world of changing appearance. Thus thinking produces being, being is an invention of thinking. What is doing the thinking if there is no thinking subject? If there are no subjects/being(s), then the self as a "doer," as a will, is not a being either. There is no thinking being; the self is a fiction (created by nothing?). The self is a fiction. Reason — the tools of this "self" — is a fiction of a fiction (the self). And philosophy is a fiction (story of *Logos*/reason and being) of a fiction (dialectics and logic) of a fiction (self). Following this reasoning, cultural production (language, science, religion, etc.) would be a fourth-level fiction, since it follows upon the fiction that philosophers have told us for millennia. At this point, we seem to have lost all meaning. Words are about other words. Or as Aristotle says, if there is no subject, there are just predicates of predicates *ad infinitum*, and there is no *thing* to be predicated. The separation of thinking and being leads to the loss of all meaning. In addition, if reason is not ontological, then significant speech becomes impossible. Nietzsche recognizes this reality when he says, "'Reason' in language — oh, what an old deceptive female she is! I am afraid we are not rid of God because we still have faith in Grammar."[76] To link reason to Be-

---

75 Nietzsche, *TI*, 483.
76 Ibid., 483.

ing/God is to acknowledge that reason is ontological and that the laws of thought — reflected in the rules of Grammar — are the laws of being. Order in language assumes order in being and a fit between thinking and being. To effectively be rid of reason as ontological, we must be rid of Grammar. But to be rid of grammar would be the loss of all significant speech and would result in silence.[77]

If the critical idea of Western philosophy is the *Logos*, and Nietzsche consciously and consistently rejects the *Logos*, then Nietzsche rejects the Western philosophical tradition. Nietzsche's anti-*logos* anti-philosophy would undermine all human cultural production of the West that is based upon reason as ontological. As anti-*logos*, he undermines the foundation of the West as based upon the *Logos* resulting in radical (tragic) skepticism, meaninglessness, madness, and ultimately silence. Nietzsche's critique of reason gives rise to a new breed of philosophers — his philosophers of the future — who press Nietzsche's denial of reason as ontological to the limits, leading to the death of everything. These philosophers of the future include continental postmodern philosophers, but also include others within the Anglo-American philosophical tradition; thus these "philosophers of the future" will be called post-Nietzschean philosophers.

---

[77] Some of the best quotes that support the thesis that Nietzsche denies that reason is ontological come from his unpublished notebooks later published by his sister as *The Will to Power*. Because these are preliminary notes — some of which are included in his published works, some of which are not — some Nietzsche scholars argue that in studying Nietzsche one should always look to his published works. Others argue that the *WP* includes ideas that fill in the blanks.

III. Nietzsche's Break

The rejection of *Logos* — reason as ontological — leads to madness and death in the form of all words being emptied of meaning, or semanticide. Post-Nietzschean philosophy rejects *Logos*. Therefore, Post-Nietzschean philosophy leads to madness and death. To demonstrate the death associated with the separation of reason from being, we will examine the end of Nietzsche's life and then turn to the effects for Western civilization of his pronouncement that "God is dead." Nietzsche's rejection of reason as ontological has personal and existential consequences in his life, resulting in madness. Richard Wolin, in his *The Seduction of Unreason: The Intellectual Romance with Fascism from Nietzsche to Postmodernism*, discusses Nietzsche's state of mind just prior to his madness as a kind of "megalomania." He notes:

> On New Year's Eve 1888 [Nietzsche] wrote to the composer Peter Gast, unambiguously alluding to the state of his sanity, that he had crossed "the famous Rubicon." There followed a postcard to Strindberg in which Nietzsche declared he was ordering a convocation of princes in Rome and having the young German emperor shot. (Strindberg's response, "Dear Doctor! It is a joy to be mad!") Partly cognizant of his own dementia, Nietzsche signed these final delusory missives, "Dionysus" and "The Crucified."[78]

For Nietzsche to refer to the crossing of the "Rubicon" concerning his sanity, it would seem that he is making a conscious move

---

[78] Wolin, Richard. *The Seduction of Unreason: The Intellectual Romance With Fascism From Nietzsche to Postmodernism*. (Princeton: Princeton University Press; 2004).

to cross over from sanity to madness. Could it be that his denial of reason and being, and all that this implies, has compelled him to madness? Is he living consistently with his philosophy, and as such entering into a phase of madness (unthinking) and silence (no speaking)? Wolin goes on to wonder:

> What was it that pushed Nietzsche over the brink? Contemporary diagnoses suggested he was suffering from tertiary syphilis. But at the time symptoms such as Nietzsche's were often misinterpreted, and the original diagnosis has not been definitively confirmed. There may well have been compelling physiological reasons for Nietzsche's "crossing the Rubicon" as he insightfully put it. But Nietzsche was also a victim of his own megalomania.[79]

Megalomania is a personality disorder associated with an obsession with, or a desire to gain, power. Nietzsche does seem to have had a deep-seated interest with power, but his interest rests first and fundamentally on the philosophical level, which is before the psychological level. So it makes more sense to speculate that it was Nietzsche's ideas that led to his madness, possibly also giving rise to megalomania. Wolin comes closer to saying that Nietzsche's philosophy drives him mad when he says:

> According to Klossowski [one of Nietzsche's biographers], Nietzsche's thoughts could no longer be communicated via reason or language. His madness expressed the fact that the philosopher had "reached the limit of the principles of identity and reality." Conse-

---

79   Ibid., 29

quently, for the last eleven years of his life, he simply lapsed into muteness. The obscure teachings that he left behind — above all, the doctrine of eternal recurrence — embodied the ultimate rejection of all inherited structures of culture and authority.[80]

Klossowski painstakingly argues through careful analysis of Nietzsche's personal correspondence that Nietzsche "believed he was pursuing, not the realization of a system, but the application of a program"[81] in the days leading up to his crossing the "Rubicon." Klossowski connects Nietzsche's madness to his rejection of the law of non-contradiction indirectly through his commitment to the doctrine of "eternal return." He says, "What the Eternal Return implies as a doctrine is neither more nor less than the insignificance of the *once and for all* of the principle of identity or non-contradiction, which lies at the base of the understanding."[82] It is not just that identity and non-contradiction are "insignificant" for Nietzsche. His whole system of philosophy begins with the break between reason and being such that reason cannot grasp being. Being cannot be known, and words do not express any being. Words are only conventional signs that lack any real significant meaning. It is the meaninglessness that drives Nietzsche to madness. Wolin comes close to understanding this when he says, "Once Nietzsche realized the illusory character of all language and human ends, *silence* became the only viable and honest response. Recourse to "consciousness" and "reason" would only falsify this profound real-

---

80 Wolin, 37.
81 Klossowski, Pierre, trans. Daniel W. Smith. *Nietzsche and the Vicious Circle*. (Chicago: University of Chicago Press, 1997), 225.
82 Ibid., 217.

ization."[83] In moving to silence, Nietzsche is most consistent with his professed philosophy. He does just what Aristotle says one who gives up the laws of thought should do. If reason does not apply to being, then significant speech is not possible. But Nietzsche also seems to commit intellectual suicide in embracing silence.

The implications of Nietzsche's philosophy are not only personal, for his life only, but his ideas have implications for all of Western, if not global, civilization. The separation between reason and being leads to intellectual suicide on a civilizational level as well. One way to enter into the application of Nietzsche's philosophy to Western civilization is through analysis of Martin Heidegger's essay, "The Word of Nietzsche: "God is Dead.""[84] Heidegger (1889-1976) is one of the earliest proponents of Nietzsche's ideas.[85] In this essay Heidegger both explains and systematizes the meaning of Nietzsche's proclamation that "God is Dead" and it is we that have killed him. He then shows the implications for post-Nietzschean philosophy given the death of God. The "Madman" quote, from *The Gay Science* aphorism 125, is lengthy, but important for the context of Heidegger's analysis:

> *The madman.* - Haven't you heard of that madman who in the bright morning lit a lantern and ran around the marketplace crying incessantly, "I'm looking for God!

---

83 Wolin, 38.
84 Heidegger, Martin, trans. William Lovitt. *The Question Concerning Technology and Other Essays*. (New York: Garland Publishing, Inc., 1977).
85 Heidegger interprets and systematizes Nietzsche's ideas in his four-volume work: *Nietzsche: Vol. I The Will to Power and Art, Nietzsche: Vol. II The Eternal Recurrence of the Same, Nietzsche Vol. III The Will to Power as Knowledge and as Metaphysics*, and *Nietzsche: Vol. IV Nihilism*, all edited by David Farrell Krell (San Francisco: Harper One, 1991).

I'm looking for God!" Since many of those who did not believe in God were standing around together just then, he caused great laughter. Has he been lost, then? asked one. Did he lose his way like a child? asked another. Or is he hiding? Is he afraid of us? Has he gone to sea? Emigrated? - Thus they shouted and laughed, one interrupting the other. The madman jumped into their midst and pierced them with his eyes. "Where is God?" he cried: "I'll tell you! *We have killed him* - you and I! We are all his murderers. But how did we do this? How were we able to drink up the sea? Who gave us the sponge to wipe away the entire horizon? What were we doing when we unchained this earth from its sun? Where is it moving to now? Where are we moving to? Away from all suns? Are we not continually falling? And backwards, sidewards, forwards, in all directions? Is there still an up and a down? Aren't we straying as though through an infinite nothing? Isn't empty space breathing at us? Hasn't it got colder? Isn't night and more night coming again and again? Don't lanterns have to be lit in the morning? Do we still hear nothing of the noise of the grave-diggers who are burying God? Do we still smell nothing of the divine decomposition? - Gods, too, decompose! God is dead! God remains dead! And we have killed him! How can we console ourselves, the murderers of all murderers. The holiest and the mightiest thing the world has ever possessed has bled to death under our knives: who will wipe this blood from us? With what water could we clean ourselves? What festivals of atonement, what holy games will we have to invent for ourselves? Is the magnitude of this deed not too great for us? Do we not ourselves have to become gods merely to appear worthy of it? There was never a greater deed - and whoever is born after us will on account of this deed belong to a higher history than all history up to now." Here the madman fell silent and looked again at his listeners; they too were silent and looked at him disconcertedly. Finally he threw his lantern on the ground so that it broke into pieces and went out. "I come too early," he then said; "my time is not yet. This tremendous event is still on its way, wandering; it has not yet reached the ears of men. Lightning and thunder need time; the light of the stars needs time; deeds need time, even after they are done, in order to be seen and heard. This deed is still more remote to them than the remotest stars - *and yet they have done it themselves!*" It is still recounted how on the same day the madman forced his way into several churches and there started singing his *requiem aeternam deo*. Led out and called to account, he is said always to have replied nothing but, "What then are these churches now if not the tombs and sepulchers of God?"[86]

Heidegger takes Nietzsche to be explaining what has happened in the history of Western philosophy in this aphorism. With the separation of reason from being, there either is no longer access to a suprasensory world, or we have realized that there is no suprasensory world. Heidegger says in the post-Nietzschean philosophy, "The suprasensory is transformed into an unstable

---

86 Nietzsche, Friedrich, and Bernard Williams. *The Gay Science*. (New York: Cambridge University Press, 2001).

product of the sensory. And with such a debasement of its antithesis, the sensory denies its own essence. The deposing of the suprasensory does away with the merely sensory and thus with the difference between the two."[87] When Nietzsche separates reason from being and endorses the flux doctrine, there is no permanent being to be sensed. In the process of Western philosophy, thinkers such as Plato held that reason applied to being, then later philosophers, such as Hegel, said reason is being, and then in a reaction to Hegel's idealism materialists said there is no being apart from sensory being. Modern philosophers such as Hume and Kant struggled to make sense of how reason and the senses were connected. As empiricism and materialism were pressed, further Nietzsche shows how reason cannot apply to being if all that exist are natural forces. Reason is a construct by humans deployed as a way of mastering and ordering the chaos of experience. Heidegger says that Nietzsche's position "culminates in meaninglessness."[88] And he says that "Nietzsche himself interprets the course of Western history metaphysically, and indeed as the rise and development of nihilism."[89] "God is dead" is the summary of the historical movement towards nihilism, according to Heidegger.[90] God, the good, and Ideas are all part of a suprasensory world, what Nietzsche and Heidegger call the "metaphysical" world. Heidegger says:

> The pronouncement "God is dead" means: The suprasensory world is without effective power. It bestows no life. Metaphysics, i.e., for Nietzsche Western philoso-

---

87 Heidegger, *Question Concerning Technology*, 53-54.
88 Ibid., 54.
89 Ibid., 54.
90 Ibid., 57.

phy understood as Platonism, is at an end. Nietzsche understands his own philosophy as the countermovement to metaphysics, and that means for him a movement in opposition to Platonism.[91]

In a very subtle move, post-Nietzschean philosophy redefines the field of metaphysics to be the study of the suprasensible world. They then deny the reality of the suprasensible world, and so do away with the study of metaphysics. This is a dishonest act of semanticide. Metaphysics is not the study of the suprasensible, but the study of ultimate reality, which may or may not include the suprasensible. If we define reality as merely sensible, then we are still doing metaphysics. It is naturalist or materialist metaphysics. By defining away the suprasensible, and tying metaphysics to the suprasensible, post-Nietzschean philosophers get away with assuming all that exists is the natural, sensible, material world.

The death of God, or the end of metaphysics as imagined by the post-Nietzschean philosophers, leads to nihilism and pragmatism. Nihilism, according to Heidegger, has "a double meaning ... on the one hand, it designates the mere devaluing of the highest values up to now, but on the other hand it also means at the same time the unconditional countermovement to devaluing."[92] There is a negative side to nihilism which consists in the devaluation of all values. This nihilism sees the emptiness of the old values of the suprasensible systems of thought of Plato and Christian theism. This strain of nihilism is carried out to its logical conclusions in postmodern deconstruction and the "death of everything." The positive strain of nihilism sets up

---

91 Ibid., 61.
92 Ibid., 68.

a new system of "values" to replace the old metaphysics of the suprasensory philosophy. It is fascinating to note that Heidegger claims that "values talk" begins with Nietzsche. He says, "But only after the dissemination of the writings of Nietzsche did talk of values become popular."[93] These new values replace the old "objective" moral standards of the suprasensible metaphysic, and are subjective and pragmatic. Heidegger explains what Nietzsche means by "values": "Nietzsche says in a note (1887-88) what he understands by value: 'The point-of-view of "value" is the point-of-view constituting the *preservation-enhancement conditions* with respect to complex forms of relative duration of life within becoming' (*Will to Power,* Aph. 715)."[94] Values are the means by which we preserve and enhance life within the realm of becoming, or the flux of the natural world. Heidegger then systematically connects becoming to the will to power, the will to power to "life," and life to values. The will is to gain power, more power, and more strength.[95] Values are the means to "will-out-beyond" the individual into society. This willing out beyond oneself is pragmatism, the notion that truth is what brings results for a given goal. In another act of semanticide, Heidegger sees post-Nietzschean truth as having "an essentially historical origin out of the modes of its essence … that which — making stably constant — makes secure the constant reserve, belonging to the sphere from out of which the will to power wills itself."[96] Truth is the conditions that allow for the preservation and exercise of power. The will to power is the "truth" of the new metaphysics of the sensible world.

---

93 Ibid., 70.
94 Ibid., 71.
95 Ibid., 78.
96 Ibid., 85.

In the new metaphysics God is dead, there is no transcendent reality, man is subjectivity constituted by a will to power, the goal of man is the preservation and enhancement of life, and this goal is carried out through values on an individual level and by the imposition of those values upon society through justice, the "function of a power having a wide range of vision, which sees out beyond the narrow perspectives of good and evil, thus has a wider horizon of *interest* — the aim, to preserve Something that is *more* than this or that particular person."[97] The common good in this new view is the "dominion over the earth" as the will to power for the preservation and enhancement of life.[98] The new, post-Nietzschean philosophy constitutes a revaluation of all values. In this new system of "values" God may still be believed in, but God becomes merely another survival or pragmatic value.[99]

Heidegger says that "The ultimate blow against God and against the suprasensory world consists in the fact that God, the first of beings, is degraded to the highest value. The heaviest blow against God is not that God is held to be unknowable, not that God's existence is demonstrated to be unprovable, but rather that the God held to be real is elevated to the highest value,"[100] where value is just a means to preservation and enhancement of life in the sensory world. Heidegger goes on to say that this blow, of changing God into a "value," is not done by non-believers, but rather is a move made by people of faith

---

97 Ibid., 91-92.
98 Ibid., 99.
99 It is interesting to note that Nietzsche influences early theorists of Religious Studies such as Max Weber, Sigmund Freud, and Claude Levi-Strauss, who reduce religion to something natural and practical.
100 Ibid., 105.

and ought to be thought of as blasphemy from the perspective of true faith. In other words, believers buy into the post-Nietzschean framework without recognizing the consequences of their belief in God. Heidegger, at the end of the essay, returns to Nietzsche's story of the Madman. He asks, "what men did when they unchained the earth from its sun...." He says:

> When Nietzsche names the relationship between the sun and the earth he is not thinking merely of the Copernican revolution in the modern understanding of nature. The word "sun" at once recalls Plato's allegory. According to the latter, the sun and the realm of its light are the spheres in which that which *is* appears according to its visible aspect, or according to its many countenances (Ideas). The sun forms and circumscribes the field of vision wherein that which is as such shows itself. "Horizon" refers to the suprasensory world as the world that truly is. That is at the same time that whole which envelops all and in itself includes all, as does the sea. The earth, as the abode of man, is unchained from its sun. The realm that constitutes the suprasensory, which as such, *is* in itself no longer stands over man as the authoritative light ... That which is, as the objective, is swallowed up into the immanence of subjectivity.[101]

Man, cut off from the sun, from the transcendent, is confined to life in Plato's cave, or to the Immanent Frame.

Heidegger thinks that his story of Nietzsche's insights about the Death of God and the revaluation of all values is an

---

101 Ibid., 106-107.

inevitable logical outworking of Western philosophy. This cannot be assumed. Nihilism is only a logical outcome of Western philosophy if one first assumes a naturalistic metaphysic. If there is no suprasensory reality, then the history of philosophy could be read as the gradual realization of that reality, but it seems that Nietzsche and Heidegger are held as captive to their conception of "truth" as those they criticize.[102] It is not a natural, historical outworking that leads to the death of God, but instead, it is the historical turning away from Theism and German Idealism by the German materialists[103] primarily, but not exclusively, which leads to the logical outcome of nihilism. Heidegger misuses historicism in his story of the Death of God. It is not a natural outworking that results in the death of God. Rather, God was killed by actors, by men like Nietzsche who are willing to power an alternative narrative. Nietzsche willed the death of God; he does not argue for it, he does not prove it; he merely wills it. Nietzsche and Heidegger miss the logical necessity — the force of reason — that determines the outcome of nihilism from the starting point of empiricism and naturalism. They miss the reality that the death of God in the history of Western philosophy is a movement that is directed by human actors pushing a view that gets accepted and propagated by power elites.

Nietzsche's rejection of reason led to personal madness, but it also leads to the Postmodern post-Nietzschean turn and cultural madness in the West. This madness is not a natural outworking of history but is an agenda pushed by post-Nietzschean philosophers to remake the world in their image. Rainer Friedrich, in a two-essay series, "The Enlightenment Gone Mad: The

---

102 Death of God metanarrative could do with a bit of deconstructing.
103 This history will be explored in Chapter 4.

Dismal Discourse of Postmodernism's Grand Narratives,"[104] says that Lyotard's *Postmodern Condition:*

> ... defines "postmodern as an incredulity towards metanarratives" and translates this incredulity into a program of dismantling them once and for all. This is generally regarded as the defining forte of Postmodernism, said to complete the Nietzschean-Heideggerian enterprise of the destruction of metaphysics. Post-modernity deems itself the death of the grand narrative.[105]

Friedrich aims to show that what postmodernism does is exchange one grand narrative for another. He also shows that the death of metaphysics and the death of the grand narrative results in the death of everything. He says:

> ...there is a discernable commonality among the various branches of postmodernism. They have in common a penchant for passing death sentences and issuing death certificates, promulgating, with either insouciant glee or ponderous gloom, the death of reason; the death of enlightenment; the death of universalism; the death of normativity and law; the death of meaning and truth — in short, the death of almost everything that the Western intellectual tradition stands for in general and that modernity has claimed in particular. With exorbitant virulence, postmodernism has turned

---

[104] Friedrich, Rainer. "The Enlightenment Gone Mad (I): The Dismal Discourse Of Postmodernism's Grand Narratives." *Arion: A Journal of Humanities and the Classics* 19, no. 3 (01 2012): 31-78. Accessed 3/18/2017. doi:10.2307/arion.19.3.0031.

[105] Ibid., 31.

against the anthropocentric and subjectivistic-individualistic terror in modernity, in particular against its focus on the thinking subject, with the denigration of the Cartesian cogito, yielding further death certificates: the death of man; the death of autonomous subjectivity; the death of the self; the death of the author. Such pervasive negativity, often speaking in apocalyptic tongues, is the chief defining feature uniting the many postmodernisms.[106]

A re-valuation of the revaluation of all values needs to take place to stop the madness. Post-Nietzschean[107] philosophers chose empiricism, naturalism, and perspectivalism. This position was not an inevitable outcome of history. It was a decisive, willful, turning away from Idealism and towards materialism. To see the Death of God as inevitable is a misreading of reality, the very thing Nietzsche and the postmodern philosophers accuse their predecessors of doing. Nietzsche and those who follow redefine metaphysics as belief in the supranatural. The result of this redefinition is to insulate their empiricist and naturalist assumptions from metaphysical critique. The post-Nietzschean philosophers attempt to carry out Nietzsche's nihilism, both through deconstruction and through revaluation, but they do so with a blind spot. They are guilty of pushing an agenda; they are involved in the power dynamics they seek to unmask.

---

106 Ibid., 31-32.
107 For reasons that will become apparent in Chapter 4, the term "post-Nietzschean" is being used rather than merely "postmodernism." Postmodernism's deconstruction is just one aspect of the outworking of Nietzsche's nihilism. The other aspect of nihilism is the positive promotion of values, which includes a broader group of actors than the continental postmodernists philosophers.

Nietzsche accuses Plato of doing creative philosophy, of being a myth-making artist, who invents a narrative about what is, and then propagates that narrative on the mass of mankind. Nietzsche does precisely the same thing with his revaluation of values.

Rather than pit one narrative against another, we can recognize that rejecting a "supranatural" reality logically leads to accepting a natural reality. This is the force of reason applied to being. Reality cannot both be supranatural and only natural in the same respect and at the same time. Either reality is supranatural, or it is only natural. We know this by the inescapable force of reason. Nihilism is not a historical inevitability, but rather a logical alternative that has been tried before and found wanting. In fact, we are at a place historically where we have seen the logical options of materialism, dualism, idealism and the contradictory view of theism to have been tried and found wanting. Where do we go from here? The options seem to be return to reason and try again or continue with the abandonment of reason and allow the Death of God and accompanying nihilism to continue to work itself out until the madness of the West results in the silence and death of the West. As mentioned previously, the post-Nietzschean philosophy is not an inevitability but was a choice, a set of values, that has been pushed by those in leading positions of power within the West. The next chapter will trace the development of Nietzsche's separation of reason from being through three strains of contemporary philosophy leading to institutionalized skepticism, or pragmatism: life within the Immanent Frame.

Chapter 4

Post-*Logos* Philosophy

It could even be possible that whatever gives value to those good and honorable things has an incriminating link, bond, or tie to the very things that look like their evil opposites; perhaps they are even essentially the same. Perhaps! — But who is willing to take charge of such a dangerous Perhaps! For this we must await the arrival of a new breed of philosophers, ones whose taste and inclination are somehow the reverse of those we have seen so far — philosophers of the dangerous Perhaps in every sense. — And in all seriousness: I see these new philosophers approaching.[1]

---

1   Nietzsche, Friedrich Wilhelm, Rolf-Peter Horstmann, and Judith Norman. *Beyond Good and Evil: Prelude to a Philosophy of the Future*. (Cambridge: Cambridge University Press, 2002).

THE PURPOSE OF this chapter is to trace the history of Nietzsche's skepticism and nihilism stemming from empiricism and materialism to contemporary philosophy. A continuation of a Nietzschean divorce of reason from being will emerge within three strains of contemporary philosophy — the continental, the analytic, and the pragmatic. These three strains of Post-Nietzschean philosophy enact Nietzsche's nihilism, both negatively and positively, and provide the underpinnings of institutionalized skepticism. We will see that this skepticism is not an inevitable and necessary historical outworking, but rather it is the logical outworking of philosophical assumptions that are promoted by historical actors. Institutionalized skepticism is the uncritically assumed philosophical position that knowledge is not possible, which becomes the basis of Western culture — Charles Taylor's immanent frame — expressed in the institutions of culture such as the family, education, the state, and its laws, economics, and religion. In a period of long-term institutionalized skepticism, pragmatism becomes the *modus operandi* philosophy. It will be argued that all three strains of contemporary philosophy are essentially pragmatic, that truth is the will to power and values are the means by which to "will-out-beyond" the individual into society. Furthermore, pragmatism is the will to power institutionalized. Thus, Western cultural skepticism is institutional pragmatism.

The current crisis of public discourse, resulting from at least a century of institutionalized skepticism, is rooted in the empiricism and materialism, or what we can call a post-*Logos* philosophy. This empiricism reaches back at least to Francis Bacon (1561-1626) and Thomas Hobbes (1588-1679), the forerunners of British Empiricism. Yet it is not until Nietzsche and the post-Nietzschean philosophers that empiricism and materialism are brought together and brought to their most consistent expression. Nietzsche's empiricism and materialism are the most consistent forms in Western philosophy. He goes several steps further than David Hume (1711-1776), Karl Marx (1818-1883), Charles Darwin (1800-1882), and Arthur Schopenhauer (1788-1860). Nietzsche goes further than Hume, as Nietzsche denies the self as a subject, by denying that there is any "being" that makes up a human being, and Nietzsche puts his philosophy into practice in a way that Hume does not. The so-called "self," for Nietzsche, is the phenomenon we call "will" that arises from opposing forces. He rejects Hume's sentiments in favor of the will to power. Nietzsche goes further than Marx and Darwin, who both affirm some sort of order and progress, which must affirm some being that "progresses" even if that being is merely material. Nietzsche denies the very idea of progress. There is no order, no progress, only chaos and disorder that is the result of the conflict of forces in this ever-changing world of flux. He goes beyond all of Philosophy from Plato to his own day by denying that reason is ontological, denying being, denying the self, and affirming what he thinks is the pre-Platonic, Heraclitan flux doctrine.

Nietzsche, unlike his predecessors, negates the whole Western philosophical tradition. Nietzsche in turn influences over 120 years of continental philosophy through the likes of Martin Heidegger (1889-1976), Sigmund Freud (1859-1939), Georges Bataille (1897-1962), Emmanuel Levinas (1906-1995), Jean-Paul Sartre (1905-1980), Jean-François Lyotard (1924-1998), Gilles Deleuze (1925-1995), Michel Foucault (1926-1980), Jacques Derrida (1930-2004), and Jurgen Habermas (1929-). These philosophers apply Nietzsche's philosophy more and more consistently, leading to "the death of everything" as seen in Chapter 3. We can conceive of the continental strain of philosophy as carrying out the application of Nietzsche's negative nihilism through deconstruction and unmasking power dynamics. This post-Nietzschean strain of contemporary philosophy, of the three strains, is the most consistent, and thus the most damaging source of institutional skepticism. This strain of contemporary philosophy is found in most of the liberal arts and soft sciences in the academy. Yet the post-Nietzschean continental strain of contemporary philosophy is not the only source of our current crisis of skepticism. The second strain of contemporary philosophy, and the second most consistent of the three is that of Pragmatism. Pragmatism can be thought of as carrying out Nietzsche's positive nihilism — the revaluation of values — by replacing the old values of the "suprasensible world" with new values. The third strain of contemporary philosophy is analytic philosophy, which is less conscious and less consistent of the three in applying empiricist and materialist principles. Yet analytic philosophy, on the whole, is also a major player in institutionalized skepticism.

The term "Post-Nietzschean" philosophy will be used to refer to the three strains of contemporary philosophy — continental, Pragmatic, and analytic. Not all strains can be directly tied to Nietzsche himself, and not every philosopher after Nietzsche is a post-Nietzschean. Those who deny the isomorphism between reason and being will be termed post-Nietzschean. Insofar as they share a common set of assumptions, they shall be called by the same name. The term "Post-Nietzschean" also recognizes the historical turn instigated by Nietzsche that is associated with the "Death of God" as discussed in Chapter 3. The post-Nietzschean world is "this" world without reference to any transcendence; it is life in the Cave; it is the immanent frame. All three strains of contemporary philosophy are post-Nietzschean insofar as they assume and further promote life after the death of God.

I. A Genealogy of Post-Nietzschean Skepticism

Richard Rorty recognizes three strains of Post-Nietzschean philosophy in America. In the analytic strain he sees philosophy as akin to science; in the continental strain philosophy is akin to poetry or metaphor, and in the pragmatist strain he sees philosophy as politics.[2] In addition, Rorty recognizes Nietzsche as a pragmatist and sees all three strains of philosophy in America terminating in pragmatism. He says:

> The context in which my essays put post-Nietzschean philosophy is, predictably enough, pragmatism. I see Nietzsche as the figure who did most to convince European intellectuals of the doctrines which were purveyed to Americans by James and Dewey. A lot of what Nietzsche had to say can be viewed as following from his claim that "knowledge in itself" is as impermissible a concept as a "thing-in-itself" and his suggestion that "[the categories of reason] represent nothing more than the expediency of a certain race and species — their utility alone is their 'truth'."[3]

---

2 Rorty, Richard. "Philosophy as Science, as Metaphor, and as Politics." *Essays on Heidegger and Others: Philosophical Papers Volume 2.* (New York, Cambridge University Press, 1991), 9.
3 Ibid., 2.

The purpose of this section of the chapter is to trace each of the three strains of Post-Nietzschean philosophy to its skeptical and pragmatic conclusion. All three strains of contemporary philosophy lead to this conclusion because they all share a family resemblance of similar problems, stemming from shared assumptions that Nietzsche also promoted. The family resemblance of shared ideas include: 1) a divorce of reason from being, or the denial that reason is ontological, 2) an embrace of empiricism and naturalism without justification, 3) the abandonment of metaphysics, 4) meaning is tied to language, making meaning relative to either the individual or to a group, 5) reason only applies to rule following in a formal language (affirmation of LNC-logical, but not LNC-ontological), 6) with the rejection of reason all "values" are attributed to sentiment or to the will to power, 7) "reason" is not absolute or authoritative and cannot serve as common ground for public discourse. Not every person within each of the three traditions holds to each of these ideas, but on the whole, each tradition affirms something akin to these ideas. But in order to examine the traditions, we must explore individual thinkers within each strain of the Post-Nietzschean philosophies.

Martin Heidegger is directly tied to Nietzsche, as we saw in the last chapter. Heidegger's reading of Nietzsche influences Jacques Derrida (1930-2004), and Michel Foucault (1926-1984) claims to be Nietzsche's disciple. We will explore the continental strain of Post-Nietzschean philosophy through these two figures as they are introduced into American academic life in the late 1960's and early 1970's. We will also explore a dissenting voice in the literary and continental stream, Allan Bloom (1930-1992), who is both influenced by and warns against the philosophy of Nietzsche. Since the continental strain comes last historically in America, these philosophers will be examined last in the chapter.

The Pragmatist philosophers, Charles Sanders Peirce (1839-1914), Josiah Royce (1855-1916), William James (1842-1910), and John Dewey (1859-1952), were all familiar with the philosophy of Nietzsche, and Royce was the first in America to introduce Nietzsche to the academy for serious study. Rossella Fabbrichesi says, "With Royce, and this is notable, Friedrich Nietzsche, in the early 1900's entered one of the most important American Departments of Philosophy: Harvard in Cambridge. Royce, the utmost forerunner of Christianity, seems to have opened the way to the dangerous Anti-Christ."[4] Nietzsche seemed welcome alongside American Pragmatism because there were many similarities between his thinking and that of the Pragmatic school. We will examine the Post-Nietzschean strain of Pragmatism through the key figures of Peirce, Royce, James, and Dewey, and then through the neo-Pragmatists: Richard Rorty (1931-2007), and Cornel West (1953-).

Nietzsche died in 1900. By this time in Germany and abroad Nietzsche is "in the air" and has influenced the popular imagination.[5] While not accepted as a "professional" philosopher, he is read by many who will become professional philosophers in the American academy. While it is difficult to tie Nietzsche as a direct influence of the analytic strain of Post-Nietzschean philosophy, there is ample evidence that key members of the

---

4   Fabbrichesi, Rossella. "The Body of the Community: Peirce, Royce, and Nietzsche." (*European Journal of Pragmatism and American Philosophy*, 2009) 9.

5   See Ratner-Rosenhagen, Jennifer. *American Nietzsche: A History of an Icon and His Ideas* (Chicago: University of Chicago Press, 2012).

Vienna Circle (1924-1936), the birthplace of analytic philosophy, had read Nietzsche. Moritz Schlick (1882-1936), founder of logical positivism and the Vienna Circle, read Nietzsche's *Thus Spoke Zarathustra*, as Kurt Rudolf Fischer observes:

> With Nietzsche, Schlick believes that modern man is in a unique situation. He explicitly appeals to what he finds to be the wisdom contained in "*Zarathustra* regarding the meaning of life ... that life has no meaning as long as it [is, sic] solely governed by *purposes* [external] to itself." When Schlick remarks that "for modern man ... the value and aim of life must be found here on earth or it cannot be found anywhere," he seems to echo an implication of the death of God proclaimed by Nietzsche.[6]

Fischer notes that though there are marked differences between the thinking of Nietzsche and that of Schlick. Schlick recognizes that we are living in a world without God in a Post-Nietzschean era. Fischer notes that Rudolf Carnap (1891-1970), also a member of the Vienna Circle, and proponent of logical positivism, had read Nietzsche. He says:

> In "The Elimination of Metaphysics through Logical Analysis of Language," Carnap declared that it was the concern of metaphysics to express a certain attitude towards life, and that Nietzsche realized this: "In the work ... in which [Nietzsche] expresses most strongly that which others express through metaphysics or

---

[6] Babich, B. (ed.). *Nietzsche, Theories of Knowledge, and Critical Theory: Nietzsche and the Sciences I*, Kurt Rudolf Fischer. "Nietzsche and the Vienna Circle," (Kluwer Academic Publishers, 1999), 120.

ethics, in *Thus Spoke Zarathustra*, he does not choose the misleading theoretical form, but openly the form of art or poetry." Carnap reads Nietzsche as sharing his own view that metaphysics and ethics are expressions of emotion.[7]

Other members of the Vienna Circle that have read Nietzsche include Ludwig Wittgenstein (1889-1951) and Bertrand Russell[8] (1872-1970). Erich Heller, in his *Importance of Nietzsche*, includes a chapter that compares the aphorisms of Nietzsche

---

7   Fischer, 122.
8   To be fair, Russell had contempt for Nietzsche. At the end of his chapter on Nietzsche in his *History of Philosophy*, he imagines a conversation between Buddha and Nietzsche before the throne of God. Each philosopher suggests his view as better for the world God will create. Russell depicts Nietzsche as inspired by Heraclitus and as embracing suffering and pain as an affirmation of life. Buddha, on the other hand is depicted as a forerunner of Jesus and endorses a life of universal love and compassion. Russell then says: "For my part, I agree with Buddha as I have imagined him. But I do not know how to prove that he is right by any argument such as can be used in a mathematical or a scientific question. I dislike Nietzsche because he likes the contemplation of pain, because he erects conceit into a duty, because the men whom he most admires are conquerors, whose glory is cleverness in causing men to die. But I think the ultimate argument against his philosophy, as against any unpleasant but internally self-consistent ethic, lies not in an appeal to facts, but in an appeal to the emotions. Nietzsche despises universal love; I feel it the motive power to all that I desire as regards the world. His followers have had their innings, but we many hope that it is coming rapidly to an end." Russell, Bertrand. *A History of Western Philosophy: And Its Connection with Political and Social Circumstances from the Earliest Times to the Present Day*. (New York: Simon and Schuster, 1945), 772-773. It is interesting to note that Russell does not primarily disagree with Nietzsche's empiricism or naturalism, but rather he objects to Nietzsche's ethics. It is also interesting to note that Russell is aware of Nietzsche's influence and he hopes that the post-Nietzschean philosophy comes to a quick end.

with those of Wittgenstein. Over and over again Heller shows the similarity of thought between the two men. Yet this quote shows that at the heart of both of their thinking is what results when reason and being are separated. Heller says: "With Wittgenstein, the decisive change of vision, which occurred between *Tractatus* and *Investigations*, seemed centered upon an event less dramatic than the death of God; namely, the vanishing of the belief in a categorical logic of language, and hence in a categorically harmonious relationship between words and world."[9] Following this "vanishing belief" Wittgenstein seems to settle into a "quietism" with respect to philosophy. This quietism is less drastic but is similar to, the silence Nietzsche falls into in the later years of his life. Silence is the logical outcome of giving up significant speech. Heller notes this reality and says, "Compared to the vast dominions that metaphysical thought had claimed in the past for its settlements of truth, there is now hardly more than a little province of 'significant' speech in a vast area of silence."[10]

While Wittgenstein seems to have taken Nietzsche seriously, Russell does not treat Nietzsche with the same seriousness. He says in his *History of Western Philosophy:*

> Nietzsche, though a professor, was a literary rather than an academic philosopher. He invented no new technical theories in ontology or epistemology; his importance is primarily in ethics, and secondarily as an acute historical critic. I shall confine myself almost entirely

---

9   Heller, Erich. *The Importance of Nietzsche: Ten Essays*. (Chicago: Chicago University Press, 1988), 150-151.
10 Ibid., 148.

to his ethics and his criticism of religion, since it was this aspect of his writing that made him influential.[11]

Russell does not see Nietzsche engaged in serious philosophy, having "invented no new technical theories on ontology or epistemology." It sounds like Russell objects to Nietzsche because he does not do philosophy in the mode of the logical positivists. Nietzsche, on the other hand, was far ahead of the logical positivists in his ontology and epistemology. It will take about 100 years of entanglement in the problems related to empiricism, the world, and language for the analytic philosophers to arrive at a position similar to that of Nietzsche's. One last quote will serve to link the thinking of the Vienna Circle to that of Nietzsche prior to looking at some of the key figures of the analytic tradition. Eckhart Kohler notes that:

> The Vienna Circle's opposition to metaphysics must be judged, in addition, against the background of a cultural uprising against absolutism, a rebellion whose spirit was perhaps most poignantly formulated by Nietzsche. Indeed, the parallels between Nietzsche and the Vienna Circle even pertain to detail: (a) the denial of an object for logic; (b) the linguistic conception of logic; (c) the assimilation of mathematics and logic; (d) the connected rejection of Kant's synthetic a priori, in mathematics as well as in physics; (e) the decisive rejection of metaphysics; and (f) a proto-existentialist conception of scientific method as a form of life.[12]

---

11 Russell, 760.
12 Uebel, Th.E. *Rediscovering the Forgotten Vienna Circle: Austrian Studies on Otto Neurath and the Vienna Circle. Vol 133 of Boston Studies in the Philosophy and History of Science.* Eckehart Kohler. "Metaphysics in the Vienna Circle." (Springer Science & Business Media, 2012), 134.

It should be clear that the Vienna Circle, the origin of analytic philosophy, shares a body of ideas that are either directly or indirectly shared with Nietzsche. We will now turn to a few key figures within the analytic tradition of philosophy, the dominant strain within the American university from the 1950's to the present, to see how these ideas unfold over time. The particular theme we will attempt to draw attention to is the denial of reason as ontological.

It must be kept in mind that analytic philosophy, by and large, has already assumed empiricism and naturalism. It is within this context that the two axioms of analytic philosophy arise: "What distinguishes analytical philosophy, in its diverse manifestations, from other schools is the belief, first, that a philosophical account of thought can be attained through a philosophical account of language, and, secondly, that a comprehensive account can only be so attained."[13] In addition, Michael Dummett says that "Widely as they differed from one another, the logical positivists, Wittgenstein in all phases of his career, Oxford 'ordinary language' philosophy and post-Carnapian philosophy in the United States as represented by Quine and Davidson all adhered to these twin axioms."[14] This focus on accounting for thought through language has been termed "the Linguistic Turn"[15] in philosophy and has been the primary focus for analytic philosophy.

---

13   Dummett, Michael. *Origins of analytical Philosophy*. (Cambridge: Harvard University Press, 1998), 4.
14   Ibid., 4.
15   See Dummett, *Origins of analytical Philosophy*, and Rorty, Richard. *The Linguistic Turn: Essays in Philosophical Method*. (Chicago, University of Chicago Press, 1992).

Gottlob Frege (1848-1925) makes possible the linguistic turn in 1884 in his *Grundlagen*,[16] where "At a crucial point in the book, Frege raises the Kantian question, 'How are numbers given to us, granted that we have no idea or intuition of them?'"[17] Frege uses his "context principle" to address the question he raises. The context principle is "the thesis that it is only in the context of a sentence that a word has meaning: the investigation, therefore, takes the form of asking how we can fix the senses of sentences containing terms for numbers. An epistemological enquiry (behind which lies an ontological one) is to be answered by a linguistic investigation."[18] The linguistic turn involves rejecting the idea that words having meaning in light of concepts that are grasped by the mind understanding being, as Aristotle conceives meaning, but rather, words have meaning in the context of sentences. Dummett makes this interesting observation with regarding Frege's "turn": "No justification for the linguistic turn is offered in *Grundlagen*: it is simply taken, as being the most natural way of going about the philosophical enquiry."[19] Dummett explains why the turn seemed a natural one to take by explaining "the presence in Frege's philosophy of deep currents driving towards the investigation of thoughts through the analysis of language. It is clear that he himself was not fully conscious of the thrust in this direction, which came from certain of his doctrines, but was impeded by others."[20]

---

16   *Die Grundlagen der Arithmetik: Eine logisch-mathematische Untersuchung über den Begriff der Zahl* (1884). Breslau.
17   Ibid., 5.
18   Ibid.
19   Ibid.
20   Ibid., 6-7.

Frege's lack of awareness of some of his assumptions has led analytic philosophy down a long road leading nowhere.

Frege and the linguistic turn assumes that thoughts can only be understood in terms of language and a linguistic community. Thoughts are not connected to being, but to language. Here we can already see the linguistic turn, in essence, is the separation of LNC-logical from LNC-ontological, as discussed in Chapter 3. In other words, the linguistic turn can only be taken if reason is not ontological. In addition, those who took the linguistic turn deny the reality of the mind, mental images, and a realist view of the world that previous British Empiricists held to. Thoughts are not about sensations, which assume a reality to be sensed, as the early Empiricists held. Thoughts are only about language, and language is within a linguistic community. That is meaning is relative to a community of language users who determine the rules of the language. "Reason," if used at all by the early analytic philosophers, refers to the logical rules of a linguistic community. The story of early analytic philosophy seems to be a cleansing of philosophy of all rational and ontological references. Yet the linguistic turn raises new problems for philosophy when we no longer have reference to being. For example: what is "meaning?" What is "truth?" And what is the relationship between "meaning" and "truth?" Is "truth" logically prior to "meaning," or vice versa?

Ludwig Wittgenstein, a student of Bertrand Russell, in his *Tractatus*, attempts to address some of these questions. Russell, who is also a proponent of Frege's logic, in his introduction to Wittgenstein's *Tractatus* says that the problems of traditional philosophy arise from a misunderstanding of "Symbolism and out of a misuse of language,"²¹ and that it is Wittgenstein's goal to help us to see these problems of language through logic and "Symbolism." He says, "Logic has two problems to deal with in regard to Symbolism: (1) the conditions for sense rather than nonsense in combination of symbols; (2) the conditions for uniqueness of meaning or reference in symbols or combinations of symbols. A logically perfect language has rules of syntax which prevent nonsense and has single symbols which always have a definite and unique meaning."²² Russell goes on to tell us that "the essential business of language is to assert or deny facts."²³ It is just this business of "fact" that will lead Wittgenstein and others to reconsider the role of philosophy. Wittgenstein will ultimately settle on the principle that the meaning of language is the use of language. Dummett explains:

> The use of an expression should be characterized, not in terms of a conception of truth-conditions that *guides* our use, but directly: we have, that is, to describe the actual use that we make of the expression — when we employ it, how we respond to another's employment of it; and this must be stated by reference to circumstances that we can recognize as obtaining — for instance, criteria that we can effectively apply. The use so described completely embodies the meaning of the expression, nothing further, concerning what is required for as statement involving that expression to be true,

---

21 Wittgenstein, Ludwig. *Tractatus Logico-Philosophicus*. (New York: Barnes and Noble, 2003), xvii.
22 Ibid., xviii.
23 Ibid., xvii.

or equivalently, the state of affairs asserted by such a statement to obtain, is required.[24]

"Meaning as use" implies that truth is what works within a given linguistic context. Rorty sees the later Wittgenstein's move to "meaning as use" as both a pragmatic move and a kind of quietism. Rorty thinks this is where analytic philosophy ultimately ends up. It will take another 100 years to come to the fullness of this realization. Donald Davidson (1917-2003), who also falls into the pragmatic strain of post-analytic philosophy, will solve the problem of "meaning" as truth conditions within the context of a sentence. Davidson's theory "will simply specify the truth-conditions of all sentences, and thereby determine the meanings of all expressions of language."[25] Wittgenstein and Davidson represent two extremes in attempting to answer the questions raised by the linguistic turn — meaning is use as determined by language users for a given purpose, or meaning is determined by a kind of formalism in logical structure. Rorty sees both paths leading to pragmatism.

There are reasons that analytic philosophy persists despite these implications. One reason analytic philosophy persists is that in its founding it is still tied up with logical positivism, a rigorous scientific empiricism with realist assumptions about reality. The implications of the divorce of LNC-logical from LNC-ontological had not been fully realized. It will take a series of problems inimical to the analytic enterprise to come to what Nietzsche begins with and what the Pragmatists and continentals have known since their inception. Russell is a realist in metaphysics, and furthermore, he is an empiricist and

---

24 Dummett, 164.
25 Ibid., 17.

a materialist. He is a logician and develops "verificationism" in which "the meaning of any empirically meaningful proposition is the method of experientially verifying it, and the decisive suggestion, already implicit in Russell's method of analysis, is that the doctrine could be used to purge science of metaphysical claims unconnected to any possibility of verificationism."[26] Russell thought that knowledge is by acquaintance through direct empirical contact with sense data. He also thought that he was going to "purge science of metaphysical claims" in the new post-Nietzschean sense of metaphysics as anything supranatural. What Russell and those in the Vienna Circle who championed his "verificationism" did not realize was that they too had bought into an ontologically unjustifiable metaphysics that assumed a "mind" that reads empirical reality through some "correspondence." The Vienna Circle was committed to a "foundationalist empiricism,"[27] which would come under further scrutiny by the logic-chopping analytics, and by the force of reason pressing the logical implications of assumptions.

Moritz Schlick and Rudolf Carnap held that the "subjective, elementary experience is the epistemological basis of scientific knowledge, and sought the reduction of the meaning of scientific propositions to their basis in experience."[28] Schlick and Carnap were still holding to an older version of Empiricism and "this element of foundationalist empiricism was the first element of the Circle's program to be abandoned" in the 1930's after critique by Otto Neurath, sociologist and fellow

---

26   Nelson, Alan, ed. *A Companion to Rationalism*. Paul Livingston. "Rationalist Elements of Twentieth-Century analytic Philosophy." (West Sussex: Wiley-Blackwell Publishing, Ltd. 3013), 381.
27   Ibid., 388.
28   Ibid., 388.

member of the Vienna Circle. After Neurath's critique of Carnap, "analytic philosophers would increasingly reject the Circle's foundationalist project and its empiricist hope of finding a basis for knowledge in immediate experience."[29] The question to be answered now becomes how to get "objective" scientific knowledge from particular subjective experience. In 1932, as a result of his conversations with Neurath, Carnap converts to physicalism,[30] the same year he writes "The Elimination of Metaphysics Through Logical Analysis of Language." The analytic philosophers now enter into a post-positivist phase, which is closer to the project of linguistic analysis started by Frege. Carnap says in his "Elimination of Metaphysics" that "modern logic" has allowed for the clarification of "the cognitive content of scientific statements and thereby the meanings of the terms that occur in the statements, by means of logical analysis" which leads to both positive and negative results.[31] The positive result "is worked out in the domain of empirical science; the various concepts of the various branches of science are clarified; their formal-logical and epistemological connections are made explicit."[32] With the "positive aspect" of Carnap's theory we can see the marriage of analytic philosophy to the sciences. He goes on to say that:

> In the domain of *metaphysics*, including all philosophy of value and normative theory, logical analysis yields the negative result that the *alleged statements in this domain are entirely meaningless*. Therewith a radical elim-

---

29 Ibid., 388.
30 Ibid., 391.
31 Carnap, Rudolph, trans. Arthur Pap. "The Elimination of Metaphysics Through Logical Analysis of Language." (Originally published in *Erkenntnis*, Vol. II, 1932), 60.
32 Ibid., 60.

ination of metaphysics is attained, which was not yet possible from the earlier antimetaphysical standpoints. It is true that related ideas may be found already in several earlier trains of thought, e.g. those of a nominalistic kind: but it is only now when the development of logic during recent decades provides us with a sufficiently sharp tool that the decisive step can be taken.

Several interesting features stand out in Carnap's quote. Analytic philosophy is not interested in metaphysics (the supranatural, that is). It is not interested in the meaningless statements in the realm of "values" or normative ethics, which are subjective in a post-Nietzschean world.[33] This move of the separation of analytic philosophy from metaphysics, values, and normative ethics was not possible in previous decades because the tools of logic had not yet been developed. What Carnap really should say is that prior to Nietzsche, the separation of LNC-logical from LNC-ontological was not in place. It is only after his rejection of reason as ontological that logic could be developed in the linguistic turn of analytic philosophy, without so-called metaphysical baggage. Only there is a price to pay for the development of logic in this direction.

Carnap is the end of the first phase of analytic philosophy; the second phase "begins with the decisive repudiation by Quine, Sellars, and Wittgenstein of this original project" of trying to find the "empirical foundations of knowledge."[34] Another key

---

33   The notion that talk about the "supranatural" as meaningless, or "values" as subjective would have probably developed even if Nietzsche had not appeared on the scene. The seeds of the ideas that Nietzsche develops to their logical conclusion are present in the thinking of Hume.
34   Nelson, 393.

figure in the second phase is Nelson Goodman (1906-1998). Goodman is a nominalist and a skeptic who presses Hume's "problem of induction" to a new level in his essay "The New Riddle of Induction." Goodman takes the laws of deduction to be unproblematic because:

> To justify a deductive conclusion ... requires no knowledge of the facts it pertains to. Moreover, when a deductive argument has been shown to conform to the rules of logical inference, we usually consider it justified without going on to ask what justifies the rules. Analogously, the basic task in justifying an inductive inference is to show that it conforms to the general rules of induction. Once we have recognized this, we have gone a long way towards clarifying our problem.[35]

There are several assumptions in Goodman's statement. First, he says that the justification of a deductive conclusion "requires no knowledge of facts...." Goodman understands the rules of deduction the same way that Aristotle does, but he departs from Aristotle in that the rules of deduction do not require knowledge of facts. Presumably, these "facts" would be some reality outside my thinking. Aristotle believes that the laws of deductive logic also apply to reality. Goodman does not. The second assumption in Goodman's statement is that we usually consider a deductive argument to be justified without going on to justify the rules. This is because Goodman thinks that the "principles of deductive inference are justified by their conformity with accepted

---

35 Goodman, Nelson. *Fact, Fiction and Forecast*. (Cambridge: Harvard University Press, 1983), 63.

deductive practice."³⁶ The deductive laws of logic are part of an accepted language community and they "work" because they conform to an "accepted deductive practice." Goodman seems to be saying that the laws of logic are merely conventional. This is definitely post-Nietzschean thinking. The third problem with Goodman's statement is that "the basic task in justifying an inductive inference is to show that it conforms to the general rules of induction." Yet Goodman finds no valid way of justifying inductive inferences. He says:

> The vast amount of effort expended on the problem of induction in modern times has thus altered our afflictions but hardly relieved them. The original difficulty about induction arose from the recognition that anything may follow upon anything. Then, in attempting to define confirmation in terms of the converse of the consequence relation, we found ourselves with the distressingly similar difficulty that our definition would make any statement confirm any other.³⁷

Hume's original problem of induction is in the area of the separation of reason from being. Goodman' "New Riddle" leaves us in a deeper skepticism than David Hume because he is more aware of the consequences of the separation of reason from being. One last observation about Goodman shows that it is clear that he falls within the category of post-Nietzschean philosophy. Hilary Putnam (1926-2016), in his forward to *Fact, Fiction and Forecast*, observes that Goodman does not think that skepticism requires the end of philosophy, as Rorty does.

---

36   Goodman, 63.
37   Ibid., 81.

Rather, Goodman proposes that we "construct" worlds: "If there isn't a ready-made world, then let's construct worlds ... If there aren't objective standards, then let's construct standards! Nothing is ready-made, but everything is to be made ... We are world-makers; we are constantly making 'new worlds out of old ones'. What we see, perceive, touch, is all in flux — a flux of our own creation."[38] This is very close to Nietzsche's notion of the philosopher as artist and world maker.

Wilfrid Sellars (1912-1989) attempts to synthesize American Pragmatism with analytic philosophy and logical positivism in a post-analytic mode. His landmark essay, "Empiricism and the Philosophy of Mind," helps to move analytic philosophy into its post-analytic phase. In this essay, Sellars critiques the assumptions of the previous verificationists, such as A.J. Ayer,[39] by showing that their commitment to "the Given" is a mistake. He argues that the:

> ... Interpretation of the status of the scientific picture of the world rests on two mistakes: (1) a misunderstanding ... of the ostensive element in the learning and use of language — the Myth of the Given; (2) a reification of the *methodological* distinction between the theoretical and non-theoretical discourse into a *substantive* distinction between theoretical and non-theoretical existence.[40]

---

38 Ibid., xv.
39 See Ayer, A.J. *Language, Truth, and Logic.* "The Elimination of Metaphysics".(New York: Dover, 1952), 33-45, where he defends a version of verificationism.
40 Sellars, Wilfrid. "Empiricism and the Philosophy of Mind." Accessed 3/13/2017. http://selfpace.uconn.edu/class/percep/SellarsEmpPhilMind.pdf, 304.

Retrieving Knowledge

The Myth of the Given assumes that there is some "reality" that is presented to the "mind" in the process of obtaining empirical knowledge. The Given is foundationalist in nature, and Sellars, in good post-Nietzschean form, sets out to expose the false assumptions that there is some "being" which our "mind" is in touch with. These conceptions of being and mind are the spooky stuff of metaphysics, understood as supranatural, that must be expelled from "scientific" investigations. Sellars also points out that the verificationists confuse methodological distinctions with substantive distinctions with regards to what exists. As part of our method we may talk about empirical "reality," but let us not confuse that kind of talk with the assumption that there is a reality that corresponds to our words. Put another way, reason does not apply to being. Sellars confirms our suspicion when he says:

> ... *Speaking as a philosopher*, I am quite prepared to say that the common-sense world of physical objects in Space and Time is unreal — that is, that there are no such things. Or, to put it less paradoxically, that in the dimension of describing and explaining the world, science is the measure of all things, of what is that it is, and of what is not that it is not.[41]

Instead of Protagoras's "man," individually, "is the measure," Sellars sees the community of scientists as the measure of all things. What the community of scientists says is what constitutes reality. Science is another language game. But it is the most important one. If this is not post-Nietzschean philosophy, then nothing is.

---

41   Sellars, 303.

The final philosopher in the post-Nietzschean post-analytic strain, and one who explicitly ends in pragmatism is W.V.O. Quine (1908-2000). Quine, taking up the project of Goodman and Sellars, critiques traditional Empiricism in his "Two Dogmas of Empiricism."[42] Quine begins the essay:

> Modern empiricism has been conditioned in large part by two dogmas. One is a belief in some fundamental cleavage between truths which are *analytic*, or grounded in meanings independently of matters of fact, and truths which are *synthetic*, or grounded in fact. The other dogma is *reductionism*: the belief that each meaningful statement is equivalent to some logical construct upon terms which refer to immediate experience. Both dogmas, I shall argue, are ill-founded. One effect of abandoning them is, as we shall see, a blurring of the supposed boundary between speculative metaphysics and natural science. Another effect is a shift toward pragmatism.[43]

Analytic truths are those truths that are supposed to be "true by definition," and synthetic statements are supposedly those that are made based upon empirical data. What Quine seems to be saying is that analytic truths, formerly considered *a priori* truths, are really no different in kind than synthetic *a posteriori* statements. The reason that this distinction cannot be made is that 1) nothing is "true by definition" if definition is a human construct and a convention of our language games, and 2) synthetic

---

42   In Kolak, Daniel and Garrett Thomson (eds.). *The Longman Standard History of Philosophy*. (New York: Pearson Longman, 2006), 1041-1053.
43   Ibid., 1041.

statements, supposedly grounded in "fact," fail to recognize that there is no "fact" of reality; there is no Given. The critique of the "second dogma" rests upon the rejection of the notion that experience delivers anything that provides meaningful content. This critique recognizes that it is not experience that provides meaning, but rather something else, such as language, that provides meaning. Quine comes very close to Nietzsche when he says the following:

> The totality of our so-called knowledge or beliefs, from the most casual matters of geography and history to the profoundest laws of atomic physics or even of pure mathematics and logic, is a man-made fabric which impinges on experience only along the edges. Or, to change the figure, total science is like a field of force whose boundary conditions are experience.[44]

Goodman, Sellars, and Quine have stated something similar to Nietzsche's flux doctrine. What Nietzsche proclaims in 1888, the analytic philosophers arrive at in the 1950's. If all is flux, then reason cannot apply to being, because there is no permanent being in which to ground a *logos*. There is no way to tie down an account. There is no rational justification. Knowledge is not possible. If we cannot know, then we are in a state of philosophical skepticism. The second phase of analytic philosophy opts to embrace science in a pragmatic move.

The final phase of analytic philosophy is carried out by Richard Rorty, who critiques the last remaining vestiges of being within the discipline in his blistering 1979 publication *Phi-*

---

44 Ibid., 1051.

losophy and the Mirror of Nature.[45] Trained as an analytic philosopher, Rorty identifies more with John Dewey and American Pragmatism. He is attributed by many as being the person who brought the Pragmatists back to life in academic philosophical circles. In addition, Rorty is comfortable speaking in the language of the continental strain of philosophy and is involved in historicism in this book akin to the method of the continentals. Rorty sees all three strains of American philosophy as post-Nietzschean and converging in pragmatism, because of course, Nietzsche is a pragmatist himself, according to Rorty. In the introduction to *Philosophy and the Mirror of Nature*, Rorty describes his project in the following way:

> This book is a survey of some recent developments in philosophy, especially analytic philosophy, from the point of view of the anti-Cartesian and anti-Kantian revolution ... The aim of the book is to undermine the reader's confidence in "the mind" as something about which one should have a "philosophical" view, in "knowledge" as something about which there ought to be a "theory" and which has "foundations," and in "philosophy" as it has been conceived since Kant. Thus the reader in search of a new theory on any of the subjects discussed will be disappointed ... The book, like the writings of the philosophers I most admire, is therapeutic rather than constructive.[46]

---

45 Rorty, Richard. *Philosophy and the Mirror of Nature*. (Princeton: Princeton University Press, 1979).
46 Ibid., 7.

It is interesting to note that Rorty does not seem to be taking aim merely at other analytic philosophers as did his predecessors; his goal is to "undermine the reader's confidence." He is involved in a kind of Nietzschean attempt to "will-out-beyond" a pragmatic therapeutic set of values from philosophy into society. This is what one would expect of the positive aspect of post-Nietzschean nihilism. If there is no being that may be known, and this leads to skepticism, we could fall into the "pessimism of weakness" and turn inward in gloomy despair, or we could embrace the "pessimism of strength"[47] and "will-out-beyond" ourselves in order to create the world of values that we envision. This is precisely what the Pragmatic, or political strain, of post-Nietzschean philosophy, proposes that we do, and it is to them that we turn next.

As it was difficult to draw a direct line from Nietzsche to the founders of the analytic school, so too it is difficult to trace the Pragmatic school directly to Nietzsche. Yet there are several convergent lines of thinking that justify calling Pragmatism post-Nietzschean philosophy. The first line of thinking that justifies bringing Nietzsche together with Pragmatism is suggested by the English translator of Nietzsche's work, Walter Kaufmann.[48] Kaufmann says:

---

47   Heidegger, "Word of Nietzsche," 68.
48   The story of Walter Kaufmann, German emigre, teaching at Princeton from 1947-1980 is very interesting. Kaufmann is instrumental in translating Nietzsche's works into English. He also writes a biography of Nietzsche in which he defends Nietzsche against popular claims that Nietzsche was implicated in Nazism. Kaufmann's translations allow for a Post-WWII academic study of Nietzsche. Jennifer Ratner-Rosenhagen tells details the influence of "Kaufmann's Nietzsche" in her *American Nietzsche*.

Nietzsche's experimentalism may seem suggestive of pragmatism; and as a matter of fact there are in his writings and particularly in those of his notes which deal with epistemological problems — a great number of passages which read like early statements of pragmatic views. This will surprise nobody who has considered the historical roots of pragmatism which must surely be sought, above all, in Darwin and Kant. The teachings of evolutionism supplied the decisive impetus which prompted the development of pragmatic doctrines at about the same time — toward the end of the nineteenth century — in England, France, Germany, and of course the United States.[49]

Kaufmann says that it was Kant's recognition that we cannot apprehend ultimate reality, fused with a Darwinian theory of evolution that gave rise to the conditions that inspire a "great number of different thinkers, including James, Dewey, Schiller, Simmel, Vaihinger, Mach — and Nietzsche."[50] Kaufmann goes on to say that Nietzsche's pragmatism was not very thought through and that John Dewey's Pragmatism is much more systematic. It should also be noted that Nietzsche believed Kant to be holding on to some form of "being" in his version of knowing the phenomenal world and his notion of the "mind," which Nietzsche rejected in the name of being consistent with the flux doctrine. In addition, Nietzsche thought Darwin's view of evolution to be too orderly and bound up in a view of progress still associated with Hegel, which he also rejected.

---

49 Kaufmann, Walter. *Nietzsche: Philosopher, Psychologist, Antichrist.* (New York: Meridian Books, 1950), 75.
50 Ibid, 75.

The second line of thinking that justifies bringing together Nietzsche with the Pragmatists is the cultural exchanges between German and American thinking at the time. Daniel Kolak and Garrett Thomson, in the introductory essay to the American Pragmatists in their *Longman Standard History of Philosophy* observe:

> That there was virtually no philosophy to speak of in the United States prior to Charles Peirce (1839-1914), his pupil William James (1842-1910), John Dewey (1859-1952), and Josiah Royce (1855-1916) is all the more remarkable, given its sudden and extraordinary proliferation throughout American colleges and universities ever since ... To get a philosophical education at the time, one had to go to Europe, and it is no surprise that all four of these great minds had strong associations, either directly or indirectly, with philosophy as it was flourishing at the time in Germany.[51]

James and Royce studied in Germany, while Peirce and Dewey studied German philosophy during their university years. As was mentioned earlier, by 1888, Nietzsche was "in the air," both in Germany and in the popular imagination of America.[52] There are several other lines of thinking that could link the ideas of Nietzsche with the Pragmatists: their shared source of inspiration from Harvard professor and Transcendentalist, Ralph Waldo Emerson (1803-1882);[53] Josiah Royce's intro-

---

51 Kolak and Thomson, 888.
52 See Ratner-Rosenhagen, *American Nietzsche*.
53 Ratner-Rosenhagen draws a tight connection between Nietzsche and Emerson in her *American Nietzsche*. Nietzsche read Emerson's work each year and had several annotated copies of the works of Emerson that he brought with him when he travelled.

duction of Nietzsche's works to Harvard, where all the Pragmatists listed above had connections either as professors or as students;[54] a common rejection of German idealism; and influence through American popular culture at the time. The link between Nietzsche and the Pragmatists will be made on the shared rejection of the isomorphism between reason and being and resulting skepticism and "positive" nihilism leading to a pragmatic willing of new "values." This line of thinking will also show the correlation between Pragmatism and the analytic thinkers as well.

Douglas McDermid, in his essay "Pragmatism", says that the Pragmatists held "pace Descartes, no statement or judgment about the world is absolutely certain or incorrigible."[55] This could be taken to mean that the Pragmatists deny that language names anything about reality, or that language does not give us knowledge of the world. McDermid says that the naturalist assumptions of the Pragmatists deliver the "idea that philosophy is not prior to science, but continuous with it. There is no special, distinctive method on which philosophers as a caste can pride themselves; no transcendentalist faculty of pure Reason or Intuition; no Reality (immutable or otherwise) inaccessible to science for philosophy to ken or limn."[56] Again, the Pragmatists, like the analytics, follow Nietzsche in the denial of the power of reason and in the isomorphism between reason and being. McDermid links the ideas of the Pragmatists with the

---

54 Royce wrote several essays about Nietzsche, one in 1917 titled "Nietzsche" was published in the *Atlantic Monthly*.
55 McDermid, Douglas. "Pragmatism." Accessed 3/16/2017. http://www.iep.utm.edu/pragmati/
56 Ibid.

post-analytic philosophers when he says that the Pragmatists do not think that the world imposes:

> ... some unique description on us; rather, it is we who choose how the world is to be described. Though this idea is powerfully present in James, it is also prominent in later pragmatism. It informs Carnap's distinction between internal and external questions, Rorty's claim that Nature has no preferred descriptions of itself, Goodman's talk of world-making and of right but incompatible world-versions, and Putnam's insistence that objects exist relative to conceptual schemes or frameworks.[57]

The world is not a "thing" to be read, but rather we (a linguistic community) choose how the world is through our descriptions. Once again, language is what determines what is "real," and language is a construct of the community, not a tool for conveying concepts of reason. Another similarity between Nietzsche and the Pragmatists[58] is an opposition to traditional forms of

---

57 Ibid.
58 Richard Rorty notes that: "Berthelot was probably the first to call Nietzsche 'a German pragmatist,' and the first to emphasize the resemblance between Nietzsche's perspectivism and the pragmatist theory of truth. This resemblance—frequently noted since, notably in a seminal chapter of Arthur Danto's book on Nietzsche—is most evident in the *The Gay Science*. There Nietzsche says, "We do not even have any organ at all for *knowing*, for 'truth'; we 'know' ... just as much as may be *useful* in the interest of the human herd." This Darwinian view lies behind James' claim that "thinking is for the sake of behavior" and his identification of truth as "the good in the way of belief."' Dickstein, Morris (ed.). *The Revival of Pragmatism: New Essays on Social Thought, Law, and Culture*. Richard Rorty. "What Difference does Pragmatism Make? The View from Philosophy" (Durham: Duke University Press, 1998). Accessed 3/31/2017. http://www.nytimes.com/books/first/d/dickstein-pragmatism.html.

empiricism, which claims that beliefs are derived immediately from perception. Rather, the Pragmatists:

> ...Aver that to perceive is really to interpret and hence to classify. But if observation is theory-laden — if, that is, epistemic access to reality is necessarily mediated by conceptions and descriptions — then we cannot verify theories or worldviews by comparing them with some raw, unsullied sensuous "Given." Hence old-time empiricists were fundamentally mistaken: experience cannot serve as basic, belief-independent sources of justification.[59]

The Pragmatists are empiricists, as was Nietzsche, and as are the later analytic philosophers, but they recognize the role of interpretation, what Dewey sees as the social construction of knowledge. There is much literature to support the Pragmatist rejection of reason as ontological, so for the sake of brevity, we will focus on a few statements by James and Dewey.

In his essay "Remarks on Spencer's Definition of Mind as Correspondence,"[60] William James takes to task old guard empiricists in a way similar to how the later analytic philosophers take the logical positivists to task. James seeks to reduce realist materialists, such as Herbert Spencer (1820-1903), Aldous Huxley (1894-1963), and W.K. Clifford (1845-1879) to pragmatists, which James sees as a more consistent naturalism. It should be noted that Spencer is a thoroughgoing evolutionist, even coining the term "survival of the fittest." James first ad-

---

59 Ibid.
60 James, William. "Remarks on Spencer's Definition of Mind as Correspondence." *The Journal of Speculative Philosophy*, Vol. 12, No. 1 (January 1878), 1-18.

dresses Spencer's conception of "Mind." James notes that "In a series of chapters of great apparent thoroughness and minuteness [Spencer] shows how all the different grades of mental perfection are expressed by the degree of extension of this adjustment, or, as he here calls it, 'correspondence,' in space, time, specialty, generality, and integration."[61] James then goes on to argue, contra Spencer, that there is no "Mind" and there is no "correspondence" between "Mind" and "reality." He says:

> In a word, "Mind," as we actually find it, contains all sorts of laws — those of logic, of fancy, of wit, of taste, decorum, beauty, morals, and so forth, as well as of perception of fact. Common sense estimates mental excellence by a combination of all these standards, and yet how few of them correspond to anything that actually *is* — they are laws of the Ideal, dictated by subjective *interests* pure and simple. Thus the greater part of Mind, quantitatively considered, refuses to have anything to do with Mr. Spencer's definition.

James points out that given Spencer's theory of evolution, if one were to trace the origin of life "back of all, the universal mother, [is] fire mist." And thus, to look for the reality of Mind through an evolutionary process "would reduce all thinking to nonentity."[62] The reality of Mind is incompatible with naturalistic evolution. Thinking is not a product of some supranatural "Mind." Rather, thinking is relative to "subjective *interests* pure and simple." Thinking is not rational.

---

61   Ibid., 2.
62   Ibid., 4.

James then interrogates Spencer's notion of "correspondence." He quotes Spencer as saying, "'Right or intelligent mental action consists in the establishment, corresponding to outward relations, of such inward relations and reactions as will favor the survival of the thinker, or, at least, his physical well-being.'"[63] Spencer sees a correspondence between right mental "inward" relations with "outward relations" for the purpose of the survival of the thinker. James thinks this is utter nonsense. First, he points out that Spencer's mind fitting reality for the purpose of survival is "frankly teleological." He notices that instead of describing "mental action," Spencer slips into a normative prescription of "right mental action." If all we have to work with is the unguided, natural, evolutionary process, there should be no teleology and no normativity. Secondly, James critiques the notion that the "inner" mental relations correspond with external relations. His critique is similar to the analytic critique of "the Given" or Rorty's no "mirror of nature." In fact, James uses the phrase "nature's mirror." Yet James is years ahead of the analytics in his critique of the correspondence theory of knowledge, writing his response to Spencer in 1878. James concludes his critique of Spencer's correspondence by saying:

> This, then, must be our conclusion: That no law of the *cogitandum*, no normative receipt for excellence in thinking, can be authoritatively promulgated. The only formal canon that we can apply to mind which is unassailable is the barren truism that it must think rightly. We can express this in terms of correspondence by

---

63   Ibid., 5.

saying that thought must correspond with truth; but whether that truth be actual or ideal is left undecided.[64]

James seems to say that there is no law of thinking that is authoritative. That is, reason is not a source of authority for human thinking. In addition, the relevant correspondence is that of our thinking to truth. But what Spencer means by truth — the correspondence between mind and matter — is not what James means by truth. James defines truth in light of his "pragmatic method":

> The pragmatic method is primarily a method of settling metaphysical disputes that otherwise might be interminable. Is the world one or many? — fated or free? — material or spiritual? — here are notions either of which may or may not hold good of the world; and disputes over such notions are unending. The pragmatic method in such cases is to try to interpret each notion by tracing its respective practical consequences. What difference would it practically make to any one if this notion rather than that notion were true? If no practical difference whatever can be traced, then the alternatives mean practically the same thing, and all dispute is idle.[65]

James notes that his method is for addressing "interminable" and unending philosophical debates. His comment represents the essence of skepticism. One can never really settle these debates because one can never really have knowledge about reality.

---

64 Ibid., 16.
65 James, William. *Essays in Pragmatism*. (New York: Hafner Press, 1948), 142.

According to James, "truth" is what works for a given purpose. We measure truth by its outcome. Truth has "cash value" for James.⁶⁶ One final quote from James will show just how close he is to Nietzsche in his pragmatism. He says:

> Pragmatism represents a perfectly familiar attitude in philosophy, the empiricist attitude, but it represents it, as it seems to me, both in a more radical and in a less objectionable form than it has ever yet assumed. A pragmatist turns his back resolutely and once for all upon a lot of inveterate habits dear to professional philosophers. He turns away from abstraction and insufficiency, from verbal solutions, from bad *a priori* reasons, from fixed principles, closed systems, and pretended absolutes and origins. He turns towards concreteness and adequacy, towards facts, towards action and towards power. That means the empiricist temper regnant and the rationalist temper sincerely given up. It means the open air and possibilities of nature, and against dogma, artificiality, and the pretense of finality in truth.⁶⁷

James promotes empiricism over rationalism and any *a priori* reasons. Yet his empiricism is "more radical" than previous forms as we saw with his critique of Spencer's older empiricism. It would seem that James' empiricism is closer to something like Nietzsche's perspectivalism. James' empiricism "turns towards concreteness," which is compatible with nominalism and "always appealing to particulars."⁶⁸

---

66   Ibid., 145.
67   Ibid., 144-154.
68   Ibid., 145.

In "Remarks on Spencer's Definition of Mind as Correspondence," James reduces the older empiricist and materialist assumptions of Spencer, Huxley, and Clifford to pragmatism by showing that they still hold an unjustifiable realist view of material reality. He argues that there is no "Mind" that is separate from the world. To know the world is to be active within the world. He denies there are *a priori* laws of thought, saying that rather the laws of thought are merely useful categories of thought. He denies that there is an objective material world that mirrors reality for us. He moves materialism closer to Nietzsche's perspectivalism. James' is a more consistent empiricism and materialism than previous thinkers. It is strange, though, that James and others feel compelled — by force of reason — to become more consistent. Why should rational consistency be a standard that compels belief and action? Wouldn't the fact that all the philosophers examined so far in this chapter are moved to be consistent prove that there is a force of reason that compels? This force of reason is more basic than material forces or the will to power. Reason is inescapable. James is not just saying that his position is merely logically possible, restricting reason to a tool for thinking. Rather, he is saying that Spencer's view of reality is logically impossible — given his commitments, his talk of "Mind" and "correspondence" do not make sense — he is saying "that cannot be!" James is telling Spencer that "your theory cannot *be* given your starting point." While denying the isomorphism between reason and being, they apply reason to being. The force of reason is compelling and inescapable. Reason is prior to experience and to the meaning and interpretation of experience.

John Dewey, influenced by Peirce and James, argues in a similar manner against the correspondence theory of truth,[69] and for empiricism.[70] In addition, countless comparisons have been made between Nietzsche and Dewey.[71] Given these similarities, it is safe to say that Dewey also denies the isomorphism between reason and being. Rather than list a litany of quotes to substantiate this claim, we will instead explore Dewey's social program that puts into practice the new "values" of a post-Nietzschean world. A post-Nietzschean world is a world of skepticism which could be responded to with what Heidegger calls an attitude of "weak pessimism" and despair, or with "strong pessimism" that sees the condition of life after the death of God as one in which we can make the world over in our own image by "taking dominion," where we will to power new values and then we "will-out-beyond" to create a new social order.

As with the analytics, Dewey recognizes that the linguistic community that we look to for our authoritative "language game" with which we "create reality" is the language of science. As Sellars said: "science is the measure of all things, of what is that it is, and of what is not that it is not."[72] So, whether empiricism is "true" or not is not dependent upon "reality," but it is the shared assumption of the scientific community, which

---

69 Dewey, John. "The Correspondence Theory of Truth is Inadequate." *In The Philosophy of John Dewey*, edited by Joseph Ratner. (New York: Henry Holt and Company, 1928).

70 Dewey, John. "The Experience of Knowing." *In The Philosophy of John Dewey*, edited by Joseph Ratner. (New York: Henry Holt and Company, 1928).

71 For example, see: Castle, Alfred. "Dewey and Nietzsche: Their Instrumentalism Compared." *Wisconsin Academy of Sciences, Arts and Letters*. Vol. 65, 1977, 67-85.

72 Sellars, 303.

is the authoritative community in the post-Nietzschean world insofar as the scientific community proscribes how we know (i.e. the "scientific method") and what we know (i.e. "the world of experience"). What the scientists tell us as authorities of the linguistic community need not be literally true in the Platonic sense; it need only to work for a given purpose.

The Pragmatist purpose is to build upon the sciences and to create a new social order, a post-Nietzschean social order. The goal of the human life in this new social order is the "enhancement of experience,"[73] which sounds very similar to Nietzsche's "preservation and enhancement of life."

The first thing that is needed in the new social order is a form of government that will best promote these goals. Dewey argues that a democratic[74] society is best. Dewey has us reflect:

> Can we find any reason that does not ultimately come down to the belief that democratic social arrangements promote a better quality of human experience, one which is more widely accessible and enjoyed, than do non-democratic and anti-democratic forms of social life? Does not the principle of regard for individual freedom and for decency and kindliness of human relations come back in the end to the conviction that these things are tributary to a higher quality of experience on the part of a greater number than are methods of repression and coercion or force? Is it not the reason

---

73 Dewey, John. *Education and Experience*. Accessed 3/16/2017. https://archive.org/details/ExperienceAndEducation, 12.

74 What is meant by "democratic society" in the pragmatist literature is taken up in Rorty, Richard. *Achieving Our Country: Leftist Thought in Twentieth-Century America* (Cambridge: Harvard University Press, 1998).

for our preference that we believe that mutual consultation and convictions reached through persuasion, make possible a better quality of experience than can otherwise be provided on any wide scale?[75]

Yet for a democratic society to function so as to maximize a "continuum of experience," education for the propagation of society through the inculcation of certain values and attitudes is necessary. Values are attained by habit, where "habit is the mainspring of human action, and habits are formed for the most part under the influence of the customs of a group."[76] Dewey thinks the physical sciences have provided much by way of knowledge, and that the physical sciences have been successful in "cross fertilization," but that the social sciences have not yet benefited from being interdisciplinary.[77] He says that the "ultimate harm is that the understanding by man of his own affairs and his ability to direct them are sapped at their root when knowledge of nature is disconnected from its human function."[78] Knowledge of nature is of some benefit, but man is *of* nature and *in* nature, and so the social sciences are necessary in order for man to understand himself in his world. Knowledge for Dewey is essentially experiential, so the social sciences study the "social experiment" of our communal life together and report back to us in scientific fashion their scientific discoveries about "us." The knowledge produced in this way is then disseminated to the public because "knowledge is communication as well as un-

---

75 Ibid., 12.
76 Dewey, John. *The Public and its Problems*. (Athens: Ohio University Press, 1928), 159.
77 Ibid., 171.
78 Ibid., 176.

derstanding."⁷⁹ Lastly, "communication of the results of social inquiry is the same thing as the formation of public opinion."⁸⁰ Public opinion is best communicated by experts. Furthermore, "The smoothest road to control of political conduct is by control of opinion."⁸¹ One could say that the goal of life is the "enhancement of experiences."

The political order that best supports this goal is democracy. Democracy is not just political; for Dewey, it is also ethical. It is a system of values that is self-perpetuating through the institutions of culture. Education seems to be the primary means of inculcating and perpetuating the values of a democratic society in which the enhancement of experience is the *summum bonum*. Dewey says that:

> An experimental social method would probably manifest itself first of all in surrender of [the notion of the unchanged perpetuation of existing institutions]. Every care would be taken to surround the young with the physical and social conditions which best conduce, as far as freed knowledge extends, to release of personal potentialities. The habits thus formed would have entrusted to them the meeting of future social requirements and the development of the future state of society. Then and only then would all social agencies that are available operate as resources in behalf of a bettered community life.⁸²

---

79   Ibid., 176.
80   Ibid., 177.
81   Ibid., 182.
82   Ibid., 201.

There are a number of relevant ideas in this quote that help us to understand a post-Nietzschean social order. First, along with the pre-Nietzschean ways of "knowing," the pre-Nietzschean institutions of culture must be jettisoned. These old institutions were also self-perpetuating and were means of propagating the old ethics that relied upon the "supranatural." With the new "experimental social method" new institutions are required. Second, the youth must be nurtured in such a way that their potentials are developed so that they may contribute to the enhancement of experience for all in what Dewey calls the "Great Community." Third, habits formed by the youth will enable them to meet their social requirements and to better the future of society. The "experiment" of this new social arrangement is not based upon anything fixed but, like a scientific experiment, is always open to revision. The very fact that knowledge is experiential, not fixed, and is based on the linguistic community, shows that the new institutions of the post-Nietzschean society are inherently skeptical. Dewey's post-Nietzschean society is pragmatic institutionalized skepticism. It is a system that perpetuates skepticism and pragmatism through all the institutions of culture, but especially through the system of public education.

Dewey thinks that "The Great Community" that these institutions will help to enhance is the local community.[83] In addition, the local community is "the Public."[84] Local may be an "occupational organization" that one belongs to. Local seems to be voluntary organizations that take the place of the family, neighborhoods, and churches of the pre-Nietzschean society.[85] Yet, in pockets of society, there is suffering, oppression,

---
83 Ibid., 211.
84 Ibid., 211.
85 Ibid., 215.

and injustice (leftover from the old society) that needs to be remedied. The way these things are remedied are through social action on the local level. The Public is the local and the Public is the active. Public life, then, becomes the life of local activism. Activism is through dialogue, presumably about what could be done to enhance the conditions of life for the greatest number of people in the community. Thus, public discourse, in Dewey's new society, is local, vocal, and is formed by and creates public opinion. Public discourse is based on shared experience, "signs and symbols," and language, i.e. communication.[86] He says that public discourse is not written but is primarily spoken words: "Their final actuality is accomplished in face-to-face relationships by means of direct give and take. Logic in its fulfillment recurs to the primitive sense of the word: dialogue. Ideas which are not communicated, shared, and reborn in expression are but soliloquy and soliloquy is but broken and imperfect thought."[87] Complete thoughts can only be formulated in the context of the community because knowledge is socially constructed, and an individual's understanding must be "fulfilled only in the relations of personal intercourse in the local community."[88] But what happens when a local community, and broader democratic society, has bought into a system of thought that keeps it within the life-denying Cave, out of touch with any possible reality outside the Immanent Frame? What if man needs transcendence for the true enhancement of life? Would Dewey's form of public discourse allow for a rational discussion about the possibility of life outside the Cave? It seems that the post-Nietzschean philosophers have taken away any means for having

---

86 Ibid., 218.
87 Ibid., 218.
88 Ibid.

a rational discussion about the possible existence of a supranatural reality. A thoughtful person will find that rather than being a "pessimism of strength" based upon positive nihilism, The Pragmatists lead to a gloomy "pessimism of weakness" and ultimately to intellectual despair.

Dewey has been a major influence on American society. His ideas have been perpetuated through the American public education system since the 1950's. Dewey's post-Nietzschean new social order is not just theoretical but is currently being put into practice in American higher education today,[89] and may be a source of the contemporary crisis of public discourse. Yet there was a time when Dewey, and Pragmatism as a whole, fell out of favor in the philosophy departments of the American University.

The story of the academic study of philosophy in America is by and large a story of German philosophy in America. Dewey falls out of favor just at a crucial moment in history

---

[89] Dewey's ideas for the Great Community are perpetuated through the American public university system today through experiential learning such as "service learning" and "civic engagement." These "values" were promoted through the 2008 white paper "A Crucible Moment" issued by the Obama administration via the Association of American Colleges and Universities in which Dewey's theory put into practice, and the values of the post-Nietzschean society are inculcated through students getting involved in the problems of the local community through social activism and community organization. See Association of American Colleges and Universities. "A Crucible Moment." Accessed 3/17/2017. https://www.aacu.org/sites/default/files/files/crucible/Crucible_508F.pdf . A critique of the New Civics of the "Crucible Moment" call to action was recently given in an alternative white paper put out by the National Association of Scholars: National Association of Scholars. "Making Citizens: How American Universities Teach Civics." Accessed 3/17/2017. https://www.nas.org/images/documents/NAS_makingCitizens_fullReport.pdf

when German and American worlds intersect, guaranteeing the entrenchment of post-Nietzschean philosophy not only in the American university, but in American political and social life up to the present. The modern university in America has always seen its task as the service to society, a pragmatic goal in the mode of Dewey's vision of education. Lenore O'Boyle, in the article "Learning for its Own Sake: The German University as Nineteenth-Century Model" says that "'Knowledge for its own sake,' ... was never a concept without ambiguity. In Germany it carried connotations of idealist philosophy, of religion, and of an ideal of aristocratic cultural fulfillment or *Bildung*. In America the words came to mean, as a rule, knowledge employed in the service of society."[90] There are three aspects to the German story that interrupt the influence of the Pragmatists between Dewey in the 1940's and the neo-Pragmatists, whose most vocal proponent is Rorty, in the 1980's, but allow for the further "Nietzscheanization"[91] of the American university.[92] These three include: 1) The rise of the German model of the university in the US beginning in the 1880's and then greatly expanding after WWII, 2) German emigres entering the US German model flagship universities, particularly in the philosophy departments, and 3) German emigres bringing Nietzsche scholarship to the US in a continental strain via Heidegger. A

---

90 O'Boyle, Lenore. "Learning for Its Own Sake: The German University as Nineteenth-Century Model." *Comparative Studies in Society and History*, Vol. 25, No. 1 (Jan. 1983), 23.
91 Allan Bloom's term from Bloom, Allan. *The Closing of the American Mind*. (New York: Touchstone, 1987).
92 Bloom tells part of this story, but it should be explored further. The influx of German emigres to the United States, many of whom have imbibed in the spirit of Nietzsche, influences all disciplines of the university.

little time will be spent exploring each of these aspects of the means by which post-Nietzschean philosophy helps to bring about institutionalized skepticism, through specific actors and actions, and subsequent life in the Immanent Frame.

Wilhelm von Humboldt (1767-1835), along with Johann G. Fichte (1762-1814), Friedrich Schleiermacher (1768-1834), and Friedrich W.J. Schelling (1775-1854), are instrumental in shaping the German university, the first of which is the University of Berlin in 1810.[93] Humboldt's goal was to teach students to think, and not just to master a craft. He thought that research is of central importance and that students learn to think by research and teaching. Lastly, he believed that knowledge was an end in itself and that in order to pursue knowledge, the university should be independent of, and not a direct servant of, the state.[94] Post-Civil War America saw much industrialization, growth, and expansion, which required an increase in the number of higher educational institutions, and a change in the kind of education previously provided by liberal arts colleges and seminaries to professional education. Between post-Civil War and the 1890's, American students were going to Europe, particularly to Germany, for graduate education. As the demand for higher education in the US grew:

> Both private and state universities were founded and supported by men who wanted to develop a wider curriculum and to expand professional and graduate education. There was a move away from the waste of

---

[93] Menand, Louis, Paul Reitter, and Chad Wellmon. *The Rise of the Research University: A Sourcebook*. (Chicago: The University of Chicago Press, 2017), 2.
[94] Ibid., 3.

resources that sectarian colleges had too often meant. A noticeable increase in the number of Americans attending German universities was clearly connected with this increased emphasis on higher levels of training. Historians, economists, scientists, doctors, all looked to Germany for a level of specialized instruction unavailable in the United States, and when they returned, these men naturally tried to establish in America some of the features of the German university they had admired.[95]

John's Hopkins University was the first "graduate school set up in America" in 1876.[96] Harvard University, America's first university, established by the Puritans in 1636, adopts the German model between 1869-1909. This change signifies that something had already shifted in the American worldview. The transition to the German model only helps to usher in and institutionalize the post-Nietzschean philosophy, which finds a foothold particularly at Harvard. Other early research universities, based upon the German model, include Cornell, Columbia, Princeton, the University of Chicago, UCLA, and the University of Michigan, all of which have some of most influential and highest-ranking philosophy departments in the US. The research university in the US does not totally preserve Humboldt's original vision. Rather, research in the US is to produce knowledge that would be of use for the purposes of the advancement of science (pragmatic) and that would be of use to the state, for the moral formation of citizens (pragmatic).[97] The university became the

---
95   O'Boyle, 21.
96   Ibid., 24.
97   Ibid., 24.

means of making "professionals" and credentialing people who would teach within the university system, serving as those who would "police" the professions. It should not be surprising to note that those who were credentialed and who were certifying others were by and large persons who had bought into an empiricist, materialist, and skeptical worldview, thus bringing about institutionalized skepticism.

When the Weimar Republic ended in 1933, German intellectuals began to emigrate to the United States, where they found a home in professorships within the German model academy.[98] Of some of the philosophers who were members of the Vienna Circle, Gustav Bergman went to teach at the University of Iowa, Carnap went to the University of Chicago, and US native, but friend of the Vienna Circle, Quine, was at home at Harvard. From Harvard, Quine would influence a number of notable analytical and post-analytical philosophers such as Goodman, Davidson, Putnam, and Rorty. Goodman would go on to teach and influence students at the University of Pennsylvania. Davidson taught at Berkeley and Stanford. Putnam taught at Harvard. Rorty taught at Princeton for 21 years, where he influenced Cornel West. It is interesting to note that Dewey is associated with some of the same institutions: The University of Michigan, the University of Chicago, and Columbia. Dewey helps to found the New School for Social Scientific Research in 1919, where many professors from Columbia join the faculty. Later in 1933, The New School adds the Graduate Faculty of

---

98 Many others emigrated to England. Notable analytic philosophers, members of the Vienna Circle, who became professors in England included Wittgenstein and Ayer. They joined Russell and Moore, making the UK another center for analytic philosophy.

Political and Social Science, which was founded for German scholars in exile.

Closely affiliated with the New School, and Columbia University is the Frankfurt School, an offshoot of the Institute for Social Research in Germany.[99] The exodus and the emigres from Germany brought Nietzsche with them. In addition, some of them brought a "dark, post-holocaust" reading of Nietzsche.[100] Hannah Arendt (1906-1975), and members of the Frankfurt school: Herbert Marcuse (1889-1979), who studied with Husserl and co-authored with Heidegger, Max Horkheimer (1895-1973), and Theodor Adorno (1903-1969) bring the "dark" Nietzsche to America.[101] It was at the time of the German emigres to America that a sharp distinction between analytic and continental philosophy began to be felt. Ratner-Rosenhagen discusses Walter Kaufmann, and his English translations of Nietzsche's works, as well as his biography of Nietzsche as being instrumental to academic philosophy paying more attention to Nietzsche as a philosopher, especially after the 1960's. She also points out the those in the continental tradition prefer the Nietzsche that is presented by Pierre Klossowski, whom Derrida, Foucault, and Lyotard read.

---

99 The Frankfurt School is influenced by post-Nietzschean social scientists Max Weber and Sigmund Freud, as well as being influenced by Karl Marx.
100 Ratner-Rosenhagen, *American Nietzsche*, 232.
101 Ratner-Rosenhagen makes a distinction between the "dark" Nietzsche of the emigres, the American Nietzsche of the Emerson and the Pragmatists, which is a more upbeat and free spirit interpretation of Nietzsche, and the "French" Nietzsche that Derrida and Foucault introduce to the Americans, which is a "death of everything" interpretation of Nietzsche.

Between the 1940's to the 1980's, John Dewey's pragmatism was on the wane while analytic philosophy was thriving in the major German model research universities, and continental philosophy was being introduced through German emigre thinkers through the Frankfurt School at Columbia and the New School for Social Scientific Research. However, in the 1980's neo-pragmatism begins to be recognized by academic philosophers with the critique of positivism, and verificationism, and the post-analytic philosophers leaning towards pragmatism. Richard Rorty is trained in the analytic school but uses post-Nietzschean philosophy in a deconstructive way to further purge the analytic school of any supranatural vestiges. Rorty is well versed in the continental philosophers and is adept in bringing analytic and continental philosophy into conversation through a kind of Nietzschean pragmatism. Following in the footsteps of Rorty in promoting a neo-pragmatism is Cornel West, West incorporates more continental thinking into his pragmatism than does Rorty. In fact, West presses Rorty in the same way that Rorty has pressed the analytic philosophers to be more consistent. West says:

> To tell a tale about the historical character of philosophy while eschewing the political content, role, and function of philosophy in various historical periods is to promote an ahistorical approach in the name of history. To undermine the privileged notions of objectivity, universality, and transcendentiality without acknowledging and accepting the oppressive deeds done under the aegis of these notions is to write a thin, i.e., intellectual and homogeneous, history — a history which fervently attacks epistemological privilege

but remains relatively silent about political, economic, racial, and sexual privilege. Such a history which surreptitiously suppresses certain histories even raises the sinister possibility that the antiepistemological radicalism of neo-pragmatism — much like the antimetaphysical radicalism of postructuralism — may be an emerging form of ideology in late capitalist societies which endorses the existing order while undergirding sophisticated antiepistemological and antimetaphysical tastes of postmodern avant-gardists.[102]

West's critique comes close to the critique of this paper insofar as he exposes the post-Nietzschean philosophers as persons having an agenda. West also has an agenda, but that is not the point. The point is that the post-Nietzschean philosophers have been deconstructing and revaluating values for about 120 years, posing as neutral critics while all the while they are partisan actors willing to power their death of God quasi-religion. It is about time the assumptions of the post-Nietzscheans were exposed so that we can get back to the business of philosophy. Before suggesting a way forward, we must take a short foray into the continental strain of post-Nietzschean philosophy and explore how they contribute to the institutionalization of skepticism. As the universities have been "pragmatized" and professionalization and credentialing take precedence, and as the professional academic philosophy departments become analytical for the service of the physical sciences, the rest of the American university — the liberal arts and the social sciences — are influ-

---

102 Rajchman, John. and Cornel West (eds.). *Post-Analytic Philosophy*. (New York: Columbia University Press, 1985), 260.

enced by the post-Nietzschean continental philosophers. It is to them that we turn next.

By way of reminder, the main argument we have been pursuing is that post-Nietzschean philosophy denies the isomorphism between reason and being. This rejection is bound with a commitment to empiricism and materialism that then leads to skepticism and ultimately to pragmatism. The continental strain has the same roots and the same outcome. The Post-Nietzschean strain of continental philosophy in America is the story of "French Nietzsche." Richard Wolin, in his *Seduction of Unreason: The Intellectual Romance with Fascism from Nietzsche to Postmodernism*[103] shows how French Nietzsche has roots in the French counter-enlightenment. French Nietzsche had been a tool of the counter-enlightenment Right but was later co-opted by the Left and synthesized with a softened version of Marxism.[104] Wolin says that:

> One of the crucial elements underlying this problematic right-left synthesis is a strange chapter in the history of ideas whereby later-day anti-philosophes such as Nietzsche and Heidegger became the intellectual idols of post-World War II France — above all, for poststructuralists like Jacques Derrida, Michel Foucault, and Gilles Deleuze. Paradoxically, a thoroughgoing cynicism about reason and democracy, once the

---

103 Wolin, Richard. *The Seduction of Unreason: The Intellectual Romance With Fascism From Nietzsche to Postmodernism.* (Princeton: Princeton University Press; 2004).

104 See also Bloom, *Closing of the American Mind*, 225-226. An interesting side note is that almost to a person Post-Nietzschean philosophers are socialist or communist. This story will have to be told elsewhere.

hallmark of reactionary thought, became the stock-in-trade of the postmodern left.[105]

French Nietzsche comes to America primarily through Derrida and Foucault being invited to speak at left-leaning, German emigre-led, flagship German model research universities during the cultural revolution of the 1960's. Derrida delivers his "Structure, Sign, and Play in the Discourse of the Human Sciences" at "Johns Hopkins University's conference on structuralism, 'Languages of Criticism and the Sciences of Man'"[106] in October of 1966, where he:

> Upended the entire premise of the conference, arguing that structuralism was rooted in a flawed Eurocentric logocentrism. The English coinage *poststructuralism* would not begin to circulate for a few more years, but, as Francois Cusset has observed, "the Americans present at Johns Hopkins in 1966 realized that they had just attended the live performance of its public birth."[107]

We will examine Derrida's "Structure, Sign, and Play" and his concept of logocentrism to see how it carries Nietzsche's program of negative nihilism to its logical next step. Ratner-Rosenhagen also notes that:

> The 1975 "Schizo-Culture" conference at Columbia University was another high-visibility event that featured French theorists, most notably Michel Foucault,

---

105 Wolin, 4.
106 Ratner-Rosenhagen, *American Nietzsche*, 266.
107 Ibid., 266.

who profiled their Nietzschean-inspired theories of cultural deviance and transgression, adding to the visibility of "the reception of Nietzsche's texts in America, traveling on a French ticket."[108]

We will explore Foucault's rejection of reason in his essay "Nietzsche, Genealogy, History," *Modern Civilization*, and *Discipline and Punish*. But prior to going to these sources, it is interesting to note that in addition to the university, and academic conferences, publication in scholarly journals is another means for the institutionalization of skepticism. Ratner-Rosenhagen notes that:

> A number of books and newly founded journals facilitate the transfer, presenting the "New Nietzsche" as an antifoundationalist revelation from France. A 1977 collection of essays, *The New Nietzsche: Contemporary Styles of Interpretation*, edited by David B. Allison, introduced a French-inspired, postphenomenological linguistic and cultural theorist who, in all his guises, assaulted the "subject" and "univocal meaning," and "no longer promised[d] a final aim, goal, or purpose" for interpretation. Now the death of God, long familiar to American readers, would be made unfamiliar with its new application as the death of "traditional logocentric hierarchy," while the will to power would be transcribed as the will to interpret texts.[109]

The "New Nietzsche," who is familiarly antifoundationalist in America through other channels, is made new through applica-

---
108 Ibid.
109 Ibid., 266.

tions to the interpretation of texts. French Nietzsche, the new American Nietzsche, enters into the academy through critique of the liberal arts and the social sciences. Nietzsche had been present in the social sciences through the likes of Freud, Weber, and Levi-Strauss, the structuralist, but the poststructuralists will press Nietzsche's anti-reason to the limits.[110]

In "Structure, Sign and Play,"[111] Derrida critiques structuralist Claude Levi-Strauss, who is already influenced by Nietzsche in his approach, in a way similar to that of Quine's post-analytic critique of analytic positivism. He presses Levi-Strauss' empiricism to its logical limits. He begins by talking about an "event," a "rupture," that has "occurred in the history of the concept of structure." He defines "structure" as the "old *episteme* — that is to say, as old as western science and western philosophy." It is not difficult to guess what this *episteme* is; it is either reason or empiricism, or both. Either way, this structure has been involved with referring "to a point of presence, a fixed origin," or in other words, the old *episteme* (knowing) has always referred to being. This reference, or presence (being), has functioned as a "center" to "orient; balance, and organize the structure...." If presence is being, and structure is knowing, then Derrida is saying that being has always served to orient our knowing. Derrida notes that "even today the notion of a structure lacking any center represents the unthinkable itself." Knowing without being is

---

110 In addition to departments of literature, Nietzsche's impact is felt in the new disciplines of the German model university of psychology, sociology, anthropology, history, and religious studies. See Smith, Christian. *The Secular Revolution: Power, Interests, and Conflict in the Secularization of American Public Life*. (Berkeley: University of California Press, 2003).
111 Derrida, Jacques." Structure, Sign, and Play in the Discourse of the Human Sciences" (1970). Accessed 3/18/2017. http://www.csudh.edu/ccauthen/576f13/drrdassp.pdf

unthinkable. Derrida then goes on to say that the "center also closes off the freeplay" of ideas.[112] Freeplay is the field of language, of infinite discourse, which excludes "totalization." Derrida says the field of language is "in fact that of *freeplay*, that is to say, a field of infinite substitutions in the closure of a finite ensemble ... there is something missing from it: a center which arrests and founds the freeplay of substitutions."[113] Freeplay is contrasted with "presence." Prior to the rupture in history, being is presence and serves as the center. Derrida says that:

> The history of metaphysics, like the history of the West, is the history of these metaphors and metonymies. Its matrix ... is the determination of being as presence in all the senses of this word. It would be possible to show that all the names related to fundamentals, to principles, or to the center have always designated the constant of a presence — *eidos, arche, telos, energeia, ousia* (essence, existence, substance, subject) *aletheia*, transcendentality, consciousness, or conscience, God, man, and so forth.[114]

After the "rupture" there is no center. The center comes to serve as a locus but not as a function. Derrida says:

> From then on it was probably necessary to begin to think that there was no center, that the center would not be thought in the form of a being-present, that the center had no natural locus, that it was not a fixed locus but a function, a sort of non-locus in which an infinite

---

112 Ibid., 1.
113 Ibid., 9.
114 Ibid., 2.

> number of sign-substitutions came into play. This moment was that in which language invaded the universal problematic; that in which, in the absence of a center or origin, everything became discourse-provided we can agree on this word — that is to say, when everything became a system where the central signified, the original or transcendental signified, is never absolutely present outside a system of differences. The absence of the transcendental signified extends the domain and the interplay of signification ad infinitum.[115]

The realization of the loss of a center seems to be the "linguistic turn" of the post-Nietzschean continental philosophers. The rupture is the historic moment when we realize that thinking does not apply to being, and that language is not about being. Derrida attributes the rupture, this "decentering," to the:

> Nietzschean critique of metaphysics, the critique of the concepts of being and truth, for which were substituted the concepts of play, interpretation, and sign (sign without truth present); the Freudian critique of self-presence, that is, the critique of consciousness, subject, of self-identity and of self-proximity or self-possession; and, more radically, the Heideggerian destruction of metaphysics, of onto-theology, of the determination of being as presence.[116]

Decentering is part of an era (Derrida's era), but it had already been at work in the "destructive discourses" of thinkers such as Nietzsche, Freud, and Heidegger. One wonders why there is a

---
115 Ibid., 2.
116 Ibid.

direction to history in which ideas are working themselves out in this way such that deconstruction occurs in Derrida's day. Is deconstruction a natural outworking of history? Is it just part of the flux of life? Or is the "rupture" a logical outworking of previous ideas being pressed to their logical limits in the name of logical consistency? The remaining pages of "Structure, Sign, and Play" are devoted to Derrida's deconstruction of Levi-Strauss' old school empiricism and materialism that is still based upon presence. By the end of the essay, Derrida sets up two possible interpretations of interpretation: 1) Interpretation is deciphering meaning: "a truth or an origin which is free from freeplay and from the order of the sign," or 2) Interpretation is freeplay: "which is no longer turned toward the origin ... and tries to pass beyond man and humanism, the name man being the name of that being who, throughout the history of metaphysics or of onto-theology ... to which Nietzsche showed us the way." These two ways of interpretation are mutually exclusive and are "absolutely irreconcilable if we were to live them simultaneously."[117] The second way of interpretation sounds like the flux theory where nothing is fixed in being.

A related concept of Derrida's, that of "trace," is also reminiscent of the flux doctrine. Though trace is not discussed in "Structure, Sign, and Play," is discussed in the *Grammatology*.[118] The notion of trace denies the existence of being and sounds very similar to Nietzsche's flux doctrine where there is no permanent being, no self, no mind. Catherine Zuckert says:

---

117 Ibid., 12.
118 Derrida, Jacques, and Gayatari Chankravorty Spivak. *Of Grammatology*. (Baltimore: Johns Hopkins University Press, 2016).

> Rather than understanding our mental activity in terms of the traditional visual metaphor, as a kind of static "seeing," Derrida urges; we should conceive the character not merely of our mental activity, but of our interaction with things in the world, more dynamically, physically, and historically as a kind of "writing". If there is nothing purely intelligible, immaterial, eternal, or present — in sum, if there is no being — everything ought to be reconceived as spatio-temporal mark, leaving or "trace" of something that is itself no longer there on something that was there before.[119]

Thus far, it should be clear that Derrida denies the isomorphism between reason and being. He critiques traditional empiricism and materialism because of their relation to the old *episteme* and commitment to presence. His position is something like the flux doctrine that denies permanent being and a permanent knowing self. All is text, and we leave trace in the text. This is not too far from Nietzsche's philosophical position. What Derrida does from here is to set out on a negative nihilistic project of radical deconstruction.

Deconstruction begins with the assumption that all is text — "the world" is text — and there is nothing outside the text.[120] This sounds similar to the analytic philosopher's "language community." Deconstruction sets itself up against "logocentrism." Which means that it is:

---

[119] Zuckert, Catherine H. *Postmodern Platos: Nietzsche, Heidegger, Gadamer, Strauss, Derrida*. (Chicago: Univ. of Chicago Press, 1996), 208.

[120] Friedrich, Rainer. "The Enlightenment Gone Mad (II): The Dismal Discourse of Postmodernism's Grand Narratives." *Arion: A Journal of Humanities and the Classics* 20, no. 1 (07 2012): 67-112. Accessed 3/18/2017. doi:10.2307/arion.20.1.0067.

> Designed to subvert the claim of any text and discourse to adequate ground — to a logos that enables it to produce a stable, determinate, decidable, and coherent meaning or truth — deconstruction operates as a totalizing negative hermeneutics. As a negative hermeneutics, patent in poststructuralism's wholesale assault on Western rationality, its grand narrative is in its origins largely iconoclastic.[121]

Logocentrism is connected with being and identity. Deconstruction's alternative to logocentrism is *differance*. With *differance* meaning is indeterminate or is deferred indefinitely. There are no universal meanings. Friedrich says that "*Differance*, then, is deconstruction's principal and originary" foundation. It is "universally operative in all texts and all discourses." It is "said to impart to language and discourse a Dionysian turbulence and disorder." Lastly, "poststructuralism seeks to show not the order but the disorder of a text."[122] Logocentrism "freezes" the meaning of words, whereas deconstruction unfreezes "cemented" meanings to freeplay and *differance*.[123] Friedrich argues that deconstruction is a:

> Totalizing (and "potentially totalitarian") Grand Narrative, deconstruction has set its sights on the *whole* of the metaphysical foundations of Western thought and *all* its discourses. In domains such as ethics, politics, and the law, deconstructive subversion is anything but innocuous: there its acid proves downright toxic. When

---

121 Ibid., 84.
122 Ibid., 86.
123 Ibid., 87.

applied to political, ethical, and juridical discourses, it creates a normative void. Then deconstruction's latent nihilism comes to the fore.

Again, we see that the consequences of the denial of the isomorphism between reason and being leads to nihilism and the deconstruction and destruction of everything.

Once Nietzsche has denied the isomorphism between reason and being, and Heidegger has laid out the difference between negative nihilism, which is destructive of all old conceptions of being, and positive nihilism, which is the revaluation of old values with the new "values," the program is set for the post-Nietzschean philosophy. Derrida implements the negative nihilist project by exposing "presence" (being) in texts, and everything is text. Foucault, following Nietzsche, implements negative nihilism through the genealogical approach. This approach is discussed in Foucault's essay "Nietzsche, Genealogy, History."[124] It should be noted that many others have appropriated the genealogical approach within the disciplines of the social sciences, history, and religious studies to carry out the program of unmasking power dynamics further.[125]

Foucault develops the genealogical method for exposing knowledge claims, which includes claims of "reason," "being,"

---

124 Rainbow, Paul (ed.). *The Foucault Reader*. (New York: Pantheon Books, 1984) 76-100.
125 For a few examples of how the genealogical method is appropriated within the discipline of religious studies, see: Asad, Talal. *Formations of the Secular: Christianity, Islam, Modernity*. (Stanford: Stanford University Press, 2003). Asad, Talal. *Genealogies of Religion: Discipline and Reasons of Power in Christianity and Islam*. (Baltimore: Johns Hopkins University Press, 1993). Masuzawa, Tomoko. *The Invention of World Religions: Or, How European Universalism Was Preserved in the Language of Pluralism*. (Chicago: University of Chicago Press, 2005).

"empirical evidence," and "the self," as will to power, or what he calls "the will to knowledge." He says:

> We should admit ... that power produces knowledge (and not simply by encouraging it because it serves power or by applying it because it is useful); that power and knowledge directly imply one another; that there is no power relation without the correlative constitution of a field of knowledge, nor any knowledge that does not presuppose and constitute at the same time power relations. These "power-knowledge relations" are to be analysed, therefore, not on the basis of a subject of knowledge who is or is not free in relation to the power system, but, on the contrary, the subject who knows, the objects to be known and the modalities of knowledge must be regarded as so many effects of these fundamental implications of power-knowledge and their historical transformations. In short, it is not the activity of the subject of knowledge that produces a corpus of knowledge, useful or resistant to power, but power-knowledge, the process and struggles that traverse it and of which it is made up, that determines the forms and possible domains of knowledge.[126]

There is no "objective" knowledge in the Socratic sense. The post-Nietzschean discovers that in a world dominated by the will to power, there is only "power-knowledge." Power-knowledge is a relationship of struggle — *agon* — between the "subject who knows," the "objects to be known," the "modalities of

---

126 Foucault, Michel, and Alan Sheridan. *Discipline and Punish: The Birth of the Prison*. (New York: Vintage Books, 1977), 27-28.

knowing" or the epistemological approach of the subject who knows or the discipline that knows, and how all three have been historically conditioned. Ultimately, Foucault says, "knowledge is not made for understanding; it is made for cutting."[127] Foucault's genealogical method is a critical historical means of exposing power dynamics. His method is directed primarily towards the social sciences. His:

> Task is to cast aside ... utopian schemes, the search for first principles, and to ask instead how power actually operates in our society. "It seems to me," Foucault expounds, "that the real political task in a society such as ours is to criticize the working of institutions which appear to be both neutral and independent; to criticize them in such a manner that the political violence which has always exercised obscurely through them will be unmasked, so that one can fight them."[128]

Foucault bypasses the question of "reason" or "truth" because he does not think these concepts can be understood outside a discursive practice that is already within a power-knowledge regime. Instead, questions of reason and being, truth and justice, are historical questions not questions about reality. How have people used these concepts to gain and maintain power?

Foucault uses the genealogical method applied to the social sciences as the locus of power-knowledge dynamics in three phases of his writing career. In the first phase, he exposes institutionalized "dividing practices," which are "modes of manipulation that combine the mediation of a science (or pseu-

---

127 Rainbow, 88.
128 Ibid., 5-6.

do-science) and the practice of exclusion — usually in a spacial sense, but always in a social sense."[129] These dividing practices give the dominant group self-identity by opposition to the minority, "other." The second phase of Foucault's exposure of power-knowledge relations is related to scientific classification and the "objectification" of the human body as "thing" to be studied. What goes by:

> Scientific classification ... arises from "the modes of inquiry which try to give themselves the status of sciences; for example, the objectivizing of the speaking subject in *grammaire generale*, philology, and linguistics ... [or] the objectivizing of the productive subject, the subject who labors, in the analysis of wealth and of economics. Or ... the objectivizing of the sheer fact of being alive in natural history or biology."[130]

Foucault attempts to show that the "discourses of life, labor, and language were structured into disciplines" not by some logical, necessary progression of history, but rather by power-knowledge disciplinary practices that normalized and embed social practices within the institutions of culture. The third phase of Foucault's work is an exploration of "subjectification," or the "'way a human being turns him or herself into a subject.'"[131] This an exploration into "self formation." The genealogical approach, following Nietzsche, is a critical history that:

> Gives rise to three uses that oppose and correspond to the three Platonic modalities of history. The first is

---

129 Ibid., 8.
130 Ibid., 9.
131 Ibid., 11.

parodic, directed against reality, and opposes the theme of history as reminiscence or recognition; the second is dissociative, directed against identity, and opposes history given as continuity or representative of a tradition; the third is sacrificial, directed against truth, and opposes history as knowledge.[132]

Following Nietzsche, we can see Foucault rejecting an "objective" mind-independent "reality," rejecting "identity," which would seem to be any permanent being, and history as "truth." Foucault follows in the footsteps of his predecessor in denying the isomorphism between reason and being. Furthermore, Foucault sees reason as the other to madness in his *Madness and Civilization: A History of Insanity in the Age of Reason*.[133] Reason is used to marginalize "the other," and what goes by the name of reason, historically, has been used to obtain and maintain power. Richard Wolin brings together both Derrida and Foucault's denial of reason when he says:

> In the concluding pages of *Madness and Civilization*, Foucault praised the "sovereign enterprise of unreason," forever irreducible to practices that can be "cured." Foucault's contrast between the exclusionary practices of the modern scientific worldview, whose rise was co-incident with Descartes' *Discourse on Method*, and the nonconformist potentials of "madness" qua "other" of reason, would help to redefine the theoretical agenda for an entire generation of French intellectuals. Even

---

132 Ibid., 93.
133 Foucault, Michel, and Richard Howard. *Madness and Civilization: A History of Insanity in the Age of Reason*. (New York: Vintage Books, 1964).

in the case of Derrida, who formulated a powerful critique of Foucault's arguments, there was little disagreement with the [sic] Foucault's central contention that Reason is essentially a mechanism of oppression that proceeds by way of exclusions, constraints, and prohibitions. Derrida's indictment of "logocentrism," or the tyranny of reason, purveys a kindred sentiment: since the time of Plato, Western thought has displayed a systemic intolerance vis-a-vis difference, otherness, and heterogeneity. Following the precedents established by Nietzsche and Heidegger, deconstruction arose to overturn and dismantle Reason's purported life-denying unitary prejudices.[134]

The post-Nietzschean strain of continental philosophy has served as a corrosive acid to all areas of scholarship, leaving no claim to knowledge untouched. Wolin goes on to say that the post-Nietzschean "hostility towards reason" is both untenable and is politically dangerous because with the mistrust of reason, logic, and argumentation, "its practitioners are left dazed and disoriented — morally and politically defenseless."[135] This leaves the continental post-Nietzschean philosophy "politically impotent." Not only does Wolin see this undesirable result of this strain of philosophy, but so does Rorty. He says: "Foucault affects to write from a point of view light-years away from the problems of contemporary society," and that he is "a stoic, a dispassionate observer of the present social order, rather than its concerned critic."[136] Rorty's concern is from the perspective of

---

134 Wolin, 8.
135 Ibid., xiv.
136 Rorty, *Essays On Heidegger*, 173.

the politics of neo-pragmatism. There are broader concerns to be addressed. If not checked, the institutionalization of nihilistic skepticism, which Foucault seems to document very clearly, will destroy what is left of the West.

One way to check the acid of the continental strain of post-Nietzschean philosophy is to use the genealogical method on itself to trace the history of the separation of reason from being in order to see how that divorce was justified, and whether that divorce was a will to power pressing an alternative vision of "truth" and "values." For instance, why should one accept Nietzsche's flux doctrine? How would one "know" that all is flux? Surely one cannot simply check. To check would be to observe empirically, to assume a form of realism. In addition, what, or whom, is doing the observing? Remember, the post-Nietzschean philosophy asserts "a process without a subject; postmodern anti-humanism [reduces] humanity to an effect of such a process, the outcome of which is not the rescue of an emancipated humankind, but 'the rescue of a very differentiated system, a kind of superbrain'; and post-modernity's linguistic-textualist ontology that turns all and everything into the effects of language."[137] One cannot observe impermanence. Rather, one can speculate that — assume that — all is flux. But on what basis? Would one assume the flux doctrine because it makes sense logically? But wait, logic does not apply to being if all is flux.

It seems then that the flux doctrine is an *a priori* commitment for Nietzsche and his followers. *A priori* commitments are the very thing that the whole host of post-Nietzschean philoso-

---

137 Friedrich, Rainer. "The Enlightenment Gone Mad (I): The Dismal Discourse Of Postmodernism's Grand Narratives." *Arion: A Journal of Humanities and the Classics* (19, no. 3 (01 2012): 31-78. Accessed 3/18/2017. doi:10.2307/arion.19.3.0031., 42.

phers are trying to rid from the discipline. We should not allow the post-Nietzschean philosophers to get away with this lack of authenticity. Instead, we should all admit that our assumptions about reality *are* assumptions, whether they are Platonist, Christian, Idealist, Materialist, or post-Nietzschean impermanence. We can learn from the post-Nietzschean that all persons have assumptions, that no one is neutral concerning "truth." Also, all of our experiences are interpretations (in light of our assumptions). However, some interpretations are more rationally consistent than others. Lastly, we do belong to linguistic communities by which we interpret the world of experience. There are "competing comprehensive doctrines," but this reality does not spell the end of reason, the end of metaphysics, the end of philosophy, and the "death of everything." Instead, it means that we need to rediscover reason, established on a firmer footing. We need to define reason and its relation to being. We then need to use reason, as all the post-Nietzschean philosophers do, to identify and to analyze assumptions. Then we should use reason to defend and to argue for our assumptions with one another in the public sphere.

II. "Philosophy" is Not Philosophy: The Rectification of the Discipline

The post-Nietzschean philosophy is a purifying discipline, whether through analytic linguistic analysis, pragmatic critique of old-school empiricism, or continental deconstruction and unmasking of power dynamics. Each strain of post-Nietzschean philosophy results in pragmatism. When combined, through negative nihilism and through the positive nihilism of willing-out-beyond, the post-Nietzschean philosophy provides the foundation for institutionalized skepticism. In sum: Post-Nietzschean philosophy provides the foundation for the social fabric of life without God. It is the immanent frame. It is Plato's Cave.

Post-Nietzschean philosophy serves as the "police officer" of epistemology and metaphysics, arresting those who cling to a pre-Nietzschean notion of reason and being. Nietzsche breaks the isomorphism between reason and being assumed since Heraclitus (*logos*) and Parmenides (*ontos*) and the origin of philosophy discussed in Chapter 1. Post-Nietzschean philosophy sets out to apply the implications of Nietzsche's break to all of life: to thinking, the self, the world, language, political life, and out beyond affecting all of the institutions of culture. The post-Nietzschean philosophers provide a world and life view that is in stark contrast with the Socratic-Platonic-Aristotelian and Christian worldviews.

Philosophy begins with the search for a *logos*, but given the materialist and empiricist assumptions, the first phase of philosophy ends in skepticism, relativism and sophism. Socrates, Plato, and Aristotle address these problematic assumptions, and develop a coherent alternative understanding of a *logos* that is grounded in reality, though they have some disagreement about the nature of that reality. The *Logos* doctrine is further developed and made more coherent by St. John and Christian theism. The Platonic-Aristotelian and theistic philosophies are epistemological and metaphysical "realists." This realism is the predominant outlook of Western philosophy until Nietzsche's critique. Aligning himself with the pre-Platonic materialist-empiricist philosophers, especially Heraclitus, Nietzsche reorients philosophy towards a rejection of *Logos* and realism. He accomplishes this reorientation, or revaluation, of philosophy by explicitly rejecting the isomorphism between reason and being — rejecting that reason is ontological. The rejection of reason as ontological instigates the linguistic turn in both its analytic and continental forms. The end of the linguistic turn in continental philosophy is the silence of madness, whereas the end of the linguistic turn in analytic philosophy is pragmatism or quietism — another form of silence. Some, like Rorty, suggest that we are at the end of philosophy.[138]

In the interest of the rectification of names, we should return to Plato's *Apology* and to *Theaetetus*. In the *Apology*, three groups bring the indictment against Socrates. These are the poets, represented by Meletus, the politicians, represented by Anytus, and the craftsmen, represented by Lycon. They are those who appear to know, but who do not, in fact, possess knowledge. They do not possess knowledge because they have been taught by the skeptical sophists and are the pragmatic men of their day. They are similar to the three contemporary schools of post-Nietzschean philosophy. The poets correspond with the continental strain - philosophy is literature. The politicians correspond with the Pragmatists - philosophy is politics. And lastly, the craftsmen correspond with the analytics - philosophy is science. In Plato's dialogues, these three groups never ascend above true opinion on Plato's allegory of the Line. They never go outside the Cave in the allegory of the Cave. This is because they never get beyond true opinion — true *doxa* — because they do not go beyond sensory data. In contrast to these three groups, Socrates

---

138 See: Rajchman, John. and Cornel West (eds.). *Post-Analytic Philosophy*. (New York: Columbia University Press), 1985. Baynes, Kenneth, James Bohman, and Thomas McCarthy. *After Philosophy: End or Transformation?* (Cambridge: The MIT Press, 1987).

Retrieving Knowledge

is represented as one who is doing philosophy. He uses reason to rise above true opinion and *doxa* to true opinion with a *logos* — knowledge. Without a *logos* one cannot have knowledge of reality. One cannot exit the Cave. Put another way, contemporary post-Nietzschean philosophy, because it is empirically based, cannot go beyond mere appearance. This philosophy confines us to life within the immanent frame.

If philosophy is a search for a *logos*, then post-Nietzschean philosophy — as anti-*logos* philosophy — is not, classically understood, philosophy at all: it is sophism. Socrates clearly distinguishes the life of the philosopher from the life of pragmatic man in the *Theaetetus*.[139] By and large, what passes for philosophy today generally falls under the category of pragmatism taught by the sophists. The sophists are pushers of institutionalized skepticism. On the whole,[140] The philosophers of the academy today are paid teachers of skepticism. The search for a *logos* ended in skepticism, due to materialism and empiricism, in the first era of philosophy, and the search for a *logos* ended again with the advent of post-Nietzschean philosophy. This time the stakes in leaving off the search for a *logos* are much higher than in Socrates' day. It is not just Athens the city-state that is at risk, but now all of Western Civilization is at risk. Furthermore, since the West influences the world, the stakes are world-significant. We need to return to a search for the *logos*. We need to return to philosophy classically done as exemplified by Socrates in the *Theaetetus*. What can we learn about the *logos*, knowledge, the good and the common good, and public discourse from Socrates? We need a rectification of names in defining philosophy.

---

139   See Chapter 2.
140   But not in each and every case.

Philosophy is not sophism. Those who teach young people how to be "busy" with life based upon "popular opinion" within the Cave — where opinion and will to power rule — are not philosophers in the classical sense.

Chapter 5

Reason and Public Discourse: What Can We Learn from Socrates?

PHILOSOPHY, AS WE now know it, can either end in pragmatism, or philosophers can return to a search for a *logos*, as the first philosophers sought to do. Socrates provides a method and example for how philosophy may return to its original search, and how this pursuit may take place as rational public discourse. Philosophy need not end in a post-Nietzschean skepticism and nihilism. Allan Bloom (1930-1992), in his *Closing of the American Mind*, sees the corrosive effect of Nietzsche's influence on American culture. He was witness to the rise of the post-Nietzschean philosophy and its effects in the university and on the culture, especially in the 1960's. He tells the story of student protests happening on the campus of Cornell, where he was teaching at the time, while he was leading a discussion with a group of students on Plato's *Republic*. Bloom reflects: "The little Greek Civilization Program a group of professors set up against the currents had just gotten under way the year of the crisis. It consisted of about a dozen enthusiastic freshmen, and we had been reading Plato's *Republic* during the entire year. We had not finished it when the university became a chaos."[1] He goes on to explain that this group of freshmen were more interested in the "story of the ambitious Glaucon, who was founding a city with the help of Socrates"[2] than in the campus protests. Bloom saw this as a profoundly encouraging event as a professor who was resisting the onslaught and effects of the post-Nietzschean philosophy. He saw Socrates as a means of resistance. He notes that the corrosion of culture is not primarily political, social, or psychological, but is fundamentally philosophical. He suggests looking to Socrates for inspiration in philosophically troubled times.

Bloom concludes *Closing of the American Mind* with a melancholy note, but with a small ray of hope. He says that the analysis he presents in his work is of:

> ... the shadows cast by the peaks of the university ... they represent what the university has to say about man and his education, and they do not project a coherent image. The differences and the indifferences are too great. It is difficult to imagine that there is either the wherewithal or the energy within the university to

---

1   Bloom, *Closing of the American Mind*, 332.
2   Ibid., 332.

constitute or reconstitute the idea of an educated human being and establish a liberal education again.[3]

Bloom sees the state of the university as bleak, but he also recognizes that the fact that we are still engaged in discussion is hopeful. He says that "the contemplation of this scene is in itself a proper philosophic activity."[4] He says the questions brought up in his book "only need to be addressed continuously and seriously for liberal education to exist; for it does not consist so much in answers as in the permanent questions."[5] The way we discuss has changed, but the questions we raise are the same perennial questions. He says that as long as we keep this conversation about perennial questions going "the hope is that the embers do not die out."[6] Bloom seeks solace and a solution in communities of true friends who will seek the truth together. He uses Plato and Aristotle as an example. They were two friends who disagreed about the nature of the good, but "their common concern for the good linked them; their disagreement about it proved they needed one another to understand it."[7] True community, for Bloom, seems to be a philosophical community. He says: "This age is not utterly insalubrious for philosophy. Our problems are so great and their sources so deep that to understand them we need philosophy more than ever if we do not despair of it, and it faces the challenges on which it flourishes. I still believe that universities, rightly understood, are where community and friendship can exist in our times."[8]

---

3 Ibid., 380.
4 Ibid.
5 Ibid.
6 Ibid.
7 Ibid., 381.
8 Ibid., 382.

Friendship, for the common good, in the context of discussing philosophical questions at the university is the way out suggested by Bloom. He concludes the book with the following:

> This is the American moment in world history, the one for which we shall forever be judged. Just as in politics the responsibility for the fate of freedom in the world has devolved upon our regime, so the fate of philosophy in the world has devolved upon our universities, and the two are related as they have never been before. The gravity of our given task is great, and it is very much in doubt how the future will judge our stewardship.[9]

What Bloom says is both true and terrifying. *The Closing of the American Mind* was published 30 years ago. Philosophy has only sunk deeper into the post-Nietzschean darkness, and the current state of the university and broader culture reflect this fact. Bloom's suggestions for communities of friends carrying on the philosophical discussion is not enough to keep the embers burning. What is needed is a re-revaluation of philosophy. What is needed is a return to philosophy classically done. What is needed is a public philosophy. However, we cannot merely go back; we must understand reason — its scope and limits — on a firmer footing. Part of the problem in the history of philosophy is the loose way in which the term "reason" is used. We must begin by defining what reason is and what reason is for.[10] Bloom's

---

9   Ibid.
10 Surrendra Gangadean has defined and developed reason in itself, reason in its use, and reason in us in his work: *Philosophical Foundation: A Critical Analysis of Basic Beliefs*. Lanham: (University Press of America, 2008).

recognition that what we face is a philosophical problem seems correct, but overcoming institutional skepticism is going to require much more than friends discussing philosophy. It is going to require doing philosophy in an entirely different way. What follows is a modest direction that may be taken towards addressing the skepticism of our day. It will take much more than what is proposed here but let this serve as a first step.

I. A Return to the Search for a *Logos*

The *Theaetetus* is a dialogue that deals with the most basic concepts of philosophy — *logos* and *ontos* — reason and being. The most basic questions of philosophy are founded upon these concepts: Can reason tell us whether God exists or not? Can reason tell us what a human being *is*? Can reason tell us what is good and what is evil for human beings? Philosophy, classically understood, begins with the isomorphism between reason and being. By way of reminder, Aristotle says:

> Let this, then, suffice to show that the most indisputable of all beliefs is that contradictory statements are not at the same time true ... But on the other hand there cannot be an intermediate between contradictories, but of one subject we must either affirm or deny any one predicate. This is clear, in the first place, if we define what the true and the false are. To say of what is that it is not, or of what is not that it is, is false ....[11]

Our thinking begins with being. The law of noncontradiction is not merely a logical rule; it is a law of being. It is logically im-

---

[11] Aristotle *Metaphysics* IV.6.1011b 13-15 & 23-24, 1597.

possible for something to both *be* and *not be* in the same respect and at the same time. To deny the isomorphism between thinking and being is to deny significant, meaningful speech. This is the first principle that must be affirmed in doing philosophy. If this first principle is denied, then meaning is lost, and we are stuck in skepticism.

The problems of contemporary skepticism must be addressed in the public sphere since these problems concern the public good. Public discourse is needed to address the issues that challenge the public good. What is public is what is shared. What is shared is common. Discourse is communication, whether written or spoken, which assumes reason/*logos*. Communication is by means of words; words express concepts; concepts are the first act of reason (*logos*). Written and spoken communication assumes rationality in human beings (again, the word/*logos*). Rationality assumes a commitment to the laws of thought. The laws of thought include The law of identity (*a* is *a*); The law of non-contradiction (not both *a* and non-*a* in the same respect and at the same time); and the law of excluded middle (either *a* or non-*a*). Rationality assumes that reason is the laws of thought and the laws of being — that there is an isomorphism between thinking and being. Lack of commitment to reason — as both the laws of thought and the laws of being — leads to the loss of significant (meaningful) speech. Loss of significant speech results in silence. A person is either committed to reason, the laws of thought and being, or one is not committed to reason and should remain silent, assuming one has integrity. One cannot both be silent (not committed to reason) and participate in discourse (committed to reason). The laws of thought are the self-evident (cannot be doubted without losing meaning) source of authority for all human beings. Therefore, the laws of thought are the self-evident source of authority for public discourse. Without reason as our source of authority, we fall back into emotivism and the will to power, which are non-rational means of persuasion and bypass the dignity of human rationality and end up in dehumanization.

If we are to meaningfully discuss contentious philosophical issues that have religious and political ramifications, common ground for public discourse will need to be established.[12] The following are necessary conditions for common ground for public discourse. 1) All engaged parties in the discussion must share a commitment to reason as the laws of thought and the laws of being. 2) All engaged parties must be willing to live with integrity the positions that they express. There must be a consistency between what one says and what one does. For example, if one commits to skepticism, one should be willing to live with the consequences of skepticism, just as Nietzsche did. 3) Those engaged in public dialogue should affirm that some things are clear to reason. Minimally, the laws of thought are clear to reason. The basic things that can be known are clear to reason, the laws of thought. If the basic things that can be known are clear to reason, they are easily knowable. Because the basic things are easily knowable, we should know what is clear to reason if we are seeking to know what is clear. If we do not know, it is because we are not seeking to know, which implies moral culpability. 4) In public discourse, it is necessary to address more fundamental questions prior to addressing less fundamental questions. For example, questions of epistemology are more fundamental than

---

12   What follows is an adaptation of Gangadean, Surrendra. "Common Ground." Logos Paper #2. Accessed 3/24/2017. http://thelogospapers.com/2-common-ground/

questions of metaphysics. Questions of metaphysics are more fundamental than questions about ethics. If agreement can be secured on the more fundamental issues, then agreement can be secured on the less fundamental issues. On the other hand, if we do not agree on the more fundamental issues, we cannot and will not agree on the less fundamental issues. These four points are necessary for common ground for public discourse. Conversation without common ground will be unproductive and will further propagate skepticism.

The goal of public discourse is to discuss what is good and desirable for the public, our shared life together. This is the common good. Human beings are rational, political animals. As political, we necessarily live in community. We cannot avoid discussing the common good for the human communities in which we live. We cannot avoid discussion of the basis for a common life together. If we are to make progress in public discourse, in overcoming skepticism and discussing the common good, we must address fundamental philosophical questions that have been neglected in the public sphere since the death of God and skepticism has crept into the institutions of culture. Skepticism makes progress in public discourse impossible. Institutional skepticism results in our agreeing to disagree and resorting to pragmatic, short-term solutions. Public discourse, for the common good, then, is public philosophy.

If we are to make progress in public discourse and find unity among communities and groups of communities in the Republic, a public philosophy must address the more fundamental issues before addressing less fundamental issues. The most fundamental issue for public philosophy to address is our approach to knowing — epistemology. Are we committed to reason, and what does a commitment to reason imply? The next level of issues to be discussed in a public philosophy are questions about ultimate reality and human nature — metaphysics. For too long we have avoided these issues in the name of post-Nietzschean philosophy. Just because 120 years of institutional skepticism has reinforced an anti-metaphysical bent in philosophy does not mean that we have to accept the unfounded claim that we are post-metaphysics. It simply is not true. We all do metaphysics, more or less consciously, and we all live by our metaphysics with more or less integrity. The third level of issues to be addressed in a public philosophy are questions about what is good for human beings, and what is evil for human beings — ethics. What is the goal of life and how may it be achieved? We cannot accept "values" pluralism and ethical relativism as a "fact." These are not facts but are the outworking of institutional skepticism. If we can address these three levels of fundamental questions, starting from epistemology, then going to metaphysics, and then addressing ethics, we may be able to address even less fundamental issues, such as religious doctrines and political platforms, in the public sphere.

The most appropriate institutional location for a public philosophy is the academy. Plato's academy began with philosophy, and philosophy is the foundation of the academy. In addition, the academy is the training ground for citizens of the Republic. Yet public philosophy cannot proceed based upon the institutional skepticism that finds its root in the philosophy departments of the academy. The academy must create space for alternative philosophical voices. This can be done through public lectures, publishing scholarly articles that question skepticism and reorient the discipline, hiring faculty members that affirm reason and that some things are clear and knowable by reason. It is possible for critique to come from within the existing philosophy departments,[13] but it is unlikely. The most likely scenario is that a critique of institutional skepticism will have to come from outside of secular academic philosophy departments. Perhaps this can be achieved through think tanks, alternative publications, and internet forums. Another source of public philosophy and critique of institutional skepticism could come from traditional liberal arts colleges and religious colleges and universities that have an interest in promoting the public good. Yet it seems that public philosophy will need momentum, numbers, and time in order for effective change in our declining public sphere. What is needed is a culture of philosophy, classically done, encouraged by groups who are united and who can prepare the future generations of students. Socrates and his students once faced a crisis of skepticism and overcame. This small group of thinkers changed the West by doing philosophy. What can we learn about public philosophy from Socrates?

II. Socratic Principles for Public Philosophy

The next section of the chapter will provide a rough sketch as to how some of the principles (whether explicitly stated or implied) derived from the *Theaetetus* may be used in developing a public philosophy to address the skepticism of our day. Let us call these "Socratic Principles." The first Socratic Principle that may

---

13 Laurence BonJour, analytic philosopher and former empiricist and coherentist, has changed his position dramatically and now argues for *a priori* reason in critique of empiricism. He is an example of how internal critique could proceed. See: BonJour, Laurence. *In Defense of Pure Reason: A Rationalist Account of* A Priori *Justification*. (Cambridge: Cambridge University Press, 1998).

be derived from the *Theaetetus*, which is applicable today, is the assumption that knowledge is possible, and the related claim: that knowledge is true opinion with an account. That Socrates is thoroughly convinced that one can know the True, the Good, the Beautiful, and the Just, is inherent in his passionate pursuit of knowledge and his unrelenting quest for definitions (*logoi*). If one does not believe that knowledge is possible, then one will not pursue knowledge for its own sake. It is evident today that the dominant view in the academy, and permeating popular culture, is that knowledge of ultimate reality is not possible.

Socrates and Theaetetus propose that "knowledge is true opinion with an account (*logos*)." We need knowledge of what "knowledge" *is*. It would seem as though there is inherent in the *Theaetetus* a circular argument; that when we ask the question, "what is knowledge?" we must already know what it is to know. This is not necessarily the case. If, as Socrates and Theaetetus contend, knowledge is certain (infallible), then Socrates demonstrates for the reader the foundation of all knowledge which cannot be doubted. Throughout the *Theaetetus*, reason as the laws of thought (the law of identity: a is a; the law of noncontradiction: not both a and *non-a* in the same respect and at the same time; and the law of excluded middle: either a or *non-a*) is assumed as indubitable and infallible. The laws of thought are the indubitable starting point for all other knowledge. The laws of thought — reason, the *logos* — make thought and speech possible. Let the second Socratic Principle state that reason, in the form of the laws of thought, is assumed as a self-evident source of common ground between Socrates, his interlocutors, and the reader (which includes all thinkers). Thus, today, reason — the laws of thought — is the self-evident source of common ground for all involved in public discourse (*logos*), where public discourse is a shared give-and-take of reasons for the judgments that we make resulting in actions.

We still do not have an "account" for the definition of knowledge as "true opinion with an account." What does it mean to have an account for true belief? In the dialogue, we come to understand "belief" to be affirming a proposition or making a judgment. This belief may be according to reality (true), or not according to reality (false). The account that Socrates and his interlocutors are pursuing is what grounds a true belief in reality. So, when one makes the judgment "all men are mortal," one can show how that statement is grounded in the nature of being. Socrates shows the reader a reliable method for grounding true opinion in reality by eliminating the opposite, or contradictory, position. In this case, the opposite (or contradiction) of "all men are mortal" is "some men are not mortal." We could ask, is it true that (is reality such that) "some men are not mortal?" No, reality is not such that "some men are not mortal"; all men die (whether this is by nature or otherwise is something to be investigated further, elsewhere). By eliminating one side of the contradiction, the other side of the contradiction ("all men are mortal") is necessarily true. Socrates demonstrates this kind of argument (*reductio ad absurdum*) multiple times throughout this and other dialogues. Thus, knowledge is gained by reason and argument such that the opposite view is impossible. By ruling out what is impossible, we are left with necessary truth. Necessary truth is infallible, or certain, truth. Certain truth is knowledge. Certainty is not merely gained by sensory impressions, which only deliver probable truth (and possible falsehood). The senses may be involved, but we grasp universals by reason. To sum up: The first Socratic Principle claims that knowledge is possible, and that knowledge is true belief with an account. An account is by reason and argument such that the opposite (the contradiction) is impossible. If we were to apply this principle to contemporary public discourse, we would want to ask for and exchange reasons with one another regarding foundational assumptions where the opposite position is impossible.

In contemporary public discourse, discussion of contentious issues — such as religion, values, and politics — is discouraged because of the multitude of "competing comprehensive doctrines,"[14] each with its own set of values and attitudes. Pragmatic solutions to "social problems" are proposed with the assumption that knowledge of any one comprehensive doctrine as corresponding with reality is impossible. Yet, with our proposed first and second Socratic Principles, a public discussion about whether knowledge is possible, what knowledge is, and how we may gain knowledge is an entryway to a larger discussion about whether knowledge about which "comprehensive doctrine" best corresponds with reality may be had. Socrates may help us to navigate contemporary skepticism that results in a permanent pluralism and a pragmatically focused public discourse.

The third Socratic Principle is that naturalism and non-essentialism are highly problematic views of ultimate reality. Socrates argues in the *Theaetetus* that there must be something permanent, eternal, and universal in which to ground an "account." In addition, Socrates implies that this being cannot be material because matter is always going through a process of change, and further, because matter is changeable there is no grounding for what is permanent in the material world. In other words, there

---

14   A phrase coined by political theorist John Rawls.

must be a non-material intelligible realm in which to ground an "account." Admittedly, more argument is needed to prove the existence of non-material being to counter contemporary materialist assumptions.[15] Plato's theory of the Forms has been largely rejected due to problems with his account of the non-physical intelligible realm. What we may take away from Socrates in this dialogue is that argument regarding the existence of a non-material reality is possible, and if we want to ground an account for knowledge, it is necessary. Though an unpopular topic, one should not shy away from discussion of non-physical reality in the public realm if that is where reason leads us.

A fourth Socratic Principle that we may infer from this dialogue, and which is explicitly developed in other dialogues, is the notion that if we can give an account of what *is*, then objectivism in ethics is possible. The Good is grounded in the True or the Real. If we can understand what reality *is* through reason, and we have an "account" of reality, we can know what a human being is. And if we can know what a human being is then we can know what is good and what is not good for humans. Ethics grounded in human nature, then, would be objective and not merely subjective. In our day, skepticism regarding what is real results in relativism regarding human nature and the Good for humans.[16] In addition, naturalism and non-essentialism results in the view that there is no essential nature for human beings. Human beings are thus infinitely malleable. The post-Nietzs-

---

15   See Gangadean, *Philosophical Foundation. A Critical Analysis of Basic Beliefs*. (Lanham: University Press of America, 2008). Anderson, Owen. *The Clarity of God's Existence: The Ethics of Belief After the Enlightenment*. (Oregon: Wipf & Stock, 2008). Koons, Robert C., and George Beeler. *The Waning of Materialism*. (Oxford: Oxford University Press, 2013).

16   See Anderson, Owen. *The Natural Moral Law: The Good After Modernity*. (New York: Cambridge University Press, 2012).

chean philosophy claims that humans have no fixed nature, and so they may determine their own nature and may determine what is good for themselves (apart from any fixed human nature). The result of ethical relativism is a lack of unity in the public sphere. Lack of unity in the public sphere leads to a lack of a common good for the Republic.

A fifth Socratic Principle to be gleaned from the *Theaetetus* is that the Sophists can be silenced utilizing reason. If knowledge is possible, and reason is common ground in public discourse, then knowledge, rather than persuasion (appeal to emotion, or the will to power), is the true source of power. Knowing the truth sets one free from falsehood. Socrates makes the distinction between the Philosopher who is free and the Sophist who is not free but is a slave to his business. The Sophist is a slave to the material world which he thinks is the only reality and the source of all that is good. He is a pragmatist and has no time for considering higher things, and even if he had the time he does not have the interest because he does not think it possible. The Philosopher is willing to patiently pursue a discussion wherever it may lead in a desire for gaining Truth by means of reason. One is not obligated to listen to those in the public realm who are unwilling to use reason but who resort to appeals to emotion or the will to power. We can infer that if a statement has no reason then there is no meaning to that statement, and if there is no meaning to that statement it cannot be true. Either the person holding to a meaningless statement ought to cease speaking, or we (fellow citizens) should not give ear to what they are saying. To summarize: One is not obligated to listen to meaningless statements.

A sixth Socratic Principle to be derived from this dialogue is that the principle of charity should be observed to promote civil public discourse. The principle of charity states that when in a dialogue one should give the best possible reading to a position with which one disagrees. The principle of charity begins with understanding one's interlocutor's position before objecting to that position. This means that one does not resort to informal fallacies, particularly the fallacy of the strawman argument. The strawman is arguing against a misrepresentation of a position rather than the actual position that a person holds. Socrates suspects that he might be caught in constructing a strawman position of Protagoras' view and he says: "'No' [Protagoras] will say: 'show a more generous spirit by attacking what I actually say'."[17] The principle of charity also implies that one should give the best possible interpretation of one's opponent's position before erecting an objection to that position. Lastly, one should be personable in public discourse. Socrates, though sometimes cantankerous, displays a generous spirit towards those with whom he interacts in the common pursuit of knowledge.

The seventh Socratic Principle to be gleaned from the *Theaetetus* is that when in doubt one should resort to the Socratic Method. The Socratic Method is a means for testing the meaning of a statement prior to affirming the truth of that statement or rejecting the statement as false. It is a method for exploration of logical possibilities. And it is a means for elimination of those possibilities that violate reason, are meaningless, and are absurd. The Socratic Method affirms that reason is the source of common ground for common public discourse and that by going through a process of reasoning with one another, assuming that

---

17   Cornford, 70.

knowledge is possible, progress may be made where there are profound disagreements.

An eighth Socratic principle for public discourse, and with particular application for settling longstanding disputes, is patience in discussion. Not only do we see Socrates patiently pursuing answers to his "what is *X*?" questions in the *Theaetetus*, but Socrates' whole life is a model for the willingness to pursue the answer to difficult questions through the process of long and repeated dialogue. Socrates' discussions did not die with him but persist over 2,300 years after his life. We may learn from the dialogues of Socrates that some difficult topics require time and much discussion before a problem may be resolved. Difficult dialogues require much time, patience, and wisdom before we reach consensus and resolution of the problem at hand. Long-lasting disputes are an indication that we have not adequately identified and addressed the root of our disagreements.

A ninth Socratic principle to be gleaned from reading the *Theaetetus* is that if "man is the measure" is false — both individually and collectively — then individuals or societies are not the determiners of what is Good for the individual or society. If the ground of the Good is not the will of "man," then there must be a standard besides the will of man that determines the Good for individuals, which then may become the common good for society. Reason, as an aspect of human nature, is the standard and ground for what is good for human beings and communities of humans. The use of reason provides meaning for human beings, which is good for human beings. If reason is the standard, and all human beings as rational beings have recourse to reason – fundamentally as the laws of thought — then reason is the common ground for determining good and evil for human beings. Knowing what is good for human nature, and how to pursue what is good for human beings in every decision of life, requires wisdom.

Lastly, a tenth Socratic principle to be inferred from the *Theaetetus* is that reason is the source of wisdom in discourse. Socrates models this wisdom in his method and means for addressing difficult topics. He uses reason, an assumed common ground between himself and his interlocutors, to ask "what does that mean?" prior to declaring the truth or falsehood of any claim. We should be encouraged to ask, "what does that mean?" when in discussion with others. To do so is to attempt to understand, by means of reason, the nature of the subject being discussed. When all parties of the discussion agree to the meaning of the terms being used, they may, like Socrates, proceed to explore implications of making certain claims. Claims which are meaningless may be eliminated. Engaging in meaningless dispute is unwise. Besides, contradictory statements may be eliminated. Socrates often advances a discussion by eliminating what is logically impossible and meaningless. In addition, he uses the *reductio ad absurdum* argument to reduce positions that are often hidden behind fine-sounding statements to the nonsense that they are. His wisdom is shown in knowing how, when, and with whom to engage in discussion. Those interested in engaging in public discourse regarding highly contentious issues ought to study the dialogues of Plato with Socrates as the teacher of wisdom. He demonstrates how to use reason humanely, productively, and skillfully.

In conclusion, the problems of skepticism and relativism, resulting from the dominant epistemology of empiricism today, were prevalent in Socrates' day. Socrates provides us with a model for pursuing knowledge using reason rather than by mere appearances and sensory perception. He argues against the view that "man is the measure," similar to the view that the Good is relative to the individual today. He shows that the view "all is flux" is deeply problematic and leads to skepticism and the lack of any grounding of an "account" for true belief. The view that "all is flux" is different than, but related to, the naturalism of our day, and may have similar implications for the grounding of an "account." Lastly, Socrates provides an argument against the view that "knowledge is perception," which is similar to the dominant epistemology of our day, which assumes that all knowledge is through sensory perception. We may take hope from the example of Socrates and the way in which he addresses these challenges. Progress in public discourse may be made by applying the Socratic Principles gleaned from the *Theaetetus* and by adopting a free Philosophic spirit that is willing to be patient and follow a discussion wherever it may lead with the goal of attaining Truth. Truth, once attained, is the bedrock for the Good and the common Good of the Republic.

Epilogue

Ancient Philosophy's Search for the *Logos* and John's Gospel

"The most incomprehensible thing about the universe is that it is comprehensible" - Einstein.

EVA BRANN, IN *The Logos of Heraclitus*, says that Philosophy begins with the two concepts of *Logos* and being (*ontos*). Brann's thesis seems essentially correct, but one could make the slightly stronger claim that philosophy begins with wondering about the causal connection between *Logos* and being. This chapter argues that Philosophy begins as the search for the *Logos*, but that the search is incomplete until the Prologue to John the Apostle's Gospel. The search for the *Logos* is a search for an explanation of the fit between thinking (or reason) and being. The first philosophers assume an isomorphism between thinking and being, and then they wonder why and how such an isomorphism exists. The explanation of the *Logos*, as an isomorphism between reason and being, is incomplete until the Apostle John introduces the element of Christian Theism and the Trinity. John's Prologue provides the most comprehensive explanation of the *Logos*. Where previous searches for the explanation for the fit between thinking and being came short and resulted in skepticism, John's Gospel successfully explains the isomorphism and provides the key to grasping Truth. His description of the *Logos* is clear, simple, elegant, and full. Where previous philosophers were groping the dark to understand the *Logos*, John's revelation is illuminating. Because of its clear explanation of the *Logos*, and the *Logos* being a fundamental feature of philosophy, John's Gospel continues to have implications for doing philosophy today.

"*Logos*" is multifaceted in meaning that grows and changes over time picking up applications and nuances as philosophers pursue with wonder the relationship between thinking and the world. The first philosophers all recognize an isomorphism between reason (in man)[1] and being in the world. None acknowledge the being of the God of theism. The failure to connect thinking with the being of God will be a source of skepticism in philosophy until John's Gospel supplies the connection between reason, being, and the being of God. Philosophy begins with the search for the *Logos* and the question: Why is the world comprehensible? What is the nature of what can be known and

---

[1] The use of "man" is meant to convey universal humanity as has been used historically.

what is the nature of the knower? Philosophy begins with this wondering.

The original meaning of *logos*, frequently used by Homer, is "collecting and laying down" and "giving an account,"[2] as in telling and relating a tale. Early use of *logos* is associated with speaking, arguing, thinking, reasoning, and writing.[3] In these early uses, *logos* is the "vehicle of human rationality."[4] *Logos* is often viewed as "thought itself as well as the utterance that tells it."[5] *Logos* relates terms and relates magnitudes (*ratios*).[6] Early usage provides a sense of *logos* as the relation between reason and words. What is assumed is that thoughts are about being, and speech expresses thoughts. Thus, *logos* mediates or relates being via speech. Logos relates thoughts in my mind to the mind of another via words. *Logos* in early usage is reason (in the mind) giving an account of being via speech or writing, mediating meaning to the reason of others.

Brann calls Pythagoras (570 - 495 BCE) a "mathematical-philosopher," reserving first "philosopher-philosopher" for Heraclitus (535 - 475 BCE). She strongly believes that Heraclitus was taught, either directly or indirectly, by Pythagoras and that Heraclitus' view of *logos* advances some Pythagorean assumptions. The Pythagorean philosophy consists of a "trinity of the cosmological principles Monad, Dyad, and Harmony, which corresponds on the moral and intellectual level to the trinity of Truth, Goodness, and Beauty. The principle of Harmony, im-

---

2   Brann, Eva. *The Logos of Heraclitus*. (Philadelphia: Paul Dry Books, 2011), p.10.
3   Ibid., p. 10.
4   Ibid.
5   Ibid.
6   Ibid.

manent in the universe, was responsible for the proportional (*analogia*) relation (*logos*) of one thing to the other."[7] Monad (one) represents unity, Dyad (many) diversity, and Harmony is the "relationship (the *ratio, logos*, in proportion, *analogia*) of one thing to another." This relation is "particularly represented by the proportion between numbers, geometrical figures, or tones in the musical scale."[8] Harmony, or *logos*, is immanent in nature and is the bond between the one (Monad) and the many (Dyad). For Pythagoras, the *logos* is an immanent principle that may be apprehended analogically via the senses. Brann says, "the deliverances of our senses are expressible through the *logoi* of our minds."[9] There is a harmonious fit between mind and world, that is, reason is ontological.

The question arises, how do the *logoi* in our minds relate to the "original sensory events?"[10] The Pythagoreans realized that the events of sensory experience could only be related to the sensory world via analogy. They are led to resolving "this dilemma by their difficult doctrine that the sense-world *was* numerical and was *constituted* of numbers and number-relations."[11] The problem for the Pythagoreans seems to be the same that will trouble other pre-Socratic philosophers: Beginning with the assumptions of materialism and empiricism leads to an inability to explain how or why there is a fit between reason and being. The materialist-empiricist foundation is not adequate to rationally justify why there is a *logos*. Why is there a *ratio*? Why

---

7   Hillar, Marian. *From Logos to Trinity: The Evolution of Religious Beliefs from Pythagoras to Tertullian*. (New York: Cambridge University Press, 2012), p. 7.
8   Ibid., p. 8.
9   Brann, p. 33.
10 Ibid., p. 33.
11 Ibid., p. 33.

is there harmony? Pythagoras answers these questions by reducing matter to number.

Heraclitus, assuming the fit between mind and world, explains the fit, not numerically, but by means of Fire.[12] Brann argues that Heraclitus' Fire is an analogy, or *analogia*, ratio-relation or proportion, which is *logos* or *logoi*. Heraclitus thinks all is material and in chaotic flux. This flux is brought to order by means of antagonistic opposition. The opposition is ordered via the *Logos*-Fire. Heraclitus builds upon the *ratio*-relation of Pythagoras. He affirms a fit between all minds (the common) and the world. He thinks the *logos* is common to all men, but that men consistently fail to see the *logos*. Brann conjectures:

> That in pondering what makes the multifarious world one, he began to think about relationality itself and to consider that a logos might fill the bill who was all at once the relater of all relations, beyond and within them, a maker of the world-order and himself in that order, a world-governor, and also the world — a doer, a sayer, and perhaps himself a listener.[13]

It also seems that the "non-sensory *logoi* govern the sensory world."[14] To summarize: *Logos* for Heraclitus is the harmony between thinking and being. There are non-sensory *logoi* that govern the sensible world. The cosmos is governed by Thinking itself, which is fundamentally rational, measurable, capable of *ratio*-relations, and common to all men, but men are deaf to the logos.[15]

---

12   Ibid., p. 34.
13   Ibid., p. 42.
14   Ibid., p. 43.
15   Ibid., p. 43.

Heraclitus sees deficiencies with those who went before him in attempting to ground the *logos* in mythological and technical terms that ultimately fail to explain causation.[16] Heraclitus' philosophy of the *logos* raises similar questions. Is the *logos* an immanent self-governing principle of the world? If so, how did the *logos* come to be in the world? Or is the *logos* a transcendent externally governing divine and personal intelligent being? Brann asks: "Is this Wisdom a 'what' or a 'who?'"[17] Does the *logos* operate as impersonal law organizing the material world? What is the origin of this ratio-relation that provides rational order? Or does the *logos* have another kind of substance? Is *logos* spirit ordering matter? Heraclitus is ambivalent as to whether *logos* is immanent or transcendent, personal or impersonal, matter or spirit.

Protagoras (490-420 BCE), a Sophist expressing skepticism regarding the nature of reality after the failures of first philosophy to ground the *logos* in the material world gets associated with the Heraclitan flux doctrine by later philosophers Plato and Aristotle. Only fragments of Protagoras' work remain. The third fragment from Protagoras concerns the *logoi*. In this fragment, he says: "There are two opposing arguments (*logoi*) concerning everything."[18] Edward Schiappa, in his analysis of the "two-*logoi*" fragment, says: "the important idea of the fragment is that there are two *logoi* in opposition about every "thing.""[19] He argues that Protagoras advances the Heraclitan flux doctrine

16   Ibid., p. 46.
17   Ibid., p. 49.
18   Cohen, S. Marc., Patricia Curd, and C. D. C. Reeve. *Readings in Ancient Greek Philosophy: From Thales to Aristotle*. (Indianapolis: Hackett Pub., 1995), p. 75.
19   Schiappa, Edward. *Protagoras and Logos: A Study in Greek Philosophy and Rhetoric*. (Columbia: University of South Carolina Press, 1991), p. 89.

with this "two-*logoi*" statement. He notes that "Sextus [Empiricus] reports that Protagoras held that "the reasons [*logoi*] of all the appearances [*phainomenon*] subsist in the matter." The two-*logoi*, on Schiappa's interpretation, makes the statement more about metaphysics than about there being two sides to every argument as in a debate. Schiappa makes the case that Plato, in the *Theaetetus*, must have had a similar understanding of Protagoras advancing a Heraclitan metaphysical position and says "when Plato discussed Protagoras' theory of knowledge in the *Theaetetus*, he cited Heraclitus (as well as Empedocles) as someone who would agree with the notion that "if you speak of something as big, it will also appear small; if you speak of it as heavy, it will also appear light; and similarly everything."" Given the quote from Plato, and the connection Schiappa makes between the thinking of Heraclitus and that of Protagoras, the two-*logoi* fragment may be speaking of the relativity of our perception of the physical world.

The two-*logoi* fragment may be taken as either 1) there are two accounts of every position, or 2) metaphysically, there are two oppositional sides to every thing. Schiappa takes the latter reading and states that with the two-*logoi* fragment:

> Heraclitus' opposites in Protagoras' use began to be treated in noncompositional manner, in terms of contrariety and contradiction rather than as strictly opposing forces of nature. Put differently, nature began to be viewed in more abstract logical patterns such as "as-P" and "as-not-P" seeing opposites as essentially linguistic (*logoi*) was a necessary step to a more abstract

conceptualization to their being seen as attributes that can be predicated with respect to "things."[20]

Schiappa seems to suggest that Protagoras' version of the flux doctrine allows for abstract logic to develop. Whereas Pythagoras and Heraclitus were noticing causal laws in nature connected to *logos*, perhaps Protagoras is noticing causal laws in thinking "p" and "non-p." Aristotle later develops the logical aspect of *logos*. Protagoras' two-*logoi* advances our understanding of *logos* in moving us towards abstract conceptualization, but he also leaves us with more questions. If all is flux and there are two oppositional sides to every thing (p and not-p) do these things in flux have any fixed or permanent being? If humans are part of the flux, is there a fixed knower? Do sensations give knowledge of anything if all is flux? Does our language name what *is*? Is language relative to our perception? Does Protagoras' view suggest nominalism? How does reason apply to being given the flux doctrine?

Plato directly addresses these questions in the dialogue *Theaetetus*. In the dialogue, Socrates sees the problem of the first philosophers, particularly Heraclitus, and how these problems result in the skepticism and relativism of Protagoras. Socrates locates the problem of first philosophy in the assumptions of materialism and empiricism. If all matter is in motion, then there is no thing that is permanent. If no thing is permanent, then no thing is fixed and knowable. Furthermore, there is no permanent knower. This is the heart of the skepticism of the Sophists and Protagoras' seeming relativism.

---

20   Ibid., p. 99.

Socrates responds to the metaphysical problem of the flux doctrine by positing a permanence in man via the soul (which has reason, emotion, and will) and by positing permanence in being via the Forms. Socrates responds to the epistemological problems of the flux doctrine (and materialism-empiricism) by defining knowledge as true opinion tied down with a *logos*, or an account. This *logos*-account is by reason and argument that rules out logical impossibilities and arrives at indubitability. Knowledge of reality is by means of *logos*. *Logos* is gained primarily through dialogue - the exchange of reasons between persons through speech. Truth (the way the world *is*) is mediated to people by *logos*. Socratic *logos* is dedicated to truth, and truth is clear, not hidden.[21] The problem with the materialist-empiricist philosophers prior to Socrates is that they attempted to gain knowledge immediately, directly, by means of the senses. Socrates advances our understanding of *logos* by developing its mediating aspect. The senses give us what appears; *logos* mediates what *is*. John Sallis brings out the mediating aspect of *logos* through examining Plato's dialogue *Phaedo* lines 99d-100a2[22]:

> After this, then, when I had failed in investigating beings ... I decided that I must be careful not to suffer the misfortune which happens to people who look at and study the sun during an eclipse. For some of them ruin their eyesight unless they look at its image ... in water or something of the sort. I thought of that danger, and I was afraid my soul would be blinded if I looked at things ... with my eyes and tried to grasp them with

---

21 Sallis, John. *Being and Logos: The Way of Platonic Dialogue.* (Atlantic Highlands: Humanities Press International, Inc., 1975), p. 31.
22 See also the Allegory of the Sun in *Republic* 506c5 - 507e3.

any of my senses. So, I thought I must have recourse to *logoi* and examine in them the truth of beings....[23]

In this section of the *Phaedo*, Socrates explains to his interlocutor why he left the study of the Physicists (materialist-empiricists) and set out on a "second voyage" through dialogue. In this quote light is that by which we see, but we don't look directly at the source of light or we will be blinded. Sallis says there are two courses leading to blindness in the quote:

> One such course is only hinted at through the analogy Socrates uses, namely, that course on which one would so elevate his vision as to seek to look directly at the sun, that is, at what makes it possible for things to be visible, or, more fundamentally, at what lets things be manifest as such ... it is primarily the light and not its source that is available to one's view.[24]

Sallis goes on to say that:

> The primary reference of Socrates' statement is, however, not to a course on which one would gaze at the sun but to a course on which one would remain completely attached to the visible things and would attempt to grasp them by the senses alone, oblivious to that source and even that illumination that lets them be manifest. Here too is blindness.[25]

Immediate propositional knowledge is impossible. Direct illumination, as in mystical experience, and immediate contact with

---
23 Sallis, p. 40-41.
24 Ibid., p. 41.
25 Ibid.

sensory data both fail to deliver objective knowledge, but rather end in blindness. The only way to have objective, propositional knowledge is mediation through the *logos*. *Logos* is like light. Light is mediator between the sun and the things illuminated. *Logos* is to reason what the sun is to the eyes. *Logos* is that by which we understand being. *Logos* makes manifest (to the understanding) what *is*.[26] Speaking (*logos*) makes manifest what is inward in thought.[27] *Logos* makes manifest what *is*, and what *is* is Truth. *Logos* brings Truth to light.[28] Socrates addresses the problems of first-Philosophy by bringing in a permanent soul in humans and permanent forms to order being. The dualism of Plato answers some of the problems of first-Philosophy, but it raises new questions: If matter is eternal, is it self-maintaining? Is Plato's Demiurge personal? Is it eternal or created? What is the ontological nature of the forms?

Aristotle (384 - 322 BCE) attempts to answer some of the objections to Platonic dualism by proposing a dependent dualism and eliminating the Forms as independent realities apart from the material world. Spirit is pure actuality, and matter is pure potentiality. Pure actuality forms the cosmos — the Unmoved Mover, who is spirit — actualizing pure potentiality (matter without form). The Unmoved Mover gives form to pure potentiality.[29] The formal cause is one sense of *logos* for Aristotle. Omer Aygün notes that *Logos* has been under-appreciated in Aristotle and that there have been scant studies on his understanding of *logos* because, contrary to previous philosophers,

---

26   Ibid., p. 50.
27   Ibid., p. 54.
28   Ibid., p. 57.
29   Gangadean, Surrendra. *Philosophical Foundation: A Critical Analysis of Basic Beliefs*. (Lanham: University Press of America, 2008), p. 94.

logos is mundane in Aristotle. Aygün finds four senses of *logos* in Aristotle: it is a standard, a ratio, reason, and speech. Human beings alone have *logos* as reason and speech. All of nature has *logos* as standard and ratio.

Socrates describes thinking as dialogue (*logos*) with oneself and was looking for *logoi* that would tie down true opinion and deliver certainty. Aristotle extends this dialogue/ discourse with nature and with the social and political worlds. Dialogue provides principles which are probable or "more than likely" but not certain. This dialogue with nature is a kind of Socratic dialectic, an interrogation, and questioning that yields probabilistic principles — or the *logos* — by which nature operates. This is science. The dialectical method may also be applied to Ethics in order to discover the *logos*, or principles, of social and political order. We see in this dialectical approach of Socrates-Plato-Aristotle a method by which man engages his mind (reason) to what appears (senses, opinions) in a questioning and interrogation until he figures out what it *is* — its nature, its *logos*. The *logos* in man identifies the *logos* in the world. Yet, how is this possible? What is the origin of this fit of *logos* in the mind with *logos* in the world?

Aygün says that *logos* for Aristotle is not divine. Aristotle preserves "*nous*" for the divine.[30] Stoic philosophers (330's BCE - 30's CE), on the other hand, will call the *Logos*, or the Word, divine. Stoic philosophy covers approximately 300 years, and views about the *logos* vary from philosopher to philosopher within the Stoic camp, but Marian Hillar provides us with a summary of what may be gleaned from Stoic philosophy con-

---

30   Aygün, Ömer. *The Middle Included: Logos in Aristotle*. (Evanston: Northwestern University Press, 2017), p. 209.

cerning the *logos*. Hillar notes that *logos* is "the power or principle that shapes and creates all things from itself ... [and] is immanent in the existing world."[31] For something to exist, in Stoic metaphysics, it must have a body. Mind is corporeal in Stoicism. *Logos* is analogous with *pneuma*, heat or breath, by which things are alive. *Pneuma* "became the vehicle of the *logos*"[32] for the Stoics. The *Logos* is "the Soul of the world, Mind and Nature, Nature, God. Nature is an artistic or creative fire, and thus God is the seminal *Logos* of the universe."[33] Hillar says that:

> The *pneuma*, though corporeal, is not matter itself. *Pneuma*, unlike other elements, pervades the universe and establishes the individual parts of it. It gives coherence and holds together other elements, unites the center of the universe with its circumference, and prevents the universe from collapsing under the heavy pull of its heavy constituents.[34]

There is a moral aspect to *logos* that manifests as "Natural law, Necessity, and Destiny. It functions at the macrocosmic and microcosmic levels as God, Providence, Craftsman, and the "right reason" at the moral level."[35] Lastly, *logos* is the "particular nature *physis*," or soul of a thing. The human soul is an "'offshoot' of the divine *logos*."[36] The *logos* for the Stoics appears to be largely impersonal, immanent, and though not identical with matter is an aspect of the material world. The *logos* is in the mind, in

---

31 Hillar, p. 34.
32 Ibid., p. 34.
33 Ibid.
34 Ibid.
35 Ibid.
36 Ibid., p. 35.

the world, and is divine. What does it mean for the *logos* to be divine? Is it spirit (but all that exists has a body for the Stoics)? Is it personal?

Philo of Alexandria (20 BCE - 50 CE) is a transitional figure between the Hellenic and Christian worlds. He is a Jewish philosopher who attempts to synthesize Judaism, Stoicism, Aristotelian Logic and Ethics, and Pythagoreanism. Hillar says:

> Philo's doctrine of the Logos is blurred by his mystical and religious vision, but his Logos is clearly the second individual in one God as a hypostatization of God's Creative Power, Wisdom. The supreme is God, and next is Wisdom or the Logos of God ... Earthly wisdom is but a copy of this celestial Wisdom ... This Logos is apportioned into an infinite number of parts in humans; thus, we impart the divine Logos. As a result, we acquire some likeness to the Father and the Creator of all.
>
> The Logos is the Bond of the universe and mediator extended in nature. The Father eternally begat the Logos and constituted it as an unbreakable bond of the universe that produces harmony. The Logos, mediating between God and the world, is neither uncreated as God nor created as men. So, in Philo's view, the Father is the supreme Being and the Logos, as his chief messenger, stands between Creator and creature. The Logos is an ambassador and suppliant, neither unbegotten nor begotten as are sensible things.[37]

---

37 Hillar, p. 69-70.

Philo's conception of *logos* is multifaceted. His metaphysics is theistic but verges on pantheism. His epistemology tends to be mystical and fideistic. He advances the search for the *Logos* beyond his predecessors by grounding the *logos* in a personal God. The Father God eternally begat the *Logos* in Philo's philosophy. In addition, the *Logos* is mediator between God and the World, and between the Creator and creature. Philo's philosophy moves us closer to John's Prologue. Before moving on to the Prologue, let us wrap up the ancient philosopher's search for the *logos*.

The era of first philosophy ends with skepticism and Sophism due to the failure to adequately ground the *logos*. Skepticism follows upon the inability of the Academics (Platonists) and Peripatetics (Aristotelians) to ground the *logos* (either in the Forms or the world via causes). The Stoics are skeptics, sharing similar materialist-empiricist assumptions of the first philosophers. Philo's mysticism is fideistic and does not provide objective knowledge of *logos* or being. What began as the search for the Truth, knowledge of ultimate reality ends in skepticism for philosophy up to John the Apostle's day. The skepticism is a result of epistemological and metaphysical assumptions that do not accord with the *Logos*. *Logos* cannot be grasped merely by the senses (Socrates blindness), nor can it be seen directly (Philo's mystical vision is Socrates other source of blindness). The *Logos* also cannot be merely material (as Socrates shows in the *Theaetetus*). What can we take from the first philosopher's search for the Truth?

The first philosophers, in the search for the *Logos*, are discovering truth. They discover truth in just the way one would expect — through wondering about the world and reasoning to the cause of its comprehensibility. Truth is truth no matter its source, but our grasp of truth may be incomplete. John's account gives a more complete account of the truth about the *Logos*. It also leaves room for an ever-deepening understanding of that Truth. The history of philosophy is a story of partial truths often ending in the dead-end roads of skepticism and fideism. Partial truths are partially satisfying, but it is Truth in its fullness that is ultimately satisfying. Philosophy is the search for Truth and begins with the twin concepts of *logos* and *ontos* — reason and being — the first philosophers believed there is an isomorphism between thought and being. This was half of the truth. John's Gospel provides the fullness of Truth by grounding the *Logos* in the being of God.

John the Apostle's Gospel (6 - 100 CE), particularly the Prologue, may be viewed as a response to the philosophical search for the *Logos*. John's account of *Logos* not only assumes that reason is ontological, but he also assumes a theistic, Trinitarian, view of God. This combination supplies what is missing in the previous philosophies. Surrendra Gangadean, in his *The Word of God*[38], recognizes a seven-fold doctrine of the *Logos* in John's Gospel. We will examine each aspect, connecting each to the prior search. In doing so, we will see how John's *Logos* doctrine advances our understanding of *Logos* beyond what has gone before. Keeping in mind the original sense of *logos* as "relating," and as Socrates' "mediating" light, we can see in each sense of *Logos* in the Prologue, that the *Logos* is mediator. John's focus, as the previous search, is on Truth. The Word/ *Logos* is Truth. Truth is rational, cognitive (propositional), mediated,

---

38 Gangadean, Surrendra. *The Word of God: The Logos is Truth*. Logos Paper #30, 2016. Accessed 4/9/2018: http://thelogospapers.com/30-the-word-of-god-the-logos-is-truth/.

corresponds with reality (*analogia*), and is revealed by God (intentionally, necessarily, and exclusively).

John's Gospel is universal in its audience. The Prologue sets the stage for doing philosophy through understanding the *Logos* as Creator, the *Logos* in man as reason, and the Logos in the created order through natural and moral law. These topics are in the realm of general revelation, and in this respect, Heraclitus was right, the *Logos* is common to all men, and Socrates is correct, the *Logos* is not hidden. Because the *Logos* is in man as reason, and in the world as natural and moral law, man can infer from the things that are made the *Logos* as Creator. However, as Heraclitus noticed, though the *Logos* is common, men are blind to the *Logos*. The history of philosophy shows that mistaken assumptions about the nature of reality is the source of this blindness to the *Logos*. The *Logos* comes to man through the prophets, the written *Logos*, and ultimately comes incarnate to redeem man from his spiritual blindness. John's *Logos* doctrine thus sets the stage for doing theology as well as doing philosophy.

John 1: 1 says "In the beginning was the [*Logos*], and the [*Logos*] was with God, and the [*Logos*] was God. He was with God in the beginning."[39] The *Logos* is eternal, was with God in the beginning, and thus is Creator. All things are made through the *Logos* (John 1:3). The *Logos* is personal and is the second person of the Trinity. In contrast, the first philosophers thought matter was eternal. Matter alone could not ground the *Logos*. Socrates-Plato-Aristotle thought matter and spirit were both eternal but failed to ground the *Logos*. The Stoics returned to materialism (and resulting skepticism), which again failed to ground the *Logos*. John grounds the *Logos* in the being of God.

---

39 All scriptural references are from Holy Bible. *New International Version*. (Grand Rapids: Zondervan Publishing House,1984).

John 1:4 says "In him was life, and that life was the light of men. The light shines in the darkness, but the darkness has not understood it." The *Logos* is in man as light — that by which we understand meaning and see truth — the light is reason. Almost all of the ancient Greeks would acknowledge the *logos* in man as reason. Heraclitus saw (though dimly) that the *logos* is clear and common to all men (light), but men were blind to the *logos* (darkness). Socrates gave us the analogy of light and sight. Reason is that by which we understand. In Christian theism, the *Logos* is in human beings as made in the image of God. Gangadean says: "The life of the Word is the light of men."[40] God has created man such that men can understand the revelation of God in the created order and the scriptures. The light of man is later called "the light of nature." This is general revelation and philosophy.

John 1:10 says: "He was in the world, and though the world was made through him, the world did not recognize him." The *Logos* is common to all, but all do not see the *Logos*. Gangadean interprets this passage to mean that "The Word of God is revealed in all his works of creation and providence. The whole earth is full of his glory. Yet no one seeks, and no one understands what is clear about God."[41] The *Logos* is in the world as the natures of things and as the moral law by which men live. Almost all of the Greeks saw the *logos* in the world, as well as the fit between man's reason and the world. Yet none of them connected the *Logos* to God the Creator. Given the Biblical worldview of Creation-Fall-Redemption, this is not surprising but is part of the fallen condition of man. Worldly philosophy is affected by the fall.

---

40 Gangadean, Logos Paper
41 Ibid.

John 1:11 says: "He came to that which was his own, but his own did not receive him" and again, John 1:6 "There came a man who was sent from God; his name was John. He came as a witness to testify concerning that light so that through him all men might believe." His own were the chosen people of God. John was the last in a long line of prophets bringing the spoken word of God. The *Logos* is the Word of God spoken and then written as scripture, as special revelation, redemptive revelation. Gangadean says that "The Word of God came to the covenant people of God in history through the prophets. The prophets were not received, but their word became Scripture, the Word of God written."[42] The Greeks recognize *logos* as both spoken and written speech, but they could not anticipate the redemptive revelation given by God to the Hebrew prophets. In this respect, John's Gospel provides something unique and far beyond what the ancients understood regarding the *Logos*. The redemptive revelation of God — God's self-revelation known through divine transmission — written as scripture, is the *Logos* of God that is the basis of Theology.

John 1:14 says: "The [*Logos*] became flesh and made his dwelling among us. We have seen his glory, the glory of the One and Only, who came from the Father, full of grace and truth." Gangadean says of this passage that the *Logos* "is the lamb of God who takes away the sin of the world. He is the risen Lord who rules to make God known."[43] The *Logos* is incarnate — as Christ — who rules and redeems by means of Truth. This is the truly unique revelation of the Christian scriptures. It comes as the fulfillment of the promise of the Hebrew Scriptures after

---

42 Ibid.
43 Ibid.

the creation and fall. God himself comes in the flesh to reveal the truth of God's infinite justice and mercy. The *Logos* incarnate comes to redeem mankind, to make all things new, and to fill everything in every way. This is the truth that is only known by God in Christian revelation.

John 16:13 says that "he [the *Logos*] will guide you into all Truth." Gangadean interprets: "Christ the Lord sends the Spirit to lead the Church into all Truth." This truth is "the historically cumulative insight summed up in the Church's Creed and Confessions [it] is the holy, catholic and apostolic faith, the basis of the unity of the faith for all who believe."[44] The *Logos* is leading the Church into all Truth via the Spirit of Truth.

Lastly, 1 Peter 1:23 and John 17:17 affirm that the *Logos* is leading each believer, via restoration through the Spirit, to the full use of reason to understand Truth. 1 Peter 1:23 says: "For you have been born again, not of perishable seed, but of imperishable, through the living and enduring word [*Logos*] of God. The *Logos* is the life of man through spiritual rebirth. Again, John 17:17: "Sanctify them by the truth; your word [*Logos*] is truth." Those who have been justified are sanctified by the truth of God, which is the *Logos* of God in all of its fullness. Gangadean says: "The Word of God is in each believer by the work of the Holy Spirit. Each believer is born again by the living Word of God .... Each believer is sanctified by the Truth. The Word of God (the *Logos*) is Truth ...."[45] The *Logos* of God is robust and life-giving. The *Logos* is common and clear to all men (Romans 1:20), but men in their unbelief rejected the *Logos* at every level. Yet, the *Logos* is full of Grace and Truth and does not leave man

---

44 Ibid.
45 Ibid.

in his fallen condition but restores him to the use of reason and the light of Truth. John's *Logos* doctrine is a summary statement of the fundamentals of both philosophy (general revelation) and theology (special revelation). John demonstrates that the mind of man is well suited to understand the nature of the revelation of the *Logos* in the world as created, and the *Logos* in the scriptures as the means of redemption. The *Logos* is Truth in its fullness and man was made for knowledge of the *Logos* in its fullness. The *Logos* is the source of light and life.

Bibliography

Anderson, Owen. *The Clarity of God's Existence: The Ethics of Belief After the Enlightenment*. Oregon: Wipf & Stock, 2008.

———. *The Natural Moral Law: The Good After Modernity*. New York: Cambridge University Press, 2012.

Aristotle, and Jonathan Barnes. *The Complete Works of Aristotle: The Revised Oxford Translation*. Princeton: Princeton University Press, 1984.

Asad, Talal. *Formations of the Secular: Christianity, Islam, Modernity*. Stanford: Stanford University Press, 2003.

———. *Genealogies of Religion: Discipline and Reasons of Power in Christianity and Islam*. Baltimore: Johns Hopkins University Press, 1993.

Association of American Colleges and Universities. "A Crucible Moment." Accessed 3/17/2017. https://www.aacu.org/sites/default/files/files/crucible/Crucible_508F.pdf

Ayer, A.J. *Language, Truth, and Logic*. New York: Dover, 1952.

Aygün, Ömer. *The Middle Included: Logos in Aristotle*. Evanston: Northwestern University Press, 2017.

Babich, B. (ed). *Nietzsche, Theories of Knowledge, and Critical Theory: Nietzsche and the Sciences I*. Kurt Rudolf Fischer. "Nietzsche and the Vienna Circle." Kluwer Academic Publishers, 1999, 119-128.

Barnes, Jonathan. *The Presocratic Philosophers*. London: Routledge and Paul, 1979.

Baynes, Kenneth, James Bohman, and Thomas McCarthy. *After Philosophy: End or Transformation?* Cambridge: The MIT Press, 1987.

Bloom, Harold. *The Closing of the American Mind*. New York: Touchstone, 1987.

BonJour, Laurence. *In Defense of Pure Reason: A Rationalist Account of* A Priori *Justification*. Cambridge: Cambridge University Press, 1998.

Brann, Eva T. H. *The Logos of Heraclitus: The First Philosopher of the West on Its Most Interesting Term*. Philadelphia: Paul Dry Books, 2011.

_____. "Pre-Socratics or First Philosophers?" *The Imaginative Conservative*, January 26, 2016. Accessed 3/16/2016.

http://www.theimaginativeconservative.org/2016/01/pre-socratics-or-first-philophers.html

Carnap, Rudolph, trans. Arthur Pap. "The Elimination of Metaphysics Through Logical Analysis of Language." Originally published in *Erkenntnis*, Vol. II, 1932.

Castle, Alfred. "Dewey and Nietzsche: Their Instrumentalism Compared." *Wisconsin Academy of Sciences, Arts and Letters*. Vol. 65 (1977): 67-85.

Cohen, S. Marc., Patricia Curd, and C. D. C. Reeve. *Readings in Ancient Greek Philosophy: From Thales to Aristotle*. Indianapolis: Hackett Pub., 1995.

DePoe, John M. "Knowledge by Acquaintance and Knowledge by Description." Accessed 4/14/2014. http://www.iep.utm.edu/knowacq/

Derrida, Jacques, and Barbara Johnson. *Dissemination*. Chicago: University of Chicago Press, 1981.

_____, and Gayatari Chankravorty Spivak. *Of Grammatology*. Baltimore: Johns Hopkins University Press, 2016.

_____. "Structure, Sign, and Play in the Discourse of the Human Sciences," 1970. Accessed 3/18/2017. http://www.csudh.edu/ccauthen/576f13/drrdassp.pdf

Desjardins, Rosemary. *The Rational Enterprise: Logos in Plato's Theaetetus*. Albany: State University of New York Press, 1990.

Dewey, John. *Education and Experience.* Accessed 3/16/2017. https://archive.org/details/ExperienceAndEducation.

_____. In *The Philosophy of John Dewey*, edited by Joseph Ratner. New York: Henry Holt and Company, 1928.

_____. *The Public and its Problems.* Athens: Ohio University Press, 1928.

Dickstein, Morris (ed.). *The Revival of Pragmatism: New Essays on Social Thought, Law, and Culture.* Richard Rorty. "What Difference does Pragmatism Make? The View from Philosophy." Durham: Duke University Press, 1998. Accessed 3/31/2017. http://www.nytimes.com/books/first/d/dickstein-pragmatism.html

Dretske, Fred. "Gettier and Justified True Belief: 50 Years On." Accessed 2/28/2017. http://www.philosophersmag.com/index.php/tpm-mag-articles/11-essays/10-gettier-and-justified-true-belief-50-years-on

Dummett, Michael. *Origins of Analytical Philosophy.* Cambridge: Harvard University Press, 1998.

Fabbrichesi, Rossella. "The Body of the Community: Peirce, Royce, and Nietzsche." *European Journal of Pragmatism and American Philosophy*, 2009.

Fine, Gail. *Plato on Knowledge and Forms: Selected Essays.* New York: Oxford University Press, 2003.

Fitzsimmons, Kelly. *Plantinga on Justification, Warrant, and the Proper Function of our Rational Faculties.* Master's Thesis, Arizona State University, 2000.

Foucault, Michel, and A.M. Sheridan Smith. *The Archaeology of Knowledge and the Discourse of Language*. New York: Pantheon Books, 1972.

———, and Alan Sheridan. *Discipline and Punish: The Birth of the Prison*. New York: Vintage Books, 1977.

———, and Richard Howard. *Madness and Civilization: A History of Insanity in the Age of Reason*. New York: Vintage Books, 1964.

Friedrich, Rainer. "The Enlightenment Gone Mad (I): The Dismal Discourse Of Postmodernism's Grand Narratives." *Arion Arion: A Journal of Humanities and the Classics* 19, no. 3 (2012): 31-78. Accessed 3/18/2017. doi:10.2307/arion.19.3.0031.

———. "The Enlightenment Gone Mad (II): The Dismal Discourse of Postmodernism's Grand Narratives." *Arion: A Journal of Humanities and the Classics* 20, no. 1 (07 2012): 67-112. Accessed 3/18/2017 doi:10.2307/arion.20.1.0067.

Gangadean, Surrendra. "Common Ground." Logos Paper #2. Accessed 3/24/2017. http://thelogospapers.com/2-common-ground/.

———. *The Word of God: The Logos is Truth*. Logos Paper #30, 2016. Accessed 4/9/2018: http://thelogospapers.com/30-the-word-of-god-the-logos-is-truth/ .

———. *Philosophical Foundation: A Critical Analysis of Basic Beliefs*. Lanham: University Press of America, 2008.

Gettier, Edmund J. "Is Justified True Belief Knowledge?" *Analysis*. Vol. 23 No. 6 (1963): 121-123.

Goodman, Nelson. *Fact, Fiction and Forecast*. Cambridge: Harvard University Press, 1983.

Gonzalez, Justo L. *A History of Christian Thought: From the Protestant Reformation to the Twentieth Century*, Vol. III, Revised Edition. Nashville: Abingdon Press, 1975.

Goodman, Nelson. *Fact, Fiction and Forecast*. Cambridge: Harvard University Press, 1983.

Guthrie, W. K. C. *History of Greek Philosophy: The Presocratic Tradition from Parmenides to Democritus, Vol. 2*. Cambridge: Cambridge University Press, 1965.

_____. *The Sophists*. London: Cambridge University Press, 1971.

_____. *A History of Greek Philosophy: The Earlier Presocratics and the Pythagoreans, Vol. 1*. Cambridge: University Press, 1962.

Habermas, Jurgen, and Frederick G. Lawrence. *The Philosophical Discourse of Modernity*. Cambridge: The MIT Press, 1992.

Heidegger, Martin, ed. David Farrell Krell. *Nietzsche: Vol. I The Will to Power and Art*. San Francisco: Harper One, 1991.

_____. *Nietzsche: Vol. II The Eternal Recurrence of the Same*. San Francisco: Harper One, 1991.

_____. *Nietzsche Vol. III The Will to Power as Knowledge and as Metaphysics*. San Francisco: Harper One, 1991.

_____. *Nietzsche: Vol. IV Nihilism.* San Francisco: Harper One, 1991.

_____, trans. William Lovitt. *The Question Concerning Technology and Other Essays.* New York: Garland Publishing, Inc., 1977.

Heller, Erich. *The Importance of Nietzsche: Ten Essays.* Chicago: Chicago University Press, 1988.

Hetherington. Stephen. "Gettier Problems." Internet Encyclopedia of Philosophy. Accessed 3/31/2017. http://www.iep.utm.edu/gettier/#H4

_____. "Knowledge." Internet Encyclopedia of Philosophy. Accessed 4/14/2017. http://www.iep.utm.edu/knowledg/

Hillar, Marian. *From Logos to Trinity: The Evolution of Religious Beliefs from Pythagoras to Tertullian.* New York: Cambridge University Press, 2012.

Hoitenga, Jr., Dewey J. *Faith and Reason from Plato to Plantinga: An Introduction to Reformed Epistemology.* New York: State University of New York, 1991.

Holy Bible. *New International Version.* Grand Rapids: Zondervan Publishing House, 1984.

Inwood, Brad, ed. *Cambridge Companion to the Stoics.* Cambridge: Cambridge University Press, 2003. "Stoic Natural Philosophy (Physics and Cosmology)," Michael White.

James, William. *Essays in Pragmatism.* New York: Hafner Press, 1948.

———. "Remarks on Spencer's Definition of Mind as Correspondence." *The Journal of Speculative Philosophy*, Vol. 12, No. 1 (1878): 1-18.

Kaufmann, Walter. *Nietzsche: Philosopher, Psychologist, Antichrist.* New York: Meridian Books, 1950.

Klossowski, Pierre, trans. Daniel W. Smith. *Nietzsche and the Vicious Circle.* Chicago: University of Chicago Press, 1997.

Kolak, Daniel and Garrett Thomson (eds.). *The Longman Standard History of Philosophy.* New York: Pearson Longman, 2006.

Koons, Robert C., and George Beeler. *The Waning of Materialism.* Oxford: Oxford University Press, 2013.

Lee, Mi-Kyoung. *Epistemology after Protagoras: Responses to Relativism in Plato, Aristotle, and Democritus.* Oxford: Clarendon Press, 2005.

Liddell and Scott. *An Intermediate Greek-English Lexicon.* Oxford: Clarendon Press, 1995.

Locke, John. *An Essay Concerning Human Understanding.* New York: Clarendon Press, 1975.

Masuzawa, Tomoko. *The Invention of World Religions: Or, How European Universalism was Preserved in the Language of Pluralism.* Chicago: University of Chicago Press, 2005.

McCall, Raymond J. *Basic Logic: The Fundamental Principles of Formal Deductive Reasoning.* New York: Barnes and Noble Books, 1952.

McDermid, Douglas. "Pragmatism." Accessed 3/16/2017. http://www.iep.utm.edu/pragmati/

Menand, Louis, Paul Reitter, and Chad Wellmon. *The Rise of the Research University: A Sourcebook*. Chicago: The University of Chicago Press, 2017.

Meyer, Matthew. "Metaphysics of Entanglement." Accessed 7/7/2016. http://www.metaphysics-of-entanglement.ox-.ac.uk/

_____. *Reading Nietzsche through the Ancients: An Analysis of Becoming, Perspectivism, and the Principle of Non-contradiction*. Boston: De Gruyter, 2014.

National Association of Scholars. "Making Citizens: How American Universities Teach Civics." Accessed 3/17/2017. https://www.nas.org/images/documents/NAS_making-Citizens_fullReport.pdf

Nelson, Alan, ed. *A Companion to Rationalism*. West Sussex: Wiley-Blackwell Publishing, Ltd., 2013.

Nietzsche, Friedrich Wilhelm, Rolf-Peter Horstmann, and Judith Norman. *Beyond Good and Evil: Prelude to a Philosophy of the Future*. Cambridge: Cambridge University Press, 2002.

_____, and Sander L. Gilman, Carole Blair, and David J. Parent. *Friedrich Nietzsche on Rhetoric and Language*. New York: Oxford University Press, 1989.

———, and R. J. Hollingdale, and Richard Schacht. *Nietzsche: Human, All Too Human: A Book for Free Spirits*. Cambridge: Cambridge University Press, 1996.

———, and Marianne Cowan. *Philosophy in the Tragic Age of the Greeks*. Lanham: Regnery Publishing, Inc. 1962.

———, and Aaron Ridley, and Judith Norman. *The Anti-Christ, Ecce Homo, Twilight of the Idols, and Other Writings*. New York: Cambridge University Press, 2005.

———, and Francis Golffing. *The Birth of Tragedy and the Genealogy of Morals*. New York: Anchor Books, 1956.

———, and Bernard Williams. *The Gay Science*. New York: Cambridge University Press, 2001.

———, and Walter Arnold Kaufmann. *The Portable Nietzsche*. New York: Viking Press, 1954.

———, and Greg Whitlock. *The Pre-Platonic Philosophers*. Urbana: University of Illinois Press, 2001.

———, and Walter Arnold Kaufmann, and R. J. Hollingdale. *The Will to Power*. New York: Random House, 1967.

O'Boyle, Lenore. "Learning for Its Own Sake: The German University as Nineteenth-Century Model." *Comparative Studies in Society and History*, Vol. 25, No. 1 (1983): 3-25.

Ophuijsen, Johannes M. Van, Marjolein Van Raalte, and Peter Stork. *Protagoras of Abdera: The Man, His Measure*. Leiden: Brill, 2013.

Plantinga, Alvin. *Warrant and Proper Function*. New York: Oxford University Press, 1993.

_____. *Warrant: The Current Debate*. New York: Oxford University Press, 1993.

_____. *Warranted Christian Belief*. New York: Oxford University Press, 2000.

Plato, John M. Cooper, and D. S. Hutchinson. *Complete Works*. Indianapolis, IN: Hackett Pub., 1997.

_____, and Francis Macdonald Cornford. *Plato's Theory of Knowledge; the Theaetetus and the Sophist of Plato*. New York: Liberal Arts Press, 1957.

_____, and H.N. Fowler. *Plato VII Theaetetus and Sophist*. Cambridge: Harvard University Press, 1977.

_____, and Seth Benardete. *The Being of the Beautiful: Plato's Theaetetus, Sophist, and Statesman*. Chicago: University of Chicago Press, 1984.

Poston, Ted. "Internalism and Externalism in Epistemology." Internet Encyclopedia of Philosophy. Accessed 3/31/2017. http://www.iep.utm.edu/int-ext/#SH3c.

Rainbow, Paul (ed.). *The Foucault Reader*. New York: Pantheon Books, 1984.

Rajchman, John. and Cornel West (eds). *Post-Analytic Philosophy*. New York: Columbia University Press, 1985.

Ratner-Rosenhagen, Jennifer. *American Nietzsche: A History of an Icon and His Ideas.* Chicago: University of Chicago Press, 2012.

Rawls, John. *Political Liberalism.* New York: Columbia University Press, 1993.

Rorty, Richard. *Achieving Our Country: Leftist Thought in Twentieth-Century America.* Cambridge: Harvard University Press, 1998.

_____. *Essays on Heidegger and Others: Philosophical Papers Volume 2.* New York: Cambridge University Press, 1991.

_____. *Philosophy and the Mirror of Nature.* Princeton: Princeton University Press, 1979.

_____. *The Linguistic Turn: Essays in Philosophical Method.* Chicago: University of Chicago Press, 1992.

Russell, Bertrand. *A History of Western Philosophy: And Its Connection with Political and Social Circumstances from the Earliest Times to the Present Day.* New York: Simon and Schuster, 1945.

Sallis, John. *Being and Logos; the Way of Platonic Dialogue.* Pittsburgh: Duquesne University Press; Distributed by Humanities Press, Atlantic Highlands N.J., 1975.

Scherer, Michael. "Is Truth Dead?" Time Magazine, March 22, 2017. Accessed 3/31/2017. http://time.com/4710614/donald-trump-fbi-surveillance-house-intelligence-committee/

Schiappa, Edward. *Protagoras and Logos: A Study in Greek Philosophy and Rhetoric*. Columbia: University of South Carolina Press, 1991.

Sellars, Wilfrid. "Empiricism and the Philosophy of Mind." Accessed 3/13/2017. http://selfpace.uconn.edu/class/percep/SellarsEmpPhilMind.pdf

Smith, Christian. *The Secular Revolution: Power, Interests, and Conflict in the Secularization of American Public Life*. Berkeley: University of California Press, 2003.

Taylor, Charles. *A Secular Age*. Cambridge: The Belknap Press of Harvard University Press, 2007.

Uebel, Th.E. *Rediscovering the Forgotten Vienna Circle: Austrian Studies on Otto Neurath and the Vienna Circle. Vol 133 of Boston Studies in the Philosophy and History of Science*. New York: Springer Science & Business Media, 2012.

Wheelwright, Philip Ellis. *The Presocratics*. New York: Odyssey Press, 1966.

Wittgenstein, Ludwig. *Tractatus Logico-Philosophicus*. New York: Barnes and Noble, 2003.

Wolin, Richard. *The Seduction of Unreason: The Intellectual Romance With Fascism From Nietzsche to Postmodernism*. Princeton: Princeton University Press, 2004.

Zuckert, Catherine H. "Nietzsche's Rereading of Plato." *Political Theory* 13, no. 2 (1985): 213-38.

———. *Plato's Philosophers: The Coherence of the Dialogues.* Chicago: University of Chicago Press, 2009.

———. *Postmodern Platos: Nietzsche, Heidegger, Gadamer, Strauss, Derrida.* Chicago: Univ. of Chicago Press, 1996

Index

a posteriori, 36-37, 224
a priori, 36-40, 133-134, 162-164, 236-237, 282n.
    commitment, 267
    innate, 121
    and Plato, 121
    truths, 224
Academy, the, 10, 12-15, 75, 204, 255, 281, 283
    authority within, 131
    German model, 248
    as location for public philosophy, 281
    Nietzsche and, 207
    philosophers of, 271
    and skepticism, 43
account, 17, 19, 25, 26n., 50
    giving an, 102, 125, 140, 151-153, 294, 300
    and logos, 57, 61, 76, 129
    philosophical, 212
    and skepticism, 291-292
    tie down with, 123-124, 225
    true opinion with, 32, 34, 36, 44, 103-107, 156-160, 283-286
    two accounts, 298. See also *Logos*
Allegory of the Cave, 113, 119-121, 145, 205, 243, 270-272. *See also* Plato
Allegory of the Line, 113, 116-120, 121, 127, 142-144, 270. *See also* Plato
Allegory of the Sun, 113, 114-116, 119-120, 196, 300-302. *See also* Plato
Analytic Philosophy, 204, 212-219

final phase of, 225
and linguistic analysis, 268
and linguistic turn, 270
and Plato's Craftsmen, 270
and post-analytic, 222
postpositivistic, 136
and Pragmatism, 222, 250
second phase of, 225
and Vienna Circle, 208, 212.
See also Philosophy
analytic tradition 135, 139
Anderson, Owen, 34n., 286n.
anti-logos, 185
    of Nietzsche, 147, 150, 171-172, 185
    philosophy, 41-42, 271
    and Protagoras, 71
anti-materialist, 111, 191-193
anti-realism, 81, 136n.
Apostle John, 35, 46, 269, 292-293
    Gospel, 46
    and Prologue, 46, 306
    and the *Logos*, 306-312
appearance(s), 55, 58, 73, 90, 106, 298
    changing, 86, 124
    immediate, 92
    intuitive, 173
    mere, 133, 291
    realm of, 120
argument:
    a priori, 36, 38, 40
    and deductive, 129, 220
    and dialogue, 156, 286
    circular, 283
    inductive, 36
    logical proof, 143

and logos, 106, 126
reason and, 91, 105, 284-285, 300
and *reductio ad absurdum*, 88, 99, 102, 127, 290
silenced through, 19, 25
and syllogism, 127
third act of the mind, 160, 171
tied down, 127
two opposing, 73, 297-298
Aristotle, 44, 302
    and deductive reasoning, 160
    and first philosophers, 55-56, 58
    and law of non-contradiction, 160-170
    and laws of thought, 17, 153, 159, 189
    and *logos*, 303
    Metaphysics, 19, 41, 163-170
    on negative proof for LNC, 163-170
    and objections to Platonism 302
    Organon, 159
    and realism, 21
    and reason as ontological, 18, 156
    and skepticism, 20, 49
atheist, 14, 33, 145
Atomists, 20, 55-60, 78-79
Ayer, AJ, 138, 248n.
    and "Myth of the Given," 222
Bacon, Francis, 202
Bataille, Georges, 203
belief, 18, 22, 76

defeaters to, 30
degrees of, 30, 121
ethics of, 34
and evidence for, 17, 28
justified true, 25-28, 31-32, 104, 107-108, 132-134
properly basic, 29, 33
and true, 57, 61, 77, 82, 110, 284
warranted true, 28, 33, 110
Beautiful, the, 25, 45, 121, 144n, 283
beauty, 33, 114, 120-121, 128, 294
Berkeley, George, 79
Bloom, Allan, 206, 273-276
Bon Jour, Laurence, 16n., 36n., 37-40, 282n.
Brann, Eva, 149-152, 172n., 173n., 292-295, 296-297
Carnap, Rudolf, 208-209, 217-219, 231, 248
Certainty, 143
and first principles, 35
and indubitability, 105
logical, 133, 163
and knowledge, 15, 23-24, 127, 133, 284
and necessity and impossibility, 127
and Plato, 123, 140
psychological, 133, 163
and Xenophanes, 57
Chisholm, Roderick, 138
Classical Philosophy, 45, 271-272, 276-277, 282
Clifford, W.K., 232, 237

common good, 45, 195, 280, 283, 287
and public discourse, 18, 271, 276, 280
and shared authority, 85
for society, 289, 291. *See also* the Good
common ground, 279
conditions for, 279
for public discourse, 8, 17, 280
lack of, 12, 18, 206, 279-290
logos and, 46, 64
and reason, 11, 17, 19, 283, 287
and Gangadean, Surrendra, 279n.
concepts, 126, 128-129, 155, 171, 278
and first act of the mind, 159
and Foucault, 263
and linguistic turn, 213
and Nietzsche, 177, 180, 231, 257
Continental Philosophy, 13, 42-43, 45, 136, 185, 202-207
and German emigres, 249-252
and Heidegger, 245
and linguistic turn, 270
Post-Nietzschean 257, 266-268
and rejection of reason, 270
and Rorty, Richard, 226. *See also* Philosophy
Darwin, Charles, 136, 203, 228, 231n.

Davidson, Donald, 212, 216
death of everything, 185, 193, 198, 204, 249n., 268
Death of God, 189. 193, 197, 199-200, 204, 280
   and Immanent Frame, 14, 145
   and metanarrative, 197n.
   and Nietzsche, 42, 238
   and Post-Nietzscheans 251
death of metaphysics, 198
death of reason, 145, 198
Deconstruction, 193, 199, 204, 250-251, 258-261, 268
deduction, 105-106, 161, 220
definition of knowledge, 21, 25, 27-28, 50, 136-139
   and Gettier, Edmund, 28
   and justified true belief (JTB), 25, 31, 107, 112, 136, 139
   and Plantinga, Alvin, 28
   and Socrates ,35-36, 94, 107-109, 130-134
   and *Theaetetus*, 44, 52-53 71 82-83, 86
   and true opinion with an account (TOA), 25, 32, 111, 124, 137
Deleuze, Gilles, 203
Democritus, 55, 58-60, 78-79
Derrida, Jacques, 203, 206, 249, 253-261
Desjardin, Rosemary, 83, 152
Dewey, John, 207, 226, 228-229, 238, 243
   and democratic society, 239

   and education, 240-241, 244-245, 248, 250
   and enhancement of experience, 239
   and social construction of knowledge, 232
   and social sciences, 240
dialectic, 119, 155, 157, 168, 175, 303
dialogue, 17, 51, 91, 96, 104, 289, 303
   and *dialogos*, 20
   and *logos*, 150, 152, 200
   and patience, 289
   and Principle of Charity, 288
   and reason, 157, 279
difficult dialogues, 289
Dretske, Fred, 140-143
dualism, 69n., 200, 302
Dummett, Michael, 212-213, 215
Emerson, Ralph Waldo, 229, 249n.
emotivism, 131, 279
Empiricism, 15, 80
   and Aristotle, 169
   British, 202, 214
   and Gettier, Edmund, 143-144
   and Modern Period, 12, 14
   moderate, 12, 23n., 36n., 84
   and naturalism, 31-32, 136
   and Nietzsche, 147, 197-199, 202-203 and *passim*
   radical, 12, 23
   and relativism, 85, 124
   and skepticism, 15-16, 19, 44, 51, 53-55 and *passim*, 86-88 and *passim*

and Socrates, 17, 21, 43, 75
epistemology, 17, 60, 80-81, 279-281, 290-291
    and Aristotle, 61, 162
    and coherentist, 81
    and empiricism, 85
    and Gettier, Edmund, 135
    and Plantinga, Alvin, 31n.
    and Plato, 21, 95, 109, 121, 127
    and Post-Nietzschean, 126, 146-17, 269
    and rationalist, 36
    and *Theaetetus*, 61, 162
ethics, 8, 11, 18, 20, 28, 74, 76, 219, 280-281, 286-287
evidence, 24, 28, 138
    and defeaters 29
    empirical, 28, 35, 40, 139-140
    externalist, 29
    and justification, 28, 138
    and reason, 17
    and senses, 25-27, 140
    strong, 138-140
    weak, 140
experience, 37, 55-57, 80, 225
    and Dewey, John, 239, 240, 241-243
    and God, 33
    and Nietzsche, 192
    and reason, 237
    sense, 25, 54, 86, 125, 218
    subjective, 55, 66, 84
Fichte, Johann G., 246
fideism, 131, 307
Fine, Gail, 81-82, 107

First Philosophers, 11, 20, 48-50, 53, 56, 293, 302, 306
    early Greek, 149
    and materialists, 59, 62, 69n., 30
    and Nietzsche 172
    and Plato, 84, 156
    and search for the *logos*, 77, 151-152, 273, 293, 306
    skepticism of, 61, 68, 299
first principles, 35, 37, 119
    and being and thinking, 164, 278
    and certainty, 35
    and science, 119
    self-evident, 162
flux doctrine, 55, 65-68, 101, 167, 267, 299-300
    and Aristotle, 169
    and Derrida, 258-259
    and Heraclitus, 13, 41, 60, 86, 98, 297
    Heraclitan-Protagorean, 156, 160
    and Nietzsche, 147, 154n., 170, 172-174, 192, 203, 228
    and Protagoras, 73, 299
    and Zeno, 86
Forms, the, 117-118, 285
Foucault, Michael, 203, 206, 253-254, 261-266
foundationalist, 80-81
Frankfurt School, 249n., 249-250
French Counter-Enlightenment, 252n.
Frege, Gottlob, 42, 213-214, 218
Freud, Sigmund, 203, 255, 257

Friedrich, Rainer, 197-200
Gangadean, Surrendra, 276n., 286n., 307-311
German:
    and Emigres to United States, 245n., 248-249, 250
    and German University model, 245, 246-248, 250, 253, 255n.
    and Germany, 229
    Idealism, 197, 230
    Materialists, 197
    and Nietzsche, 207, 231n.
    and Philosophy, 229, 244
Gettier, Edmund, 25, 29, 32, 134, 133-144
    and examples, 27-28, 31, 111, 136, 139, 141,
    formulation of knowledge, 109, 111n., 142
    and fourth condition, 143
    and Justified True Belief, 27, 32, 133-144
    and weak justification, 27, 34
God, 14-15, 110, 145, 208, 293
    being of, 308
    belief in, 29-35
    death of, 192, 195-197, 199-200, 238, 251, 280
    existence of, 29, 277, 293
    and the *Logos*, 46, 306, 308-311
    and Nietzsche, 184-185, 186, 189-190
Good, the, 123, 130, 275, 286, 289
    and Allegory of the Sun, 114-116, 120-121
    and Beatific Vision, 120
    and Beauty, 120
    and Christian tradition, 170
    as common, 280
    as highest, 116
    and knowledge, 61, 97, 116, 121
    and philosophy, 75
    and the True, 286, 291. See also Common Good
Goodman, Nelson, 220-225, 248
Gorgias, 20, 49-50, 62, 68-70
Gospel of John, 46, 293
    and Prologue, 292, 307-312. *See also* Apostle John
Habermas, Jurgen, 203
Harvard University, 229, 247
Heidegger, Martin, 42, 203, 206, 237, 245, 257
    and Frankfurt School, 249
    and nihilism, 261
    and "The Word of Nietzsche: God is Dead," 189-197
Heraclitus, 16, 20, 58, 294, 296, 308-309
    and flux doctrine, 41, 60, 62-65, 68, 98, 104, 169
    and intuitive perception, 174-175
    and *logos*, 148, 150-151, 15-157, 159, 269, 297
    and *logos*-fire, 296
    and Nietzsche, 170, 172, 173n., 174, 177. *See also* First Philosophers; Flux Doctrine
Hobbes, Thomas, 202
Hoitenga, Dewey, 82-83, 107, 110

Hume, David, 33, 38n., 79, 192, 203, 220-221
Huxley, Aldous, 232, 237
Idealism, 192, 197, 199-200, 230
Immanent Frame, 14, 145, 196, 200, 202, 205, 243, 246, 269, 271. *See also* Taylor, Charles
impossibility, 91, 98, 168
    of knowledge, 62
    and necessity, 127
    of non-being, 153
    of the opposite, 106
induction, 38, 160
    a priori support for, 40
    justification of, 38
    and New Riddle of, 220-221
    problem of, 38, 220
isomorphism, 13, 45, 148-149, 174, 177
    between reason and being, 12-13, 39, 42, 101-102, 204
    between thinking and being, 17-18, 21, 154, 179
    denial of, 148
    and knowledge, 112
    Nietzsche and denial of, 42, 171, 180, 182-183
    and Parmenides, 157
    and Post-Nietzschean denial of, 144, 204
    rejection of, 41, 159
    and Western Tradition, 169. *See also* reason
James, William, 42, 207, 229, 232-238
judgment, 58, 90, 92-95, 98, 119, 173, 284
and knowledge, 106, 125
and perception, 72, 92
and propositions, 126, 128, 158-159, 284
and reason, 54, 284
and statements, 107
and true, 93, 129
justification, 24, 138, 141
and evidence, 24, 28
and Gettier, 25, 28, 141-143
maximal, 34
and Plantinga, 28
and *prima facie*, 27
and rational, 33, 61, 69n.,225
and strong, 31, 33-34
and *ultima facie*, 31
and weak, 27-28, 31-32, 34
Justified True Belief, 25-28, 31-32, 104, 107-112, 137
Kant, Immanuel, 192, 228
Kauffmann, Walter, 227-228, 249
Klossowski, Pierre, 187-188, 249
Knowledge:
by acquaintance, 22, 81-83, 217
and belief, 102, 107
and certainty, 15, 23, 283-284
and correspondence, 217, 233-234
and fallibility, 23-24
and infallible, 105, 283
objective, 44, 74, 262, 286, 302, 306
and perception, 87, 89, 92, 101,240
Post-Nietzschean formulation of, 112

and power, 263-264
and propositional, 22-23, 25, 49, 51, 81
social construction of, 232, 243
language games, 42, 238, 244
law of excluded middle, 11, 128-129, 158, 160, 278, 283. *See also* laws of thought
law of identity, 11, 128, 158-159, 167, 181, 278. *See also* laws of thought
law of non-contradiction, 11, 158, 160, 162, 188, 278
    LNC, 127-129, 164-170
    PNC, 163. *See also* laws of thought
laws of thought, 17-19, 36-37, 94, 133, 278-279, 283
    and Aristotle, 159-164, 189
    compelling, 127, 237
    denial of, 168-169, 171, 174, 181
    and isomorphism, 237
    and laws of being, 18, 41, 148, 278
    reason as, 11, 17, 19, 21, 35, 94, 128-129, 158, 289
    self-evident, 37. *See also*, law of excluded middle; law of identity; law of non-contradiction
Lucippus, 58
Levi-Strauss, Claude, 255, 258
Levinas, Emmanuel, 203
linguistic turn, 43-43, 212-214, 216, 219, 257, 270
Locke, John, 79
logic, 68, 157, 210, 214
    and Aristotle, 159, 220-221, 305
    modern, 218-219
    Nietzsche's critique of, 149, 181-183
Logical Positivism, 36n., 208, 216, 222
Logical Positivists, 211-212, 232
logocentrism, 42, 253, 260-261, 266. *See also* Derrida, Jacques
logos:
    and account, 50, 76, 106, 140, 158
    and a *logos*, 11, 17, 20, 21, 84, 76
    and being, 75, 153, 156-157, 170
    common to all, 64, 296, 308-309, 311
    definition of, 106-107
    and eternal, 64
    and intelligence, 65, 158, 160
    and law, 65, 153
    and *logoi*, 73, 106
    and reason, 76, 106, 158, 160
    search for a, 43-44, 45-48, 64, 68, 77, 271
    and tying down, 123, 159, 300. *See also* the *Logos*
Logos, the, 65, 75, 158, 271
    as aspect of being, 106
    and Christian theism, 269, 293, 297
    as common ground, 46, 64, 296

and Nietzsche, 147, 183, 185
objection to, 44
and Plato, 43, 157
and reason, 17, 44, 160, 283
rejection of, 43
and Western Philosophy, 147, 148-150, 185, 292. See also *logos*
Lyotard, Jean-Francois, 198, 203, 149
madness:
  and Foucault, 265
  and Nietzsche, 42, 43, 151n., 171, 182, 186-188, 197
  as other to reason, 265
  of Post-Nietzschean philosophy, 131, 148, 186, 199
  and rejection of *Logos*, 186
  and silence, 270
  of the West, 185, 200
"Man is the measure," 89-90
  and Protagoras, 52, 54-55, 68, 71-76, 86-87
  and science is the measure, 223
  and Socrates, 91-94, 98, 289, 291
  and *Theaetetus*, 52 104, 124. See also Protagoras
Marx, Karl, 203, 249n., 252
Marxism, 252n., 252
Materialism, 15, 21, 59-60, 145, 200, 237
  and ancient philosophy, 62-63
  assumptions of, 295, 299
  and atomic theory, 58

and empiricism, 15-17, 19, 252, 258-259
and Nietzsche, 131, 192, 202-203
and nominalism, 53
and physicalism, 218
and Post-Nietzschean philosophy, 199
and Socrates, 76, 105, 111. See *also* materialists
materialism-empiricism-skepticism, 136, 306
materialists, 41, 43, 59-60, 62, 69, 192, 197, 232. See *also* Atomists; First philosophers; Pre-Socratic; Materialism
matter, 15, 54, 60, 63, 76, 85, 99, 130, 285, 299, 302
meaning, 45, 131, 158, 213-215, 225, 287
  cemented, 260
  and definition, 61
  loss of, 162, 184
  and *logos*, 21, 65, 293, 294
  and meaningless, 18, 98, 131, 148, 165, 185, 188, 219, 288
  names and, 10
  reason and, 19
  significant, 165, 188, 278
  survival of, 111, 214
  and thinking, 37
  as use, 216-217
  words and, 8, 101, 144, 157, 166-167. See *also* nihilism
meaninglessness, 148, 185, 192
  of public discourse, 131

of speech, 165. *See also* nihilism
Metaphysics (Aristotle), 17, 19, 37n., 41, 55-56, 62, 159-161, 163-170
metaphysics, 11, 14, 20, 193, 280-281
   abandoned, 130, 206
   and Analytic philosophy, 219
   elimination of, 218
   end of, 193, 268
   history of, 258
   naturalistic, 197
   and Nietzsche, 147
   and Platonism, 40
   Post-Nietzschean, 40, 130, 217, 269
   realist, 21, 216
   and supranatural, 223
   and suprasensory, 191-193
   tradition of, 171
   and ultimate reality, 193
Meyer, Matthew, 146-149, 159-161, 163, 165, 168, 171
mind, 60, 233, 312
   denial of, 214, 226
   first act of, 128, 158-159, 177, 213
   and *logos*, 152-154, 160, 294, 303-304
   non-material, 99
   non-physical, 76
   second act of, 128
   third act of, 159-160
Modern Period, 12, 20-21, 84, 145, 147, 170
naming, 17, 167

Naturalism, 85, 161, 206, 285-286, 291
   Darwinian, 136
   ontological, 161
Neo-Pragmatism, 250-251, 267
Neurath, Otto, 217
Nietzsche, Friedrich:
   and anti-Christ, 171, 207
   and anti-Logos, 41-42, 148, 150, 171-172, 185
   Birth of Tragedy, 176
   and becoming, 147-148, 170, 172-174, 179-180, 182
   Beyond Good and Evil, 181-182
   and Christian tradition, 170-171
   Ecce Homo, 151n., 171n.
   Gay Science, 189-191
   Human All Too Human, 179
   and intuitive perception, 172-175, 177
   Madman, 189-191
   and madness, 42, 151, 171, 182, 185-188
   and megalomania, 186-187
   and new philosophers of the future, 13, 42, 185
   and nihilism, 182, 292
   "On Truth and Lying," 172-179
   and perspectivism (perspectivalism), 147-148, 169, 199, 231, 236-237
   Pre-Platonic Philosophers, 155-156, 170, 172

and rejection of Western
philosophical tradition, 147-
150, 155, 171-172, 185, 203
and revaluation of values, 42,
127, 173, 200, 204
and tragic worldview, 146-
147, 149, 156
Thus Spake Zarathustra, 208
nihilism, 68, 192-193, 197, 200,
261
negative, 193, 202, 204, 253,
261, 268
positive, 193, 202, 204, 230,
244, 261, 268
and Nietzsche, 199, 202
Post-Nietzschean, 227, 273
nihilistic, 182, 192
Nominalism, 53, 84, 236
and Goodman, Nelson, 220
and James, William, 236
and non-essentialism, 85, 89,
285-286
nominalist, 219-220
One and the Many, 70, 77
ontological, 147-149, 159-169,
170, 172, 295
and being, 153-154
and isomorphism, 12-13, 18,
21, 39, 41-42, 45, 148-149,
154, 157
and LNC (PNC), 127, 163,
168, 214, 216, 219
and *logos*, 147
reason as, 18-19, 43-44, 130-
131, 133, 154-157, 172-174
reason not as, 183-186, 203,
206, 212, 232, 270. See also
logos; *ontos*

ontology, 161, 210-211, 267
ontos, 11-12, 48, 84, 112, 277, 307
opinion, 50, 56-57, 65, 70, 83-84,
123-129
and *doxa*, 111-113, 118-119,
123, 271, 303
false, 122, 142
true, 17, 19, 25-26, 102-103
Parmenides, 16, 20, 53, 66-69
and being, 67, 147-150, 153
and Heraclitus, 62, 159, 174,
269
and *Logos*, 153-157, 175
and Nietzsche, 175
and non-being, 67
Peirce, Charles Sanders, 207, 229,
238
perception(s), 57-59, 84, 97, 99-
106
faculties of, 15
intuitive, 173-174, 175, 177
knowledge as, 54-55, 72-75,
86-92, 12, 291
knowledge not, 133, 140-143
relativity of, 54, 71, 298
sensory, 112, 114, 118-120,
157, 291
pessimism 227, 238, 244
Philo of Alexandria, 305-306
Philosopher(s), 11-17, 124, 192,
237, 271
Analytic, 23n., 25, 104, 144,
211, 214, 218, 225-227
Continental, 252, 257
First, 20, 46, 48, 50-63, 68-77,
293
as free, 95, 97, 287
as lovers of wisdom, 52

and poets, 177, 179, 270
Post-Analytic, 230-232, 248, 250
Post-Nietzschean, 36, 40-43, 126, 130-136, 149, 185, 193, 197, 201-203
Pragmatist, 207, 273
Stoic, 303-304
survival of, 111. *See also* Poet; Politicians
Philosophy, 49, 75, 130-131, 136, 150, 185
  American, 13, 42, 185, 226
  Analytic, 136, 204, 208, 212, 219, 222
  Classical approach to, 45, 271, 276, 282
  contemporary, 16, 21, 200, 202, 204-206
  Continental, 45, 249-251, 270
  death of, 10, 16, 43, 68
  discipline of, 10-11, 131
  end of, 77, 221, 268, 270
  history of, 11-12, 45, 48, 84, 197, 276, 307-308
  and John's Gospel, 293
  Post-*Logos*, 201-202
  public, 19, 44, 46, 276, 280-282
  Socratic, 53, 176, 179
  as search for a *logos*, 11, 44, 77, 271, 273, 292
  as therapy, 43, 226-227
  and wondering, 292-293, 306. *See also* Philosopher
Plato, 11, 17-19, 21, 44, 81-86
  Allegory of the Cave, 113, 116-120, 121
  Allegory of the Line, 113, 116-120, 121
  Allegory of the Sun, 113, 114-116
  and dialogues, 49, 51, 270, 284, 286, 289-290
  Meno, 50, 107, 111, 121-124
  Phaedo, 300-301
  Republic, 94, 112-113, 121, 274, 300
  and knowledge as true opinion with an account, 111-112, 124, 131-133, 135, 137
Platonic, 109-111, 169
Platonism, 36, 40-41
Plantinga, Alvin, 28-34, 108, 110, 134
Poets, 177, 179, 205, 270. *See also* Philosopher
political correctness, 7-8
Politicians, 64, 270. *See also* Philosopher
politics, 18, 49, 95, 205, 266-267, 270
Post-analytic, 216, 222, 224, 231, 248-251, 255. *See also* Analytic; Philosopher
Postmodern, 21, 169, 185-186, 193, 197-199, 267
  thinking, 148, 161
Postmodernism, 198-199
Post-Nietzschean, 12-13, 15, 21, 31-32, 81, 144-145
  definitions of knowledge, 109-112, 126

era, 109
philosophers, 40-43, 46, 130-131, 149, 161, 252
philosophy, 131, 204, 227
social order, 239, 242
power dynamics, 42, 199, 204, 261, 263, 268
Pragmatism, 12, 16, 42, 136, 230, 244, 250-251
American, 207, 222, 226, 228, 230, 237, 250
institutional, 202
and Nietzsche, 227-228, 236, 250
and nihilism, 193, 204
and philosophy, 205, 227, 270
and relativism, 20
and skepticism, 13, 200, 202, 242, 252
and Sophists, 271-272
and "willing out beyond," 194. *See also* Neo-Pragmatists; Pragmatists
Pragmatists, 216, 226 229-237, 244-245, 249, 270. *See also* Pragmatism
presence, 42, 255-259, 261. *See also* Derrida, Jacques
Principle of Charity, 288
principles, 131, 152, 160-164, 303
first, 35, 37, 119
Socratic, 44-45, 282, 285, 291
universal, 46
proof, 90, 106, 143, 164-166
properties, 160, 167-168, 171
Protagoras, 16, 20, 49, 58, 71-76, 86-89, 297

and anti-*logos*, 71
and flux doctrine, 73-74, 88
and "man is the measure," 71, 73, 76, 90, 93, 89, 223
and relativism, 68, 86, 124
and skepticism, 71, 74-75, 93
as Sophist, 62, 72, 96, 105
and *Theaetetus*, 51-54, 63, 76, 87, 104
and two-*logoi*, 73, 297-299
public, 8, 11-12, 16, 18-19, 40-46, 85, 121, 242-243, 280-290
and common authority, 84-85
good, 271, 272, 282
philosophy, 19, 44, 276, 281-282
public discourse, 7-8, 10, 12, 17-18, 35, 40-46, 79-80, 88, 202, 244, 279-281, 284-285
public life, 16, 44, 46, 49, 157, 243
Putnam, Hilary, 221-222
Pythagoras, 294-296, 299
Quietism, 270
Quine, W.V.O., 36n., 212, 219, 224-225, 248, 255
Rationalism, 16n., 36, 40-41, 81, 236
and Socrates, 12, 84, 130. *See also* Reason
Rawls, John, 285
Realism, 12, 81, 84, 136, 267, 269. *See also* Anti-realism; Realist
Realist, 214-216
Reason:
and argument, 25, 33, 88, 91, 105, 284-285, 300
and Aristotle, 163-170

and authority, 18-19, 21, 235, 278-279
and being, 11-13, 19, 39, 41-42, 277, 293, 307
and common ground, 11, 19, 46, 283, 287-290
disengaged, 14, 145
instrumental, 14, 42
and laws of thought, 11, 17, 18-19, 21, 35, 41, 127-130, 169, 171, 181, 278-279, 283, 289
and logos, 11, 21, 36, 44, 171, 303
as ontological, 19, 131, 133, 148-149, 161, 169-170, 203, 206, 270, 295
and public discourse, 7, 11, 12, 41, 273
Rectification of Names, 9-10, 19, 44, 46, 144, 270-271
reductio ad absurdum, 87, 99, 127, 129, 284, 290
relativism, 17, 20, 53, 68, 71, 286, 299
epistemological, 125
ethical, 74, 85, 281, 287
and truth, 76, 290, 299
revaluation, 109, 178
and deconstruction, 199
of philosophy, 270-276
of Plato, 41, 135-136
of the definition of knowledge, 109
of values, 42, 127, 173, 195-196, 199-200, 261

Rorty, Richard, 42-43, 135, 205, 207, 225, 231, 250
Royce, Josiah, 207, 229
Russell, Bertrand, 22, 42, 209, 214
Sartre, Jean Paul, 203
Schelling, Friedrich W.J., 246
Schleiermacher, Friedrich, 246
Schopenhauer, Arthur, 203
science, 26, 80, 176, 183, 205, 218, 223-225
and Allegory of the Line, 116-119
physical, 119, 127, 240
social, 240, 249, 251, 255, 261, 263
sciences, 80, 118, 204
Scientific Method, 80, 211, 239
Schlick, Moritz, 208, 217
self-evident, 30, 37, 162, 164, 279, 283
Sellars, Wilfred, 23n., 219, 222-225
semanticide, 8-11, 18, 43, 144, 186, 193-194
significant speech, 42, 165-170, 184-185, 189, 210, 278
silence, 99, 148, 165, 187-200, 210
of madness, 42-43, 185, 270
silenced, 19, 287
skepticism:
contemporary, 12, 15-17, 19, 278, 285
crisis of, 20, 204, 282
essence of, 15, 235
institutional, 13-14, 16, 43, 204, 277, 281-282
institutionalized, 200, 202, 204, 242, 246, 248, 269-271

philosophical, 20, 79-80, 225
problem of, 17, 79, 84
radical, 62, 68, 147
Socrates:
and flux doctrine, 60, 65-66, 89, 98-99, 140, 300
and knowledge, 17, 21, 23, 25-27, 105, 125-127
and *logos*, 17, 64, 68, 75, 103, 106-107, 123, 300, 303
and materialism, 70, 285
as means of resistance, 274
and method, 12, 45, 130, 273
and philosopher, 95-97, 271, 287
and public discourse, 19, 44, 84, 285
and reason, 12, 76, 84, 101, 118, 309
and *reductio ad absurdum*, 99, 102, 284, 290
and relativism, 76
and skepticism, 17
and Sophists, 43, 92, 95-97
and soul, 99-100, 105, 113, 302. *See also* Socratic Method; Socratic Principles
Socratic Method, 76, 105, 111, 128, 288
Socratic Principles, 44-45, 282, 285, 291
Sophism, 17, 20-21, 43, 74, 271-272, 306. *See also* Sophists
Sophists, 11, 43, 48-50, 72, 287
contrasted with Philosopher, 95-97

and institutionalized skepticism, 271
as not free, 287
and Orator, 95-97
and pragmatism, 157, 270-271
and skepticism, 68, 77, 86, 299. *See also* Sophism
soul, 67, 100-102, 104-107, 304
activity of, 100
non-physical, 99
permanent, 300, 302
rational, 63, 116
and spirit, 105, 297, 302, 305
Spencer, Herbert, 232
Stoics, 304-306, 308
substance, 167-169, 171, 184, 297
supranatural, 40, 199-200, 217, 219n., 223, 233, 244, 250
suprasensory, 191-193, 194-196, 197
Szasz, Thomas, 8
Taylor, Charles, 14-15, 145, 202
Thales, 16, 150
Theism, 46, 69n., 193, 197, 200, 293, 209
transcendent, 14, 145, 195-196, 297
True, the, 26, 45, 283, 286
true opinion, 25-26, 102-104, 112-113, 122-123, 270-271
and scientific reasoning, 119, 127, 142
sufficient for action, 122-123, 143

true opinion with an account, 17, 25, 32, 44, 103-105, 111, 132-133, 283-284
    and *logos*, 83, 127, 156. *See also* Knowledge; Plato
Truth, 215, 310-312
    and *Alethia*, 102, 111-112, 144
    as relative, 73-74, 92
    correspondence theory of, 137, 234, 238
    eternal, 132, 140
    necessary, 105, 129, 284
    and pragmatic method, 235
    relativity of 58, 71, 74-77
    system of, 129. *See also* True
Tsu, Hsun, 9
University, American, 212, 244-245, 247-249, 251
values, 8, 111, 131, 194-196, 199, 219, 227, 241
    devaluation of, 193
    highest, 195
    new, 194, 204, 238
    revaluation of 42, 109, 127, 196, 200, 204, 261
Verificationism, 217, 222, 250
Vienna Circle, 42, 208, 211-212, 217-218, 248
Von Humboldt, Wilhelm, 246
West, Cornel, 207, 248, 250
West, the, 7-8, 10, 185, 271, 282
    death of, 43-44, 145, 200
    destruction of, 267
    and *Logos*, 153
    and madness, 197, 200
    survival of, 111, 131. *See also* Western
Western:
    Civilization, 7, 10, 186, 189, 271
    Nietzsche's rejection of, 147-148, 155-156, 172, 203, 269
    Philosophy, 15, 21, 79-80, 149, 185, 191-192, 197
    philosophical tradition, 147, 150, 169, 171-172
    tradition, 151n.
Will to Power, 85, 131, 267, 272, 287
    and truth, 202
    and Nietzsche, 147, 170, 173n., 203,
    and Heidegger, 194-195, 227
wisdom, 96, 128, 289, 290
    and philosophers, 5
    and Sophists 49, 72, 90, 92
Wittgenstein, Ludwig, 43, 209, 215
    Investigations, 210
    and linguistic context, 216
    and meaning as use, 215-216
    and Quietism, 210
    Tractatus, 210, 214
Wolin, Richard, 186-188, 252, 265-266
wondering, 294, 306
Xenophanes, 55-58

www.ingramcontent.com/pod-product-compliance
Lightning Source LLC
Chambersburg PA
CBHW032026290426
44110CB00012B/693